CRITICAL CARE

OBSTETRICAL

NURSING

Edited by

Carol J. Harvey, RNC, MS
Project Director
Center for High Risk and Critical Care Obstetrics
Department of Obstetrics and Gynecology
The University of Texas Medical Branch
Galveston, Texas

AN ASPEN PUBLICATION®
Aspen Publishers, Inc.
Gaithersburg, Maryland
1991

Library of Congress Cataloging-in-Publication Data

Critical care obstetrical nursing /
edited by Carol J. Harvey.
p. cm.
Includes bibliographical references and index.
ISBN: 0-8342-0235-2
1. Obstetrical nursing. 2. Pregnancy,
Complications of—Nursing. I. Harvey, Carol J.
[DNLM: 1. Critical Care—in pregnancy. 2. Obstetrical Nursing.
3. Pregnancy Complications—nursing. WQ 240 C9338]
RG951.C75 1991
610.73'678—dc20
DNLM/DLC
for Library of Congress
91-14430
CIP

The authors have made every effort to ensure the accuracy of the information
herein, particularly with regard to drug selection and dose. However, appropriate
information sources should be consulted, especially for new or unfamiliar drugs
or procedures. It is the responsibility of every practitioner to evaluate the
appropriateness of a particular opinion in the context of actual clinical situations
and with due consideration to new developments. Authors, editors, and the
publisher cannot be held responsible for any typographical or other errors found
in this book.

Editorial Services: Ruth Bloom

Library of Congress Catalog Card Number: 91-14430
ISBN: 0-8342-0235-2

Printed in the United States of America

3 4 5

To
William C. Mabie, MD,
who patiently and generously
taught me how to take care of
critically ill pregnant women.

Table of Contents

Contributors

Mary Lou Adams, RN, MSN
Director of Maternal Child Health
formerly, Maternal Child Clinical Nurse
 Specialist
Jackson-Madison County General Hospital
Jackson, Tennessee

Roxelyn G. Baumgartner, MS, RN
Clinical Nurse Specialist
Pulmonary Critical Care
Vanderbilt University Medical Center
Nashville, Tennessee

Mary Ellen Burke, RN, MS
President
Perinatal Resources
Rumford, Rhode Island

Kitty Cashion, RNC, MSN
Clinical Nurse Specialist for Outreach
 Education
Division of Maternal-Fetal Medicine
Department of Obstetrics and Gynecology
University of Tennessee College of Medicine
Memphis, Tennessee

Karen Dorman, RNC, MS
Coordinator of Clinical Research
Division of Maternal-Fetal Medicine
Department of Obstetrics and Gynecology
Baylor College of Medicine
Houston, Texas

Mildred Gillihan Harvey, RNC, MSN
Clinical Nurse Specialist
Baptist Memorial Hospital East
Affiliate Faculty, College of Nursing
University of Tennessee at Memphis
Memphis, Tennessee

Lisa K. Mandeville, RN, MSN
Assistant in Obstetrics
Administrative Coordinator
Maternal/Fetal Medicine
Vanderbilt University Medical Center
Nashville, Tennessee

L. Kay Medford, RN, MSN
OB Regionalization Coordinator
Erlanger Medical Center
Chattanooga, Tennessee

Susan Pozaic, RNC, MS
Director of Perinatal Services
Children's Hospital Home Care
Buffalo, New York
 and
Senior Consultant
Harvey, Troiano, and Associates, Inc.
Memphis, Tennessee

Melissa C. Sisson, RN, MN
Director, Labor and Delivery
Northside Hospital
Atlanta, Georgia

Nan H. Troiano, RN, MSN
Co-Director of Critical Care Obstetrics
Maternal/Fetal Division
Critical Care Obstetrics
Vanderbilt University Medical Center
Nashville, Tennessee

Foreword

The practice of obstetrics has undergone a remarkable evolution during the past 25 years. In many instances these advances have hinged on the introduction of new technologies and their application to obstetrics. The advent of sonography allowed us, for the first time, a window through which to examine the intrauterine contents and thus opened up the entire field of antenatal diagnosis. Similarly, the development of the flow-directed pulmonary artery catheter transformed a research tool into a reliable clinical instrument available at a patient's bedside to monitor cardiovascular status. First reported in the *New England Journal of Medicine* in 1970, this landmark article by Swan, Ganz, and Forrester signaled the birth of the modern critical care era. As these technologies achieved widespread implementation and application, the need to certify the competence of health care providers in their use was recognized. Formal recognition of the subspecialty of maternal-fetal medicine occurred in 1972, with authorization to certify for added qualifications in critical care approved by the American Board of Medical Specialties in 1983. The explosion of both information and interest in these areas has led to the creation of the Society of Critical Care Medicine and the Society of Perinatal Obstetricians, both within the last 10 years.

The key to successful bedside implementation of any advanced medical technology is the availability of skilled and knowledgeable nursing personnel. *Critical Care Obstetrical Nursing* by Carol J. Harvey and associates is a comprehensive state-of-the-art review of critical care obstetric nursing. Throughout the textbook attention is given to the physiologic changes in pregnancy that render the pregnant woman unique and different from her nonpregnant counterpart. This is an excellent reference source compiled by highly qualified and experienced nurses who practice their specialty daily at the patient's bedside and who have been directly involved in advancing the sciences of critical care obstetrics. This text should be a part of the reference library of every critical care obstetric unit and readily available to both the nurses and physicians charged with caring for these women.

Gary D. V. Hankins, MD
Chairman and Program Director
Department of Obstetrics and Gynecology
Wilford Hall, USAF Medical Center
San Antonio, Texas

Preface

High-risk obstetrics has taken on a new complexion in the past 5 years. Common in the care of these patients is the use and interpretation of advanced hemodynamic technology. Women with chronic disease who were once discouraged from attempting pregnancy are now presenting to obstetric health care providers and inpatient obstetric services. These societal and epidemiologic changes in the obstetric population have placed new demands on nurses and physicians who practice obstetrics.

Traditional preparation and training for obstetric nurses has been void of critical care theory and practice. Likewise, training for critical care nurses has been lacking in instruction on the physiologic parameters of high-risk pregnancy. Historically, critical illness in pregnant patients has produced frustration for staff and patient alike, as fragmented care from several subspecialists was the only option available.

To overcome these obstacles, organizations have been developed and national conferences have been held, and published resources are becoming available. In the past 10 years, our medical colleagues have formed the Society of Perinatal Obstetricians; more recently, a special interest group for critical care obstetrics was formed within this society. Nurses are also developing our own networks; there are national meetings on the care of these high-risk women, and the Organization for Obstetric, Gynecologic and Neonatal Nursing (NAACOG) special interest group on critical care obstetrics will meet for the first time in 1991.

Critical Care Obstetrical Nursing was designed to meet the need for a published resource to assist the nurse caring for the high-risk, critically ill obstetric patient. It is the product of a coordinated effort by several nursing specialists in critical care and obstetrics.

Carol J. Harvey, RNC, MS

xiii

Acknowledgments

I would like to acknowledge the contributors for their hard work on their individual sections. I would also like to acknowledge the work of Mary Lou Mraz, technical writer, whose contribution has been invaluable, and who is responsible for getting this book to press. Special acknowledgment is made to Garland D. Anderson, MD, Chairman of the Department of Obstetrics and Gynecology at the University of Texas Medical Branch, without whose support this book would not have been possible. Finally, I would like to thank the nursing and medical staffs of the obstetrics service at the University of Texas Medical Branch, who have been extremely supportive of this project and who inspire and encourage me to never stop learning.

Chapter 1

Physiologic Changes of Pregnancy

Mildred Gillihan Harvey

INTRODUCTION

Fertilization initiates the physiologic changes that accompany pregnancy. As the maternal body makes adaptations to meet the needs of fetal physiology, the functioning of most of the maternal organ systems is affected, often in interrelated ways. Ovarian and placental hormones govern the majority of these changes, either directly or through secondary effects. The presence and mechanical effects of the growing uterus and fetus also produce some maternal alterations. These functional adjustments begin in the first week of gestation and continue throughout pregnancy, labor, delivery, and the puerperium. Understanding and appreciation of the normal physiologic adaptations to pregnancy are important for the management of all pregnant women.

HORMONAL CHANGES

The maternal body increases the production of certain hormones to maintain the pregnancy and to provide the fetus an optimum environment. The placenta produces several of these hormones, some of which are unique to pregnancy, while the endocrine glands (the ovaries and the pituitary, thyroid, and adrenal glands) also increase their respective hormone secretions.

Placental Hormones

Endocrine alterations of major and minor importance are brought about by development of the placenta. The trophoblast of the placenta produces large amounts of the protein hormones human chorionic gonadotropin (HCG) and placental lactogen (HPL), as well as the steroid hormones progesterone and

1

estrogen. The trophoblast also synthesizes a thyroid-stimulating hormone, a corticotropin (chorionic adrenocorticotropic hormone [ACTH]), and hormones of lesser importance.

The protein hormones are present only during pregnancy, as a result of the functioning placenta. They play a specific role during gestation and then disappear with separation of the placenta. The steroid hormones estrogen and progesterone are produced by the ovaries as well as the placenta and are present in nonpregnant women. Larger amounts are available during pregnancy because of synthesis by the placenta. Placental production of these steroids is dependent upon precursors derived from the fetal and maternal circulations.

Human Chorionic Gonadotropin

HCG appears very early in gestation. The main function of HCG is to maintain the corpus luteum during the early weeks of pregnancy, thereby producing enough progesterone to preserve the pregnancy until the placenta produces adequate amounts of progesterone on its own.

HCG has biochemical similarities to luteinizing hormone (LH) and has been used as an LH substitute in the treatment of certain infertility problems. HCG induces ovulation in an ovary that has been primed with follicle-stimulating hormone (FSH), when infertility is due to anovulation.

HCG is secreted into the maternal circulation and is excreted by the renal system. Assays of HCG form the basis for the majority of tests for pregnancy. This hormone is detectable a few days after implantation, via a sensitive radio-immunoassay test using antibodies against the ß subunit of HCG. HCG reaches peak levels between the 12th and 13th weeks of gestation. Thereafter the levels fall, reaching a low level around the 20th week of gestation. This low level plateaus and is maintained until the placenta is delivered. The hormone disappears rapidly after delivery of the placenta, within 3 to 4 days postpartum.[1] Significantly higher titers of HCG are found in multiple gestation, erythroblastosis fetalis, hydatidiform mole, and choriocarcinoma.

Human Placental Lactogen

HPL, also known as human chorionic somatotropin (HCS), has both lacto-genic activity and an immunochemical resemblance to human growth hormone. HPL can be detected in the serum as early as the sixth week of gestation. Serum levels rise steadily, keeping pace with placenta development. The concentration in maternal blood is approximately proportional to placental mass and reaches a high concentration in late pregnancy. The half-life of HPL is very short, so production must be abundant to produce high serum levels. Blood levels should closely reflect production level. HPL disappears rapidly after delivery of the placenta.[2] Practically no HPL is found in the fetal circulation, in the urine of the mother, or in the urine of the newborn.

HPL affects maternal and fetal metabolism, both directly and indirectly, to supply the fetus with needed nutrients for growth and development by decreasing the maternal utilization of glucose, which provides food for the fetus. HPL promotes maternal lipolysis, which results in an elevated maternal plasma level of free fatty acids. The mother then uses the available free fatty acids rather than carbohydrates for energy. This allows more glucose to be available for the fetus. HPL also affects protein metabolism so that the fetus has more amino acids available for use.

HPL is a physiologic antagonist of insulin and contributes to the diabetogenic effect of pregnancy. The anti-insulin effect of HPL causes increased peripheral resistance to insulin. This leads to the need for the mother's pancreas to secrete additional insulin. The increased level of maternal insulin promotes protein synthesis, ensuring a source of amino acids for the fetus.[3]

HPL is not involved in actual milk secretion after delivery but prepares the breasts for lactation by stimulating breast growth and development.

Estrogen

The placenta produces large amounts of the estrogen hormones during gestation, at levels that continually increase. Estrogens have many functions during pregnancy (Table 1-1). The hyperestrogenic state of pregnancy abruptly ceases with delivery of the placenta.

The common estrogens in the human are estradiol-17ß, estrone, and estriol. The placenta secretes mainly estriol, while the ovaries secrete mainly estradiol. In nonpregnant women, the ratio of estriol to estrone plus estradiol is about equal. During pregnancy there is a large increase in the ratio of estriol to the other estrogens. This reflects estriol biosynthesis in the placenta.[4] Estriol is detectable in material serum at 9 weeks' gestation.

Production of estrogens by the placenta is different from that in the ovary. The placenta alone cannot synthesize estriol. Essential precursors are provided by the adrenal glands of the fetus. These precursors are transported to the placenta for the final conversion to estriol. Thus there is an interdependence between the placenta and the fetus in the production of estrogens. The biosynthesis of these hormones is dependent on intact and functioning fetal adrenal glands and the fetal pituitary gland; the presence of a live fetus is necessary for its continued production.

Estriol is excreted in the mother's urine after conjugation in the maternal liver. Urinary excretion of estriol rises slowly until the 12th week of gestation. It then increases more rapidly in a steady upward curve. Because estriol production is dependent on the fetal-placental unit functioning adequately, measurement of

Table 1-1 Functions of Estrogen during Pregnancy

1. controls the growth and function of the uterus
   a. produces hyperplasia and hypertrophy of the uterus to accommodate developing pregnancy
   b. increases blood supply to the uterus
2. produces breast development through increase of alveolar ductile tissue
3. causes alterations in connective tissues
   a. increases mobility of nipple tissues
   b. relaxes pelvic joints and pelvic ligaments
4. produces a softening effect on the collagen tissues of the cervix in late pregnancy, to "ripen" the cervix
5. increases the maternal sensitivity to the P_{CO_2} level
6. affects the composition of blood
   a. decrease in total plasma proteins
   b. increase in fibrinogen concentration
   c. decrease in fibrinolytic activity
   d. leukocytosis of pregnancy
   e. increase in serum-binding proteins
7. produces skin changes
   a. striae gravidarum
   b. telangiectases
   c. palmar erythema
   d. hyperpigmentation
8. promotes sodium and water retention by kidney tubules
9. decreases the secretion of hydrochloric acid and pepsin
   a. digestive upsets
   b. nausea
   c. decreased absorption of fat

---

maternal urinary estriol has been used as a clinical index of fetal and placental well-being. However, variations in estriol secretion occur from day to day, and a single measurement is meaningless. Therefore, several times weekly measurements are necessary. Fluctuations in daily estriols will occur, but the values may be graphed to reflect a trend. Falling values of 50% or more indicate possible fetal-placental jeopardy and necessitate further studies. Because of the difficulties of accurately determining completeness of the specimen and eliminating technical error, many centers use the nonstress test and biophysical profile rather than estriol level determinations for fetal surveillance.

Progesterone

Progesterone is the hormone essential for maintaining pregnancy. In the first few weeks of pregnancy, the corpus luteum produces the progesterone needed for pregnancy maintenance. Soon after implantation, the placenta begins to produce progesterone, and by the 10th week of gestation it produces adequate amounts so that the corpus luteum is no longer required for progesterone production.

Placental production of progesterone steadily increases as the placenta develops. Production of placental progesterone requires the use of maternal rather than fetal precursors—that is, maternal cholesterol. The functions of progesterone during gestation are discussed in Table 1-2.

Progesterone actions and estrogen actions generally oppose each other. The actions of the two hormones thus usually balance out.

Pituitary Hormones

Prolactin

There is a marked increase in the plasma levels of prolactin during the course of pregnancy. Following delivery, plasma levels of prolactin decrease, even in the lactating mother. During lactation there are spurts of increased prolactin secretion in response to the infant's sucking.

The action of prolactin to produce milk is suppressed by progesterone. Delivery of the placenta removes this suppression, and lactation can proceed. Prolactin mediates lactalbumin synthesis.[5]

REPRODUCTIVE SYSTEM

Ovary

Ovulation ceases during gestation, and the maturation of new follicles is arrested. As mentioned above, the corpus luteum is needed for progesterone manufacture during the first 10 weeks of gestation; thereafter it may continue to produce hormones, but it plays a minor role. Degenerative changes begin in the corpus luteum around the 28th week of gestation.

Uterus

The uterus undergoes a remarkable transition to adapt to pregnancy.

Size

The uterus changes from a small, almost solid organ to one capable of holding the term fetus, placenta, and amniotic fluid.

The weight of the uterus increases to 20 times its prepregnant weight—from 60 g (2 ounces) to 1000 to 1200 g (2 to 2½ pounds) at the end of a full-term gestation. The capacity of a uterus increases from 10 mL or less to 4.5 to 5 L.

Table 1-2 Functions of Progesterone during Gestation

1. inhibits the contractility of smooth muscle
   a. uterine myometrium
      1) allows blastocyst to implant and develop
      2) protects against expulsion of developing pregnancy
   b. gastrointestinal tract
      1) reduces tone in gastrointestinal tract
      2) constipation
      3) heartburn
   c. renal system
      1) urinary stasis
      2) ureter dilatation
   d. vascular system
      1) edema
      2) venous dilatation
2. affects central nervous system to produce maternal complaints of being sleepy and tired
3. affects metabolism
   a. increases body temperature
   b. lays down maternal stores of body fat
4. stimulates the loss of sodium in the urine, which in turn increases aldosterone production to conserve sodium
5. provides for alveolar development
6. inhibits the action of prolactin as breasts prepare for lactation (Milk production begins only after delivery of placenta.)
7. decreases sensitivity to oxytocin
8. stimulates respiratory center to increase the respiratory rate, to reduce the P_{CO_2} level

---

This uterine enlargement is accomplished by hyperplasia, hypertrophy, and stretching. The uterine wall is thickened and enlarged by marked hypertrophy and stretching of the muscle cells. The strength of the uterine wall is reinforced by an increased amount of fibrous and connective tissue. Blood vessels and lymphatics increase in number as the uterus grows and hypertrophy of the nerve supply to the uterus occurs.

Hyperplasia is most prominent during the first 6 weeks of gestation, with some hypertrophy and considerable hyperemia present. This phase of myometrial growth is a result of stimulation by estrogen and progesterone, rather than the effect of the conceptus, for this enlargement occurs even with an ectopic pregnancy. Estrogen primes the myometrium by promoting protein synthesis, thus increasing water content and some mitotic activity. Progesterone can then greatly enhance uterine mitotic activity.

After the first trimester, hyperplasia diminishes. Hypertrophy is predominant in the myometrial changes during the mid-trimester. During the last trimester, stretching accounts for the remaining increase in size. Mechanical distention caused by the growing fetus provides a patent stimulus for hypertrophy, stretching, and an increase in vascularity. In the last weeks of gestation, stretching and thinning of the uterine wall occur because of the rapid growth of the fetus and the resultant increase in intrauterine pressure.

Shape and Position

The uterus becomes too large to remain in the pelvis after the 12th week of gestation. A steady growth continues as pregnancy advances, with a slight rotation to the right. Tension is exerted on the broad and round ligaments as the uterus ascends.

The abdominal wall provides support for the uterus. The uterus grows toward the abdominal wall, displacing the intestines laterally and superiorly, especially when the woman is standing. When the pregnant woman lies supine, the enlarged uterus rests upon the vertebral column and the adjacent great vessels, the inferior vena cava and the aorta. The uterus is quite mobile, as the lower segment is the only portion firmly anchored to the cervical connections.

Contractility

Uterine contractions, which occur as often as three to four per minute during ovulation, are suppressed during pregnancy by progesterone. After the 12th week of gestation, irregular and painless uterine contractions of low intensity may be detected. The relaxed uterus becomes firm for a few seconds and then becomes relaxed again. These are called Braxton Hicks contractions. They become more frequent and regular during the last few weeks of gestation. They may occur as often as every 10 to 20 minutes and may cause some discomfort and be mistaken for labor. Uterine contractility may be enhanced during febrile states, urinary tract infections, and orgasm.[6] The frequency and intensity of uterine contractions increase as term gestation is reached and progesterone levels decline. The myometrium likewise becomes more sensitive to oxytocin.

Uterine Blood Flow

Uterine blood flow (UBF) increases progressively during pregnancy. Approximate ranges of the increase are (1) 10 weeks' gestation—50 mL/min, (2) 16 weeks' gestation—75 mL/min, (3) 28 weeks' gestation—185 mL/min, and (4) 40 weeks' gestation—500 mL/min.[6]

These figures do not reflect actual values except to demonstrate that the progressive increase for the number was obtained from anesthetized women in the supine position. Both anesthesia and supine position decrease cardiac output and thereby decrease uterine blood flow.

The major source of the uterine blood supply is the uterine arteries, which branch off the internal iliac arteries. The uterine arteries lie along the broad ligaments and enter the uterus close to the level of the internal os of the cervix. They then ascend on each side of the uterus and form a network of spiral arterioles to provide the blood supply to the uterus. The blood vessels increase considerably in both size and number during gestation.

There is a major decrease in uterine vascular resistance since UBF rises despite minor changes in maternal blood pressure. Major expansion of the uterine vascular beds, especially in the area of the intervillous space, contributes to this decreased vascular resistance in the uterine circulation. Changes also occur in the vessel walls to further decrease uterine vascular resistance. The spiral arteries lose some of their constrictive ability and therefore decrease their vascular resistance. Fortunately, proximal segments of the uteroplacental arteries retain their vasoconstrictive abilities.[7]

The increase in estrogens and progesterone that accompanies pregnancy probably contributes to the increased UBF during pregnancy. Endocrine factors are probably responsible for the changes in the walls of the blood vessels.

The uterine venous system makes great adjustments for pregnancy. Uterine veins increase in size and may dilate up to 60 times larger than in the prepregnant state. This enlargement produces adequate venous drainage for the large uteroplacental blood flow. The ovarian veins also enlarge. Changes in the blood vessels are quickly reversed after delivery.

Cervix, Vagina, and Outlet

The increased vascularity and edema of the cervix and lower reproductive tract, along with hypertrophy and hyperplasia, result in numerous changes. As early as a month to 6 weeks after conception, the cervix is softened (Goodell's sign), and there is cyanosis of the cervical and vaginal mucosa (Chadwick's sign). Later changes include increased vaginal secretions, discernible vaginal artery pulsations, universal edema with a decrease in the vaginal rugations, and possibly vaginal and vulvar varicosities.

Substantial cervical hypertrophy occurs with gestation. Cervical mucosal glands proliferate. A honeycomb structure called the mucous plug is formed, with the spaces filled with thick mucus, which obstructs the cervical os. Cervical erosions in pregnancy represent an extension of the proliferating endocervical glands. Inflammation is rarely the cause of erosions during pregnancy.

The major component of the cervix is connective tissue, rich in collagen fibers. In late pregnancy, the cervix contains less collagen than in the prepregnant state, and the collagen fibers are swollen and loosely connected. As labor approaches, further softening of the cervix occurs. With cervical dilatation, the mucous plug is expelled.

Vaginal and cervical secretions increase. A somewhat thick, white discharge is characteristic. The pH is acidic, varying from 3.5 to 6, as a result of increased production of lactic acid from glycogen in the vaginal epithelium. This acidic environment alters the growth of pathogenic bacteria in the vagina.

Breasts

Hormonal influences cause profound changes in the breasts during pregnancy. In anticipation of lactation, the breasts are prepared anatomically and physiologically. Breast growth is accelerated as the number and size of the ducts and lobules increase. Alveolar hypertrophy causes feelings of tingling, heightened sensitivity, and fullness as early as the second month of pregnancy.

Vascularity increases, and veins become visible just beneath the skin. The nipples and areolae become larger and more deeply pigmented. Montgomery's glands appear as small elevations in the areolae. These glands or follicles are hypertrophic sebaceous glands and produce a natural lubricating oil for the breasts.

The increased ductal growth and sprouting are attributed to estrogen, and the increased lobular development is attributed to progesterone. Prolactin stimulates the glandular production of colostrum, and by the second trimester placental lactogen begins to stimulate the secretion of colostrum. Colostrum, a thick yellowish fluid, can often be expressed at this time with breast massage. By the end of pregnancy, many women leak colostrum.

Although development of the breasts for lactation is functionally complete by the end of the second trimester, there is a hormonal inhibition of lactation until after delivery of the placenta.

CARDIOVASCULAR SYSTEM

Changes that occur in the cardiovascular system during pregnancy are so significant and extensive that this system is described as hyperdynamic during gestation. Hemodynamics are altered to protect both mother and fetus. The mother's normal functions continue as her body adapts to meet the demands of pregnancy and provide nutrients and elimination for the fetus (Table 1-3).

Table 1-3 Summary of Cardiovascular Changes during Gestation

Parameter	Direction of Changes	Average Change
Blood volume	⇑	35%
Plasma volume	⇑	45%
Red cell volume	⇑	20%
Cardiac output	⇑	40%
Stroke volume	⇑	30%
Heart rate	⇑	15%
Workload of heart	⇑	40%
Total peripheral resistance	⇓	15%
Mean arterial blood pressure	⇓	15 torr
Systolic blood pressure	⇓	3–5 torr
Diastolic blood pressure	⇓	5–10 torr
Central venous pressure	No change	
Femoral venous pressure	⇑	15 torr

Heart

The progressively enlarging uterus elevates the diaphragm, displacing the heart to the left and upward. This displacement results in a slight anterior rotation. The extent of the posterior change varies in patients according to body build, uterine size and position, and strength of abdominal muscles.[8]

Cardiac volume increases about 10% (75 mL) between early and late pregnancy. This increase probably occurs as a result of cardiac hypertrophy and increased cardiac filling because of increased blood volume and cardiac stroke volume.

Auscultatory changes occur during normal pregnancy. While the second heart sound remains normal, there is a pronounced splitting of the first heart sound, and a third heart sound is common.[8] A systolic murmur is present in 90% of pregnant women. This murmur disappears soon after delivery. The increased breast vasculature produces a continuous murmur in some women. There are no characteristic changes in the electrocardiogram (ECG) with pregnancy.

The heart rate increases 10 to 15 beats per minute by the 14th to 20th weeks of pregnancy and remains at that rate until delivery. Heart rate slows following delivery to accommodate the decreased volume load at this time. This decrease may persist for the 1st week postpartum.

Hemodynamics

Cardiac Output

Cardiac output increases 30% to 50% during gestation. This increase in cardiac output occurs rather rapidly in pregnancy. It increases 20% to 25% during the first trimester, reaches a peak level by the end of the second trimester, and remains at this level until term. Normal cardiac output at term is 6.2 ± 1.0 L/min.[9]

Values in cardiac output vary according to the maternal position. During late pregnancy, cardiac output is less in the supine position than in the lateral recumbent. At term, cardiac output in the supine position is less than that of a nonpregnant woman. Cardiac output in the sitting position is intermediate between supine and lateral recumbency. The decrease in cardiac output in the supine position is due to obstruction of the inferior vena cava by the gravid uterus, with a resultant decrease in venous blood return to the heart.

Changes in heart rate (HR) or stroke volume (SV) will affect the cardiac output (CO). The increase in cardiac output with gestation is the result of an increase in both the heart rate and stroke volume. In the first half of pregnancy, the increased cardiac output is due mainly to increased stroke volume. In late pregnancy, the increased cardiac output is due mainly to an increased heart rate.

Increased cardiac output during pregnancy imposes an increased workload on the mother's heart. The workload is proportional to the cardiac output and mean arterial blood pressure. Since mean arterial blood pressure is altered very little during pregnancy, the basal workload of the mother's heart increases practically to the same degree as the cardiac output. If the cardiac output increases 40%, then the basal workload of the heart increases 40%.

Physical activity and exercise add to the basal workload of the heart. In early pregnancy, the energy cost of exercise for the pregnant woman is similar to that for the nonpregnant woman. Exercise increases cardiac demand. However, during late pregnancy, the energy cost increases for the gravida because of her extra weight, greater cardiac demand, and greater ventilatory response to exercise. Therefore, identical activity for the woman in late pregnancy produces a greater workload for her heart.[9]

Normal, healthy expectant mothers adjust readily to the additional workload of pregnancy, even with added exercise. But if the pregnant woman has a cardiac problem, the added workload can precipitate complications, especially between the 26th and 34th weeks of gestation, when blood volume reaches its peak and cardiac load reaches a high level.[10]

During labor and delivery, maternal hemodynamics are further altered depending on maternal position, type of anesthesia, and method of delivery.

With each uterine contraction, 300 to 500 mL of blood is expelled from the uterus, temporarily increasing systemic blood volume and raising central venous pressure. Labor in a lateral recumbent position produces fewer hemodynamic changes than in the supine position. In the supine position, the inferior vena cava is occluded by the gravid uterus. In addition to this venous obstruction, labor contractions in the supine position produce occlusion of the distal aorta and/or the common iliac arteries. This allows the arterial blood from the left ventricle to be circulated only to the upper half of the vascular tree.

Anesthesia modifies the cardiovascular response to labor and delivery significantly. Patients who receive local or paracervical anesthesia show a progressive rise in cardiac output during labor. Patients who receive caudal (epidural) anesthesia show a more stable cardiac output. Anesthesia does not modify the profound changes that accompany the bearing down efforts of delivery. All patients show large increases in cardiac output from the second stage to delivery.[11]

Cesarean delivery eliminates the increase in cardiac output that accompanies the bearing down efforts but cannot prevent the significant increment that follows delivery.

Immediately after delivery there is a dramatic rise in cardiac output. The contracted uterus shunts blood from the uterine vessels into the systemic circulation; the uterus is emptied of the fetal-placental unit, releasing that blood into the systemic circulation; and pressure from the heavy, gravid uterus is relieved, allowing blood flow from the lower extremities to improve and increase the venous return to the heart. This results in approximately a 1000-mL autotransfusion at the time of delivery.

A blood loss larger than the normal 300 to 500 mL reduces total blood volume. The loss at cesarean section is approximately 1000 mL, which results in a reduced autotransfusion and fewer hemodynamic changes.

An average increase in cardiac output of about 13% occurs after delivery and persists for about 1 week. The increased cardiac output is prolonged if the mother is breastfeeding.[12]

Blood Pressure

Blood pressure falls somewhat in the first trimester, reaches its lowest levels in the second trimester, and then rises toward the prepregnant level during the last 2 months of gestation. Average values for the decrease range 3 to 5 mm Hg for systolic pressure and 5 to 10 mm Hg for diastolic pressure. The pulse pressure widens slightly during the first two trimesters but returns to prepregnant values at term.

Venous pressures in the legs increase progressively during pregnancy, but arm and central venous pressures do not. This effect is due to the compression of the pelvic veins and inferior vena cava by the uterus. The elevated femoral pressure returns to its normal level at delivery.

Systemic Vascular Resistance

Systemic vascular resistance (SVR) is decreased during pregnancy. The two most important factors that reduce peripheral vascular resistance are dilatation of peripheral blood vessels and the presence of the placental vascular system.

The placental vascular bed is a low-resistance network that utilizes a large portion of the maternal cardiac output. Uterine veins increase enormously in size and number during gestation. Uterine vascular resistance is greatly decreased during pregnancy, facilitating the profound increase in uterine blood flow during pregnancy.

Progesterone produces relaxation of smooth muscles, including the muscular walls of blood vessels. The vascular tone is then decreased, and the vessels dilate to increase their capacity. This increased ability for vasodilatation increases the peripheral blood flow.

Regional Distribution of Blood Flow

Uterus. Uterine blood flow increases progressively and receives about one third of the extra volume at term. This flow is facilitated by the low-resistance network of the uteroplacental circulation.

Kidneys. The kidneys have an increased blood flow of about 400 mL/min. The increased blood flow begins early in pregnancy, to enhance elimination.

Breasts and Pelvic Organs. Blood flow to the breasts and pelvic organs also increases. Hyperemia of the cervix and vagina is seen. Increased blood flow to the breasts is demonstrated in the newly visible veins, glandular growth, and engorgement.

Venous Pooling and Edema of the Legs

The relaxed walls of the veins facilitate a progressive increase in the capacity for pooling blood in the lower part of the body, especially when the woman is in an upright position. Varicose veins in the legs and vulva and hemorrhoids can develop as a result of vasodilatation, increased pressure, and stagnation of blood. Although the hypervolemia of pregnancy fills the increased vascular area in the legs to keep the circulation normal, venous pooling reduces the amount of venous return to the heart.

The upright position during the last half of pregnancy produces increased venous pressure in the femoral and other leg veins because of the pressure of the gravid uterus. This increases the capillary pressure in the legs. During this same period of pregnancy, there is a fall in the plasma colloid oncotic pressure. These two factors permit fluid to shift from the capillaries to the extravascular space, leading to edema of the feet and legs. Dependent edema of the legs is therefore common during pregnancy. Dependent edema can be minimized by avoiding standing or sitting for long periods of time, by walking around frequently, and by sitting with the feet elevated several times a day. Positioning in the lateral recumbent position mobilizes the fluid. Pedal edema usually worsens during the day and is alleviated during the night.

Postural Hypotension and Syncope

Compensatory mechanisms usually counteract the effects of gravity when the recumbent woman stands so that blood does not pool in the legs. However, the pregnant woman has a greater tendency for pooling of venous blood, and her compensatory mechanisms may not be able to restore normal circulation as quickly as is necessary. She may, therefore, experience marked hypotension and syncope when she stands up because of the decreased blood return to the heart and decreased cardiac output.

A supine hypotensive syndrome with dizziness, pallor, tachycardia, sweating, nausea, and hypotension can occur when the pregnant woman lies on her back (supine position). The heavy, gravid uterus compresses the descending aorta and inferior vena cava. This results in a pooling of blood in the legs, a decrease in venous return to the heart, a fall in cardiac output, and hypotension. The blood pressure may drop precipitously, and severe hypotension with shock may develop. This can result in fetal distress because of the decreased perfusion to the uteroplacental-fetal unit. Turning the mother to her side immediately will quickly restore the pooled blood to the circulation.[4]

All pregnant women do not develop signs of severe hypotension in the supine position, but the potential exists. When a pregnant women must lie on her back, a large towel or small blanket should be folded and placed under either hip to position the uterus off the large vessels.

When the aorta is compressed by the enlarged uterus, pressure in the uterine arteries is reduced. Maternal blood pressure is usually measured in the brachial artery in the arm. The brachial artery is not affected by the compression of the descending aorta. Therefore, measurement of blood pressure in the brachial artery is not indicative of the uterine arterial blood pressure. Blood pressure in the uterine arteries can be extremely low even when the maternal blood pressure measures normal.[7]

Labor in a lateral position provides optimum uteroplacental-fetal perfusion. When the woman changes from the supine to a lateral position, there may be a 30% to 50% increase in cardiac output and in uterine and renal blood flow.

Blood Volume

Maternal blood volume increases markedly during gestation. Expansion in blood volume can be detected by the 12th week. It reaches a maximum volume by 32 to 34 weeks' gestation and maintains that level until after delivery. Blood volume then falls and returns to the prepregnant level within 2 to 3 weeks postpartum.

The rise in total blood volume averages 30% to 40%, with a mean of 35%. The increase in total volume for a single pregnancy is between 1000 and 1500 mL. The rise in total blood volume for multiple gestation is much greater. Rovinsky and Jaffin[13] reported a progressive rise from a level of 42% at 21 to 24 weeks' gestation to a peak rise of 67% at 37 to 40 weeks' gestation. The expansion in blood volume results from an increase in both plasma volume and red cell mass.

Hypervolemia of pregnancy is the result of major changes in fluid balance. Elevated levels of estrogens and progesterone increase plasma renin activity and aldosterone levels to promote sodium retention and an increase in total body water. Tubular sodium reabsorption rises.

During a normal pregnancy about 950 mEq of sodium along with an additional 6 to 8 L of total body water is retained, 4 of which are extracellular.[14] This increase in extracellular volume is required for optimal uteroplacental perfusion.

Relaxation of the venous walls increases the capacity of the veins to provide space for the increased plasma volume and body water. The expanded volume also helps to compensate for the poor venous return from the lower extremities.

RESPIRATORY SYSTEM

Respiration includes the transfer of oxygen from the air to the blood in the pulmonary capillaries and the transfer to and consumption of oxygen by the peripheral tissues. Respiratory adjustments are made during pregnancy to meet both maternal and fetal needs. The fetus must obtain oxygen and eliminate carbon dioxide through the mother. The maternal oxygen requirements increase in response to the increased growth and metabolism in the maternal body.

Even before there is much upward pressure exerted by the enlarging uterus, the diaphragm rises about 4 cm, causing a decrease in the length of the lungs. To compensate for this shortening of the lungs, the transverse and anteroposterior diameters of the chest enlarge by 2 cm. The lower ribs flare out progressively during pregnancy, and the substernal angle widens 50% (from 70° in the first trimester to 105° at term). Overall, the increase of the thoracic cage circumference during pregnancy is 5 to 7 cm. The result is that essentially there is no change in the overall volume in the lungs. The increase in circumference compensates for the decreased length.[15] These changes in chest configuration begin early in pregnancy, before the possibility of mechanical pressure from the uterus. This suggests that hormonal involvement as well as enlargement in uterine size is responsible for these changes.

Breathing is more diaphragmatic than costal at any stage of pregnancy than in nonpregnant women.

Respiratory Function

Vital capacity, the maximum volume of gas that can be expired after a maximum inspiration, and maximum breathing capacity, the maximum voluntary ventilation, are not changed significantly in normal pregnancy. Lung compliance and specific airway conductance are also unchanged (Fig. 1-1).

There is a progressive increase in tidal volume, the volume of gas that is exchanged with each breath, that begins in the first trimester. There is only a slight rise in respiratory rate. Ventilation is increased due to the pregnant woman's breathing more deeply and a slight increase in respiratory rate.[15]

Minute ventilation, the volume of gas expired per minute, increases about 50% by the end of pregnancy as a result of the increase in tidal volume and respiratory rate. This increased alveolar ventilation at term is hyperventilation. The maternal $PaCO_2$ is usually decreased to about 32 torr. Maternal alkalosis is not present because of a compensatory increase in renal excretion of bicarbonate. This results in a decreased serum bicarbonate level of about 4 mEq/L (from 26 to 22 mEq/L).[16] Hyperventilation results from the direct action of progesterone on the respiratory center. The decreased level of $PaCO_2$ in the maternal blood facilitates removal of fetal carbon dioxide to the maternal circulation. This higher fetal $PaCO_2$ concentration produces a gradient to the lower maternal $PaCO_2$.

During labor, particularly during transition and the second stage, ventilation may be increased as much as 300% as compared to the nonpregnant state.[16] Hypocarbia ($PaCO_2$ of 20 torr or less) and alkalemia can develop. The use of either proper breathing techniques (for the Lamaze patient) or epidural anesthesia help prevent this hyperventilation, which is largely caused by the pain felt during labor. This rapid, deep breathing during pregnancy enhances gas anesthesia, as more rapid induction and recovery from inhalation anesthesia occur.[15]

During the second half of pregnancy, the functional residual capacity, the volume of gas that remains in the lungs at the end of a normal expiration, becomes progressively smaller as the enlarging uterus elevates the diaphragm. The functional residual capacity is the volume of gas that is mixed with the inhaled air (tidal volume). Therefore, an increased volume of inhaled air is

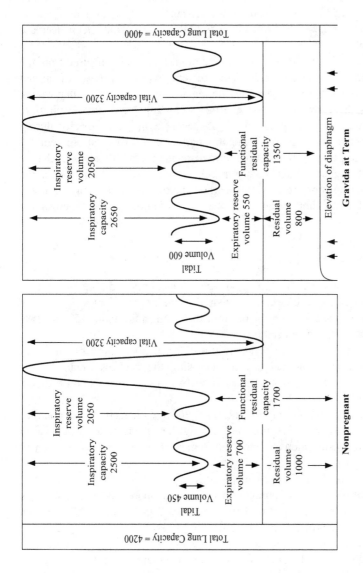

Figure 1-1 Pulmonary volumes and capacities during pregnancy, labor, and the postpartum period. *Source:* Reprinted from *Principles and Practice of Obstetric Analgesia and Anesthesia*, p 24, by JJ Bonica with permission of FA Davis Company, © 1967.

mixed with a smaller volume of gas in the lungs. This facilitates more efficient gas mixing. Thus alveolar ventilation is increased 65% to 70%.[16]

Airway resistance or conductance is not increased even with the reduced functional residual capacity. Usually there is increased airway resistance to airflow, with a smaller airway lumen. However, during pregnancy the increased progesterone level relaxes the bronchiolar smooth muscle, which helps decrease airway resistance.

Inspiratory capacity, the maximum volume of air that can be inspired from the resting expiratory level, increases. This offsets the decrease in functional residual capacity so that vital capacity, the maximum volume of air that can be expelled from the lungs by forceful effort following maximum inspiration, remains unchanged during pregnancy.[15] A decrease in vital capacity during pregnancy warrants investigation for a pulmonary or cardiovascular problem.

Adaptations in pulmonary function during pregnancy facilitate gas exchange to the fetus. A higher oxygen concentration is delivered to the placenta, the oxygen is given up more readily, and carbon dioxide is more easily removed from the fetal circulation because of the concentration gradient across the placenta.

Oxygen Consumption

There is a progressive increase in oxygen consumption during pregnancy, both at rest and during exercise, as compared to the nonpregnant state. By late pregnancy the increase is from 31 mL/min to 50 mL/min, about 15% to 25% more than in the nonpregnant state.

At term the fetus and placenta are responsible for about 50% of this extra oxygen consumption; maternal tissues, including the cardiovascular system, respiratory system, renal system, and reproductive system (uterus and breasts), use the other 50%.

During labor oxygen consumption increases 300% with each uterine contraction, from 250 mL/min to 750 mL/min. During the second stage of labor, the average oxygen consumption is almost 200% more than that of the term woman before labor begins.[16]

During gestation, the affinity of maternal hemoglobin for oxygen decreases, and the affinity of the fetal hemoglobin for oxygen increases. This facilitates oxygen exchange from mother to fetus by increasing the amount of oxygen released to fetal tissues at any level of maternal PaO_2.[17]

The decrease in functional residual capacity lowers the oxygen reserve. Endotracheal intubation of the pregnant woman is associated with a more sudden, severe drop in PaO_2 with only a short period of apnea. Increased oxygen consumption during labor aggravates the danger of the rapid development of hypoxia.[15]

Dyspnea

Dyspnea, the conscious need to breathe, develops in many pregnant women. Shortness of breath is considered a common discomfort of pregnancy. Dyspnea needs to be differentiated from hyperventilation, which is unconscious and effortless.

Dyspnea does not appear until after the first trimester. It may appear during exercise or at rest and may occur episodically. The heightened awareness of the need to breathe and the increased breathlessness on exertion appear to be due to the increased sensitivity of the respiratory center to the decreased alveolar carbon dioxide concentration.

Physiologic dyspnea is benign. Pathologic causes of dyspnea in pregnancy include severe anemia, pulmonary edema, acidosis, hydramnios, and cardiac problems.

RENAL SYSTEM

The mother's kidneys must handle the increased metabolic and circulatory requirements of her body and excrete the fetal waste products. Hormonal influences and alterations in other body systems affect renal function. Changes in renal function are so profound that they are only surpassed by those of the cardiovascular system.

The kidneys play a very vital role in maintaining homeostasis. The kidneys sustain electrolyte balance and acid-base balance, excrete waste products, regulate the extracellular fluid volume, and conserve essential nutrients. To accomplish these important functions, approximately 1000 to 1200 mL of blood flows through both kidneys each minute. This blood flow contains 500 to 600 mL of plasma that is filtered through the 2 million glomeruli in 1 minute. This glomerular filtrate, normally protein-free plasma, is modified through tubular reabsorption and tubular secretion.

Tubular function includes the processes that change the glomerular filtrate into urine. Almost all the filtered water, electrolytes, amino acids, and inorganic salts is reabsorbed. Unneeded and unwanted substances are excreted in about 1500 mL of urine each day.

Anatomy

The kidneys enlarge somewhat during gestation. This is probably due to hypertrophy and hyperemia rather than the development of new nephrons.[18] The renal pelves, calyces, and ureters become dilated as early as the 10th week of gestation. This is long before the uterus enlarges enough to cause mechanical compression. The dilatation is thought to be due to the smooth muscle relaxing effects of progesterone. In later pregnancy, the progressively enlarging uterus causes mechanical pressure on the ureters and bladder.

The ureters become more dilated and elongated. Kinking may be present. Hydronephrosis and hydroureter result because of the pressure exerted by the gravid uterus. Little change in the lumen of the ureters is seen below the pelvic brim. The dilatation of the right renal pelvis and ureter is greater than that on the left. This unequal dilatation is due to the cushioning of the left side.[18]

After the fourth month of pregnancy the bladder is affected. The increasing size of the uterus, along with the hyperemia of all pelvic organs and the hyperplasia of all muscle and connective tissues, elevates the trigone and causes thickening of the interureteric margin. This process progresses as pregnancy advances, and a marked deepening and widening of the trigone results.

After engagement occurs, the bladder is pushed forward and upward, changing its normally convex surface into concave. This makes diagnostic procedures difficult. The length of the urethra increases. Pressure from the presenting part can interfere with drainage of blood and lymph from the base of the bladder, making the area edematous, easily traumatized, and susceptible to infection.

Function

Blood flow through the kidneys increases between 25% and 50% during gestation. This is a rise from the nonpregnant level of 1000 mL/min to 1250 to 1500 mL/min.

The glomerular filtration rate (GFR) (the amount of plasma filtered by the glomeruli of both kidneys per minute) increases by approximately 50%. This is a rise from the nonpregnant level of 100 to 125 mL/min to as high as 140 to 170 mL/min.[19]

The renal plasma flow (RPF) (the volume of plasma flowing through the kidneys every minute) increases by approximately 35%. This is a rise from the nonpregnant level of 500 to 600 mL/min to between 700 and 900 mL/min.

Both the GFR and RPF begin to rise after the 12th week of gestation; the eventual peak rates for each (as measured in the lateral recumbent position) are maintained until term. Studies done with the pregnant woman in the supine position report a decrease in GFR and RPF in late pregnancy.[6]

These changes are considered mainly to result from the growth hormone effect of placental lactogen. Other factors include the increase in blood volume of pregnancy; an increased cardiac output with a lowered peripheral vascular resistance in the kidneys, to accommodate the increased flow; and possibly the elevated levels of plasma cortisol.[20]

Since the GFR increases by a greater proportion during pregnancy than does the RPF (50% as compared to 35%), the proportion of plasma that is filtered increases (filtration fraction). Therefore, the serum protein concentration in plasma is lower by about 1 g/L. This change decreases the plasma oncotic pressure by about 20%. This decreased colloid oncotic pressure facilitates the increased filtration of plasma by the kidneys.

As a result of the increased GFR and RPF, the renal clearance of many substances is elevated during pregnancy, with a corresponding decrease in serum levels (Table 1-4).

Creatinine, urea, and uric acid are excreted more effectively in pregnancy. Serum values for these substances are only about two thirds of the nonpregnant values. Therefore, values that are considered normal for other adults usually signify decreased renal function during pregnancy.[19]

Sodium Retention

The sodium content in the body is kept within very narrow limits by the regulatory functions of the kidneys. Increases in sodium intake or losses of sodium are compensated by changes in tubular reabsorption to keep the sodium level carefully balanced. Tubular reabsorption is quickly adjusted to changes in the filtered load of sodium.

In normal persons, the regulatory mechanisms function well. Balance is maintained even with marked changes such as vomiting, diarrhea, sweating, or marked dietary changes. Regulation of the sodium balance during pregnancy is

Table 1-4 Summary of Changes in Selected Blood and Urine Laboratory Values

		Nonpregnant	*Pregnant*
Blood	Serum creatinine	0.67 mg/dL	0.46 mg/dL
	Blood urea nitrogen	13 mg/dL	8.2 mg/dL
	Uric Acid	4.5 mg/dL	3.1 mg/dL
Urine	Creatinine clearance	65–145 mL/min	150–200 mL/min
	Urea		⇑
	Uric acid		⇑
	Amino acids		⇑
	Water-soluble vitamins		⇑
	Glucose		⇑

more difficult than in the nonpregnant state. There is a tendency to sodium depletion. This can become a major problem if salt is restricted or diuretics used.

There is a gradual, cumulative retention of sodium during pregnancy, reaching a total serum value of 950 mEq as blood volume increases.[14] This increased amount does not change the maternal electrolyte balance; rather, it maintains it. The average daily diet contains 100 to 300 mEq; therefore, getting the recommended daily increase of 3 mEq is easy.

The retained sodium is necessary to meet fetal needs and to maintain the maternal isotonic state. Increased sodium is necessary to maintain the expanded fluid volume. During gestation the increased interstitial and intravascular fluid volumes require additional sodium to provide a normal isotonic state.

The increased GFR in pregnancy is accompanied by a corresponding increase in tubular reabsorption of sodium, since depletion would otherwise occur.

Progesterone stimulates the excretion of sodium, while aldosterone enhances the tubular reabsorption of sodium. Since progesterone production is greatly increased during pregnancy, increased amounts of aldosterone I and II are necessary to counterbalance the effects of progesterone. Renin, a proteolytic enzyme, is secreted by the juxtaglomerular apparatus of the nephrons. Renin activates renin substrate to produce angiotensin. Angiotensin regulates aldosterone secretion by the adrenal cortex. Aldosterone then stimulates the tubular reabsorption of sodium.

Hormones that stimulate sodium retention include estrogen, placental HCS, prolactin, and cortisol.[19]

The decrease in plasma albumin and the low serum colloid oncotic pressure during pregnancy, in conjunction with decreased vascular resistance, enhance the excretion of sodium.

Glycosuria

During gestation there is no glomerular-tubular balancing mechanism for glucose and amino acids such as the one for sodium. Glycosuria occurs frequently in normal pregnancy. Glycosuria occurs as a result of the greatly increased GFR combined with the inability of the renal tubules to increase reabsorption enough to keep up with the increase in glomerular filtration.[19] The tubular maximum for glucose reabsorption does not change in pregnancy; therefore, excess glucose is excreted in the urine. The incidence of glycosuria increases as pregnancy advances.

While glycosuria is considered somewhat normal in pregnancy, it cannot be ignored. Physiologic glycosuria must be differentiated from pregnancy-induced diabetes mellitus. Some authorities feel that glycosuria in pregnancy that is not due to diabetes mellitus denotes a pre-existing deficiency in tubular function that is aggravated by gestation.[19]

Proteinuria

Proteins (albumin, globulin) are abnormal in the urine. Proteinuria is an important sign of renal disease. Protein excretion in the nonpregnant state is abnormal when the total daily excretion exceeds 150 mg. During normal pregnancy, more protein may be excreted because of the increased GFR. An amount over 250 mg/d is considered abnormal during pregnancy and may denote the presence of preeclampsia, renal disease, or urinary tract infection.

GASTROINTESTINAL SYSTEM

Changes in the function of the gastrointestinal system during gestation present a diverse picture. The appetite increases to provide nutrients for mother and fetus. Nausea and vomiting may occur, especially in the first trimester. Gastrointestinal motility is reduced, with resultant problems, including heartburn, constipation, and flatulence. Intestinal secretion is reduced, and digestion is slowed; however, absorption of nutrients is enhanced. These alterations are due mainly to the increased levels of progesterone and estrogen during pregnancy, with the increasing size of the gravid uterus contributing to some of the changes.

Mouth

Hyperemia of the gums occurs frequently, making the gums bleed easily. Gingivitis with edematous, spongy gums may occur, with increased tooth mobility and some loosening of attachment. The pH of the saliva decreases, and the frequency of dental caries may increase. Increased salivation (ptyalism) occurs in some gravidas.

Stomach

The position of the stomach is changed because of the enlarging gravid uterus. This alters the angle of the gastroesophageal junction, and the lower esophageal sphincter may be displaced into the thorax. This frequently causes incompetence of the gastroesophageal pinchcock mechanism so that the gravida is prone to passive regurgitation and aspiration during general anesthesia or during unconsciousness from any cause. Gastric motility and emptying time are also reduced during gestation. This further increases her risk of pulmonary aspiration, with the development of the acid aspiration syndrome.

These changes also commonly lead to heartburn, which is due to regurgitation of gastric contents into the esophagus. Relief measures include small, frequent meals, remaining upright for 2 hours after eating, and avoidance of spicy and fatty foods.

The hormone gastrin, produced by the placenta, raises the acid, chloride, and enzyme contents of the stomach during pregnancy to levels above those of the nonpregnant state. Studies show that parturients having an elective cesarean section after an overnight fast still have greater than 25 mL of gastric juices with a pH less than 2.5 present in the stomach at the time of surgery.

Small and Large Intestines

Increased progesterone levels during pregnancy produce a general relaxation of tone of the entire gastrointestinal tract. Motility of the small and large intestines is decreased. Increased progesterone levels also cause an increase in water absorption from the colon, producing dryer, firmer stools. Flatulence and constipation are common problems during pregnancy. Relief measures for constipation include a high-fiber diet, exercise, adequate fluid intake, and good bowel habits. Relief measures for flatulence include avoiding gas-forming foods, fats, and large meals. Increased activity and regular bowel habits also help.

Nausea (Morning Sickness)

Nausea, with or without vomiting, is common in early pregnancy and occurs to some degree in about one half of all pregnant women. Symptoms vary from slight nausea on awakening to persistent and frequent vomiting throughout the day. Nausea and/or vomiting may appear at any time of the day, but it is most common in the morning hours and thereby is termed "morning sickness." It usually occurs during the first trimester and ends between the 12th to 14th weeks of gestation. The high level of HCG during the first trimester is thought to be the primary cause, along with the increased levels of estrogens.

Relief measures include eating small, frequent meals, eating dry crackers before arising in the morning, consuming something sweet (fruit or fruit juices) before arising, and avoiding spicy or acidic foods and foods with strong odors. Most pregnant women discover what works best for them and manage until the nausea and vomiting are relieved after the first trimester. Severe nausea and vomiting sometimes occur. Hyperemesis gravidarum (pernicious vomiting of pregnancy) can lead to dehydration and starvation. This condition is a severe complication and is life threatening for mother and fetus.

Hemorrhoids

Hemorrhoids are a common problem in late pregnancy and the early puerperium. Many factors contribute to the development of hemorrhoids, including hyperemia, general pelvic congestion, and obstruction of venous return to the heart by the gravid uterus, causing increased hemorrhoidal vein pressure. Hard stools and straining with constipation aggravate this situation. Hemorrhoids can be especially severe following delivery after a long second stage of labor with extended pushing efforts. Once hemorrhoids occur, a hot sitz bath followed by application of a local anesthetic ointment will help to relieve the discomfort. Correcting constipation will help to improve the problem.

HEPATIC SYSTEM

Liver

During normal pregnancy, liver size and morphology do not change. However, liver function during gestation is altered, as evidenced by changes in values for liver function tests. Many of the changes in serum values during gestation would be suggestive of liver disease in the nonpregnant individual.[21]

Gallbladder

High progesterone levels during the second and third trimesters result in decreased gallbladder activity, causing the gallbladder to become hypotonic and distended during pregnancy. Emptying is slow, and after the 12th week of gestation volume during fasting and after a meal is twice as large for the pregnant as for the nonpregnant woman.[22] Retention of cholesterol crystals can then occur because of the faulty emptying of the gallbladder, leading to an increased incidence of gallstone formation.[22]

METABOLIC CHANGES

Profound metabolic changes occur in pregnancy to allow growth and development of the fetus and to buffer it from internal and external environmental stresses. Higher levels of circulating insulin and relative fasting and nocturnal hypoglycemia occur with normal pregnancy. Maternal metabolic homeostasis continues in the presence of high serum concentrations of placental lactogen, estrogens, progesterone, ACTH, cortisol, and lipids, in addition to quantitative shifts in amino acid and lipid levels.[23]

The placenta plays a central role in metabolism. It has the capacity to synthesize steroid and peptide hormones, to modulate and transport nutrients to the fetus, to transfer gases and water, to eliminate waste products of fetal metabolism, and to facilitate maternal metabolic adaptations to the different stages of pregnancy.

The fetus also participates in its growth and development, probably by determining the metabolic use of maternal nutrients.

Weight Gain

The increased maternal metabolism and organ growth, along with fetal growth and development, create the need for additional energy during gestation. Pitkin[24] reports that caloric expenditure is not evenly distributed during gestation. It increases only slightly during the first 9 weeks of gestation, then increases sharply and remains fairly constant until term.

This results in a relatively steady calorie expenditure during the last 30 weeks of gestation, so that the cumulative energy cost of gestation has been calculated as 75,000 kcal. Dividing this figure by 250 days gives 300 kcal/day.

Weight gain represents energy intake that exceeds energy expenditures. The total weight gain of the normal gravida at term is usually between 24 and 30 pounds. However, the pattern of the weight accumulation is more important than the weight gain itself. The usual pattern shows a gain of 2 to 4 pounds during the first trimester, followed by a steady, progressive gain of 0.8 to 1.0 pound per week during the second and third trimesters.[25]

The components and pattern of weight gain are illustrated in Figure 1-2. Weight gain in the second trimester shows dominant growth in the maternal body (blood volume expansion, uterus and breast enlargement, body stores and fluid). Weight gain during the third trimester shows dominant fetal growth (fetus, placenta, and amniotic fluid) (Table 1-5).

Numerous studies have demonstrated a strong correlation between total weight gain and birth weight. The underweight gravida is at high risk for a low birth weight infant, as is the gravida with inadequate weight gain during pregnancy. Recent studies do not support the correlation of excessive weight gain and preeclampsia. Excessive weight gain results in excessive fat deposition that can be difficult to lose following delivery.

Maternal weight loss during pregnancy is not recommended since potential maternal ketonemia may occur if there is inadequate carbohydrate intake to meet fuel requirements. Maternal ketonemia results in fetal ketonemia since ketones cross the placenta readily. Fetal ketonemia is associated with mental retardation.[3]

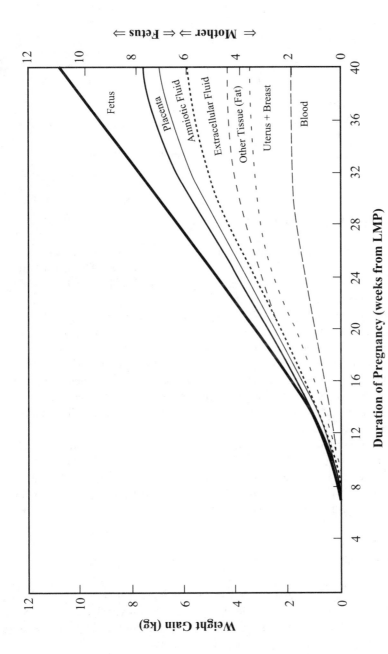

Figure 1-2 Pattern and components of average maternal weight gain during pregnancy. *Source:* Reprinted with permission from *Clinical Obstetrics and Gynecology* (1976;19[3]:491), Copyright © 1976, JB Lippincott Company.

Table 1-5 Weight Gain

Fetus	7 1/2
Placenta	1 1/2
Amniotic Fluid	2
Uterus	2 1/2
Breasts	1
Blood	3 1/2
Fluid Retention	2
Body Stores	4–8
	24–28

MUSCULOSKELETAL SYSTEM

During pregnancy there is a softening and relaxation of the interosseous ligaments of many joints as a result of both estrogens and relaxin. This causes an increased mobility of the sacroiliac, sacrococcygeal, and symphysis pubis joints. There is a tendency to develop flat feet.

The increased size and weight of the gravid uterus shift the gravida's center of gravity. Balance is then maintained by increasing the normal amount of lumbar lordosis via a forward tilt of the pelvis, which strains the sacroiliac joints. Low back pain is therefore common in pregnancy in the last trimester. If the abdominal muscles were in poor tone prior to pregnancy, the abdomen will protrude noticeably as the uterus enlarges, necessitating an even greater degree of forward tilt of the pelvis and leading to increased strain at the sacroiliac joints and progressive lordosis.

Relief measures include (1) "walking tall," with pelvis tilted forward, buttocks tucked under, shoulders held back, and head held up; (2) use of good body mechanics; (3) the pelvic rock exercise; (4) wearing medium- to low-heel shoes; (5) use of a firm mattress or bed board; and (6) wearing a maternity girdle when extreme lordosis or multiple pregnancy is present.

NERVOUS SYSTEM

Normal pregnancy is not associated with characteristic changes in the nervous system. However, some pregnant women report discomforts that are associated with this system. Major problems are associated with neurologic complications not considered normal physiologic changes of pregnancy.

Headaches

Many pregnant women complain of minor headaches during the first and second trimesters. The pain is usually frontal and mild. The cause is probably hormonal since in most cases no other cause is present; however, some headaches are due to stress, eye strain, sinusitis, or emotional factors. Tension headache is more common when anxiety or emotional distress is present. Severe headache after the 20th week of gestation can occur with preeclampsia. The headache in preeclampsia is caused by cerebral edema resulting from vasoconstriction.

Dizziness

Dizziness and even vertigo can occur in early pregnancy in the healthy woman as a result of pooling of blood in the lower legs, viscera, and pelvic areas, especially after prolonged sitting or standing in a warm room. Hypotension results in transient cerebral oligemia, and fainting or feelings of dizziness occur. When dizziness occurs, the woman should put her head lower than her knees or lie in the lateral recumbent position. Hypoglycemia during the first trimester can also result in the woman's feeling lightheaded and shaky.

Paresthesias (Numbness and Tingling of Fingers and Toes)

Paresthesias of the fingers and upper extremities can occur if lumbar lordosis is extremely exaggerated. When this posture is accompanied by flexion of the head and neck and slumping of the shoulders, traction is placed on the ulnar and median nerves. This can cause aching, numbness, and weakness of the arms and hands.

Paresthesias of the toes and legs can occur if the heavy gravid uterus exerts pressure on the femoral veins and nerves, thus interfering with circulation to the lower extremities. Excessive hyperventilation results in lowered PCO_2 levels. This can cause vasoconstriction and tingling in the hands.

Edema involving the peripheral nerves in the arms and hands can result in carpal tunnel syndrome. The edema compresses the median nerve beneath the carpal ligament of the wrist. Paresthesias and pain that can radiate to the elbow occur. The dominant hand is usually the most affected.

Cerebrovascular Events

Pregnancy increases the risk of cerebrovascular events, particularly those of an ischemic nature. Reports include transient ischemic attacks, reversible ischemic neurologic deficits, cerebral infarction, and intracranial hemorrhage.[26]

Rupture of cerebral and splenic artery aneurysms is most likely to occur in females under 45 years of age during pregnancy. The chance of rupture increases with each week of gestation, since the vascular walls are weakened by pregnancy hormones, with a profound effect on arteries with an abnormal tunica media.

INTEGUMENTARY SYSTEM

Increased Blood Flow

Blood flow to the skin increases during pregnancy, especially in the extremities. Pregnant women complain of being warm and have difficulty tolerating heat. Their skin feels warm to touch, and their hands are usually clammy. Blood flow to the skin in pregnancy is estimated to be around 500 mL/min. Blood flow to the hands increases six to seven times over that in the nonpregnant state. Many pregnant women note an increase in fingernail growth as a result of this increased blood supply.

Increased blood flow to the skin begins in the first trimester, to eliminate the heat produced by the increased metabolism of the mother and fetus. Peripheral vasodilatation and an increase in the number of capillaries are involved in this increased blood flow. The skin temperature rises during gestation.

Vascular spiders and palmar erythema may develop. Hemangiomas may form on the face and hands; pre-existing ones may enlarge. Local vascular effects are probably due to elevated estrogen levels.

Hair Growth

The character of hair growth changes with pregnancy. There may be increased hair growth on the scalp, face, and body. As more hair is growing, fewer hairs are ready to fall out. Following delivery, which removes the placental hormones, growth of new hairs slows, and older hairs fall out in large numbers, especially the scalp hair. During pregnancy the active growth phase of hairs is prolonged; in the puerperium the stimulus to prolonged growth is removed, and hair is shed. The increased flow of blood to the skin is responsible for the growing phase.[27]

Striae Gravidarum

Striae gravidarum (stretch marks) may occur in the skin of the abdomen, breasts, hips, and upper part of the thighs. They are usually most pronounced on the abdomen. Striae are the result of distention of the skin in these areas by the enlarging uterus and breasts and by fat deposition, along with softening and relaxation of the dermal collagenous and elastic tissues during the last months of pregnancy.

Pigmentation

The nipples and areolar areas of the breasts become darker. The linea alba, the whitish line that divides the abdomen longitudinally from sternum to symphysis, becomes darker and is then known as the linea nigra. The line reverts to its white color following delivery.

Chloasma

Chloasma (mask of pregnancy) appears as irregularly shaped brown blotches on the face, with a masklike distribution on the cheekbones and forehead and around the eyes. Chloasma usually disappears after the pregnancy but may reappear with excessive sun exposure or with the administration of oral contraceptives.

Changes in skin pigmentation are thought be to caused by elevated serum levels of the pituitary hormone melanocyte-stimulating hormone (MSH), which begin increasing after the second month of gestation. Estrogen and progesterone also stimulate melanin deposition.

CONCLUSION

Profound and dramatic changes occur in maternal physiology as a result of pregnancy. The normal healthy woman is able to adapt to these changes without difficulty. However, the normal alterations of pregnancy can lead to severe problems for the pregnant woman at risk.

The normal 38- to 40-week pregnancy provides a relatively short period of time for the maternal body to adjust to the many and profound adaptations. However, even greater adjustment is necessary for the changes that occur during labor, as they occur in a remarkably short period of time. Adaptations continue following the pregnancy, as the body returns to its prepregnant state over approximately 6 weeks' time.

The majority of maternal physiologic alterations to pregnancy have been discussed in this chapter to increase the nurse's understanding of the physiology of pregnancy. This knowledge is the basis for providing care to the critically ill obstetric patient.

REFERENCES

1. Marrs RP, Mishell DR Jr. Placental trophic hormones. *Clin Obstet Gynecol.* 1980;23:721-735.
2. Tyson JE. Changing role of placental lactogen and prolactin in human gestation. *Clin Obstet Gynecol.* 1980;23:737-747.
3. Felig P. Body fuel metabolism and diabetes mellitus in pregnancy. *Med Clin North Am.* 1977; 61:43-66.
4. Pritchard JA, MacDonald PC. *Williams Obstetrics.* 16th ed. New York: Appleton-Century-Crofts; 1980:151.
5. Lawrence RA. *Breastfeeding: A Guide for the Medical Profession.* St. Louis: CV Mosby; 1980.
6. Martin C. Physiologic changes during pregnancy: the mother. In: Quilligan EJ, Kretchmer N, eds. *Fetal and Maternal Medicine.* New York: John Wiley & Sons; 1980:141-179.
7. Bieniarz J, Yoshida T, Romero Salinas G, Curuchet E, Caldeyro Barcia R, Crottogini JJ. Autocaval compression by the uterus in late human pregnancy, IV: circulatory homeostasis by preferential perfusion of the placenta. *Am J Obstet Gynecol.* 1969;103:19-31.
8. Gibbs CP. Maternal physiology. *Clin Obstet Gynecol.* 1981;24:525-543.
9. Clark SL, Cotton DB, Lee W, Bishop C, et al. Central hemodynamic assessment of normal term pregnancy. *Am J Obstet Gynecol.* 1989;161:1439-1442.
10. Ueland K, Novy MJ, Peterson EN, Metcalfe J. Maternal cardiovascular dynamics, IV: the influence of gestational age on the maternal cardiovascular response to posture and exercise. *Am J Obstet Gynecol.* 1969;104:856-864.
11. Ueland K, Hansen JM. Maternal cardiovascular dynamics, III: labor and delivery under local and caudal analgesia. *Am J Obstet Gynecol.* 1969;103:8-18.
12. Novy MJ. The puerperium. In: Benson RC, ed. *Current Obstetrics and Gynecologic Diagnosis and Treatment.* 5th ed. Los Altos, CA: Lange Medical Publications; 1984:839-868.
13. Rovinsky JJ, Jaffin H. Cardiovascular hemodynamics in pregnancy, I: blood and plasma volumes in multiple pregnancy. *Am J Obstet Gynecol.* 1965;93:1-15.
14. Lindheimer MD. Current concepts of sodium metabolism and use of diuretics in pregnancy. *Contemp OB/GYN.* 1980;15:207-216.
15. Bonica JJ. *Principles and Practice of Obstetric Analgesia and Anesthesia.* Vol. 1. Philadelphia: FA Davis; 1967:21-29.
16. Gutsche BB. Maternal physiologic alterations during pregnancy. In: Shnider SM, Levinson G, eds. *Anesthesia for Obstetrics.* Baltimore: Williams & Wilkins; 1979:3-11.
17. Bauer C, Ludwig M, Ludwig I, Bartels H. Factors governing the oxygen affinity of human adult and foetal blood. *Respir Physiol.* 1969;7:271-277.
18. Beydoun SN. Morphologic changes in the renal tract in pregnancy. *Clin Obstet Gynecol.* 1985;28:249-256.
19. Davidson JM. The physiology of the renal tract in pregnancy. *Clin Obstet Gynecol.* 1985;28:257-265.
20. Ueland K, Ueland FR. Physiologic adaptations to pregnancy. In: Knuppel RA, Drukker JE, eds. *High-Risk Pregnancy: A Team Approach.* Philadelphia: WB Saunders; 1986:148-172.
21. Bynum TE. Hepatic and gastrointestinal disorders in pregnancy. *Med Clin North Am.* 1977;61:129-138.
22. Braverman DZ, Johnson ML, Kern F Jr. Effects of pregnancy and contraceptive steroids on gallbladder function. *N Engl J Med.* 1980;302:362-364.
23. Hollingsworth DR. Maternal metabolism in normal pregnancy and pregnancy complicated by diabetes mellitus. *Clin Obstet Gynecol.* 1985;28:457-472.
24. Pitkin RM. Nutritional requirements in normal pregnancy. *Diabetes Care.* 1980;3:472-475.

25. Pitkin RM. Nutritional support in obstetrics and gynecology. *Clin Obstet Gynecol.* 1976;19:489-513.
26. Wiebers DO, Whisnant JP. The incidence of stroke among pregnant women in Rochester, Minnesota, 1955 through 1979. *JAMA.* 1985;254:3055-3057.
27. Rook A, Dawber R. *Diseases of the Hair and Scalp.* Boston: Blackwell Scientific Publications; 1982:123-124.

Chapter 2

Invasive Hemodynamic Monitoring in the Critically Ill or High-Risk Obstetric Patient

Roxelyn G. Baumgartner

Invasive hemodynamic monitoring is a valuable tool that is beneficial in the evaluation and management of high-risk and critically ill obstetric patients. Invasive hemodynamic monitoring is accompanied by a certain risk to the patient; however, when its use is indicated, it provides essential information unavailable by other techniques. The nurse should have a thorough understanding of the monitoring equipment and procedures and should pay careful attention to detail. Such informed, meticulous nursing care greatly improves the benefit/risk ratio associated with invasive monitoring.

INDICATIONS FOR USE

Rapidly evolving knowledge concerning the high-risk obstetric patient supports the use of invasive hemodynamic monitoring to guide and evaluate therapy in selected cases. Invasive hemodynamic monitoring, using pulmonary artery or other catheters, provides the health care team with objective, precise data permitting evaluation of cardiac function. First introduced in the 1970s, the pulmonary artery catheter has become an integral tool in the modern management of hemodynamic instability. The efficacy of invasive hemodynamic monitoring in the high-risk obstetric patient was first reported in 1980.[1]

Clinical indications for pulmonary catheterization in the high-risk obstetric patient are listed in Table 2-1. Three forms of shock are included in this table: hypovolemic, septic, and cardiogenic. Hypovolemic shock associated with unresponsive oliguria or pulmonary edema may be caused by uterine rupture, placental abruption, cesarean section with hemorrhage, postpartum hemorrhage, or ectopic pregnancy. A pulmonary artery catheter (PAC), which provides immediate information concerning pulmonary resistance, guides large-volume

35

Table 2-1 Indications for Pulmonary Artery Monitoring in Obstetrics

1. persistent oliguria
2. shock
   a. hypovolemic
   b. septic
   c. cardiogenic
3. cardiac disease class II or IV
4. pulmonary edema
5. adult respiratory distress syndrome
6. hypertensive crisis
7. sepsis

fluid replacement to help prevent pulmonary edema or monitors the resolution of existing pulmonary edema.

Sepsis constitutes a major cause of maternal death.[2] Septic shock caused by septic abortion, pyelonephritis, intrauterine pregnancy with ruptured colon, chorioamnionitis, cesarean section with endoparametritis, or postpartum endometriosis warrants hemodynamic monitoring. Volume resuscitation and vasopressor therapy are guided by a PAC with cardiac output monitoring capabilities.

Obstetric patients with heart disease are at risk for cardiogenic shock secondary to the stress of pregnancy, labor, and delivery. During the second half of pregnancy, patients have markedly elevated blood volume and cardiac output. Labor and delivery cause major increases in intravascular volume and place further demands on the heart. Therefore, patients with a history of mitral or aortic stenosis, rheumatic heart disease, cardiomyopathy, myocardial infarction, or angina should be monitored invasively to follow cardiac output and to determine preload and afterload hemodynamic status, to assist in detecting early stages of pulmonary edema associated with heart failure.

One of the most important uses of invasive hemodynamic monitoring in the obstetric patient is to differentiate hydrostatic pulmonary edema and permeability pulmonary edema.[2] Hydrostatic pulmonary edema results from left ventricular failure, left ventricular overload, elevated systemic vascular resistance, or a low colloid osmotic pressure.[3] The decision to use diuretic, inotropic, or afterload reduction therapy and the evaluation of such interventions are based, in part, on numerical data obtained using pulmonary artery and intra-arterial catheters.

Permeability pulmonary edema can result from damage to the pulmonary alveolar capillary membrane secondary to sepsis, pneumonia, or blood transfusion hypersensitivity reaction. If the source of injury is not corrected, further damage to the alveolar membrane can lead to adult respiratory distress syndrome (ARDS). Treatment for noncardiogenic pulmonary edema includes management of left ventricular preload with PAC monitoring to minimize protein and water flux into the pulmonary interstitium and alveoli, which can occur despite normal cardiac function. Patients with ARDS usually receive mechanical ventilation to control hypoxemia and to allow time for the lungs to heal. Intra-arterial catheters allow repeated blood gas analysis, which is essential for the care of ARDS patients.

Finally, patients with severe preeclampsia may benefit from PAC monitoring. Although most patients are managed clinically using noninvasive protocols, Clark and Cotton[3] and Cotton et al[4] recommended hemodynamic monitoring in severe preeclampsia, such as that associated with hydralazine-unresponsive hypertension, persistent oliguria after fluid challenges, and pulmonary edema.

In summary, invasive pressure monitoring is useful in the assessment, intervention, and evaluation of care in the high-risk obstetric population. Fortunately, most obstetric patients are young and healthy, can withstand major insults, and can recover after delivery, despite complications.

HEMODYNAMIC PHYSIOLOGY

Hemodynamic monitoring provides the health care team with directly measured numerical data on four physiologic indicators of cardiac function: preload, myocardial contractility, heart rate, and afterload.

Preload is the first determinant of cardiac output and is defined as the amount of blood in the ventricles at end-diastole. It is the maximum volume of blood moving through the heart. Preload is measured as central venous pressure (CVP) on the right side of the heart and pulmonary capillary wedge pressure (PCWP) on the left side of the heart. Preload is increased by crystalloid and colloid infusions and by position changes. It is decreased by diuretics, vasodilators, and position changes.

The second determinant of cardiac output is contractility. The Frank-Starling law is the foundation of the principles involved in a discussion of contractility. Experimentally, Drs. Frank and Starling took one cardiac muscle fiber and found that when it was stretched, the cardiac muscle fiber contracted. When stretched further, the fiber contracted at a greater force, up to a certain point beyond which greater stretch yielded a lesser return (Fig. 2-1). Clinically, we can relate contractility to cardiac output; as the left ventricle contracts, it ejects a certain amount of blood into the periphery. Fiber length can be related to preload: As more blood is added to the left ventricle, each cardiac muscle fiber must stretch to accommodate the increase in volume (Fig. 2-1). In summary, the

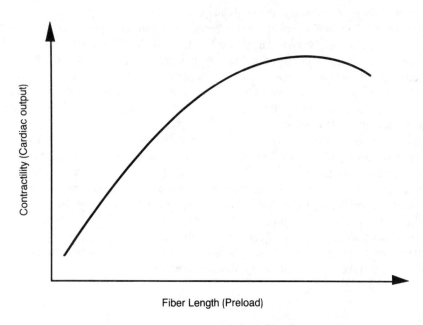

Figure 2-1 The relationship of myocardial contractility (cardiac output) to fiber length (preload).

Frank-Starling law states that the left ventricle responds to stretch in a manner similar to the isolated muscle fiber. The greater the left ventricular preload, the greater the cardiac output, up to a point where an increase in volume yields a lesser return. Cardiac output is a reflection of myocardial contractility and is equal to the heart rate times the stroke volume.

While inotropic drugs such as dopamine hydrochloride or dobutamine increase myocardial contractility, correction of maternal hypovolemia is preferable to inotropic therapy during the antepartum and intrapartum period; experimentally, dopamine hydrochloride has been found to decrease uterine blood flow in both healthy and hypotensive pregnant sheep.[2]

Heart rate is the third determinant of cardiac output, and heart rate does not change dramatically with pregnancy.[2] Sustained tachydysrhythmias may occur secondary to fever, hypovolemia, pain, or hyperthyroidism, and these should be treated. Importantly, tachycardias negatively affect cardiac output by decreasing diastolic filling and coronary artery perfusion time.

Finally, afterload is the fourth determinant of cardiac output and is defined as the resistance the blood meets when ejected from the ventricle. It is measured as pulmonary vascular resistance on the right side of the heart and systemic vascular resistance (SVR) on the left side of the heart. Clinically, left ventricular afterload is a reflection of the patient's systemic blood pressure. SVR more accurately indicates left ventricular work than does blood pressure, but because the latter is equal to the cardiac output times the SVR, control of the patient's blood pressure is used as the clinical measurement. In pregnancy, SVR is normally low, although in hypertensive disorders it can be abnormally high.[5]

In summary, the inter-relationships of preload, myocardial contractility, heart rate, and afterload are complex. The detection and monitoring of subtle changes and trends with pulmonary artery and intra-arterial catheters in the high-risk obstetric patient can direct patient care.

ELECTRONIC INSTRUMENTATION

Proper equipment preparation for hemodynamic monitoring ensures accurate data to guide treatment and avoids complications associated with line placement. Therefore, particular attention to detail and thorough knowledge and understanding of the monitoring system are essential. The flushing of pressure tubing prior to insertion, establishing a zero reference point, and both zeroing and calibrating the pressure transducer are important preinsertion tasks. All hemodynamic monitoring systems include three major components: (1) a transducer that converts physiologic pressures into electrical energy, (2) an amplifier that increases the volume of the signal being measured, and (3) a monitor screen that displays in digital and graphic form the converted physiologic signal.[6]

Rigid high-pressure monitor tubing transmits physiologic pressures without damping the waveform, and this portion of the line should include a continuous flushing mechanism to ensure line patency (Fig. 2-2). The monitoring tubing is completely flushed with heparinized fluid (normal saline or 5% dextrose and water) prior to catheter insertion. The fluid transmits physiologic pressure change from the catheter tip through the length of tubing to the transducer. Loose connections and air bubbles in the monitor tubing or transducer will cause the recorded waveform to be damped and therefore inaccurate. Proper line maintenance is critical for accuracy.

A physical reference point, the phlebostatic axis, is used when measuring pulmonary artery and intra-arterial pressures to relate readings to pressure changes within the heart. Specifically, the phlebostatic axis is the reference point on the chest wall that corresponds to the level of the right atrium. With the patient supine, the phlebostatic axis is measured at the fourth intercostal space along the midaxillary line (Fig. 2-3).

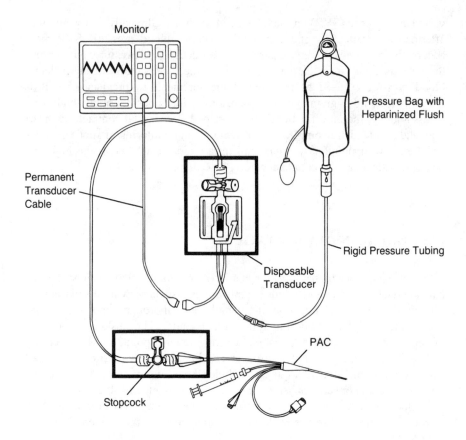

Figure 2-2 Components of hemodynamics monitoring system: pressurized tubing, pressure transducer, and hemodynamic monitor (converts physiologic signals into electronic signals).

In essence, the transducer must be told where to take a reading. The transducer is kept stationary and is vented to the atmosphere at the phlebostatic axis. The transducer negates atmospheric pressure, identifies the reference point, and provides a baseline for the pressure monitoring system during the zeroing procedure. Most new monitoring systems calibrate the transducer during the zeroing procedure to a specific predetermined calibration factor simultaneously, to ensure accuracy of the equipment. When the machine is properly zeroed/calibrated, it is assumed that the readings obtained accurately represent real pressures within the heart. Zero/calibration procedures are described in the instruction manual provided with the monitoring equipment.

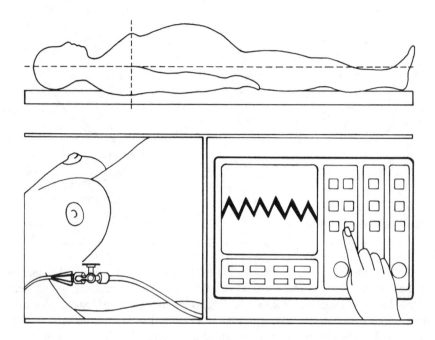

Figure 2-3 Location of the phlebostatic axis.

PULMONARY ARTERY CATHETERS

PACs are made of polyvinyl chloride and are available in several different sizes and types. Adult sizes range from 7 French to 8 French. Classically the thermodilution PAC has four lumina: distal, proximal, balloon, and thermodilution (Fig. 2-4). The distal port, which exits at the catheter tip, is connected to a transducer for continuous pulmonary artery (PA) readings. Special pressure monitoring tubing allows 3 mL of heparinized fluid to flush the port continuously each hour, to maintain line patency.

The proximal port is located in the right atrium (RA) and therefore can measure continuous RA pressures when attached to a transducer. This port is used intermittently to introduce injectate for cardiac output measurements.

The balloon port is located 1/2 inch from the catheter tip; the inflated balloon does not occlude the distal port. Inflation and deflation of the balloon is used to obtain PCWP readings. Deflation of the balloon should be passive; actively pulling back on the syringe tends to pull part of the latex balloon into the exit site and decreases its life expectancy.

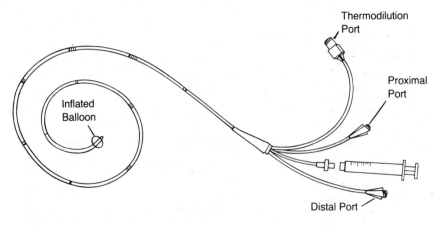

Figure 2-4 Pulmonary artery catheter.

The thermodilution port includes a thermistor located 5 cm proximal to the tip of the catheter. This thermistor measures the PA blood temperature and cardiac output injectate temperature. Since 1971, repeated indirect bedside testing of cardiac output has been available using the thermodilution PAC. Clinically, 5 to 10 mL of either chilled (0°C) or room temperature normal saline or 5% dextrose and water is injected through the proximal RA port of the PAC. The thermistor at the PAC tip measures baseline PA blood temperature and the subsequent decline in temperature after the injection. A bedside computer records and stores the temperature change over time and uses it to calculate cardiac output. Normal cardiac output is 4 to 7 L/min, but in the second half of pregnancy it increases by 30% to 45%.[2] Normally, cardiac output is proportional to body size, a fact reflected in the wide range of normal values. Maternal and fetal well-being depend on a normal cardiac output; therefore, it is essential that deviations from the norm be detected.

PACs with an extra RA port are convenient for administering vasoactive drugs when one of the proximal ports is being used for measurement of cardiac output.

The relatively new fiberoptic PACs continuously monitor mixed venous oxygen saturations (SVO_2). Normal SVO_2 is 70% to 80%. SVO_2 measures oxygen utilization at the tissue levels, allowing one to monitor hemodynamic stability. A decrease in SVO_2 may be related to an acute fall in cardiac output, an increase in metabolic rate, or a hemorrhage. Likewise, stabilization of cardiac output and an increase in SVO_2 can be a prognostic sign associated with clinical improvement. During pregnancy SVO_2 increases because of the increase in cardiac output in excess of oxygen utilization. In labor, the SVO_2 is reduced during contractions but returns to its nonlaboring value between contractions.

The need for a pacemaker is not common in the obstetric population, but there are pacing PACs that are used in emergencies for severe, hemodynamically unstable bradycardias that are unresponsive to atropine.[7]

Usually insertion of a flow-directed PAC is done at the bedside, and catheter advancement is assessed through pressure and waveform changes on the monitor screen. In some cases, for example in patients with severe mitral stenosis where high pulmonary pressures inhibit blood flow, fluoroscopy is helpful in directing catheter placement.

PAC insertion sites depend on physician preference but include jugular, sub-clavian, antecubital, and femoral sites. Introducer catheters ease percutaneous insertion. After the large-bore introducer line (approximately 8.5 French) is established percutaneously, the less rigid PAC is threaded through the dia-phragm of the introducer. Prior to insertion, maintenance fluids for the RA and introducer ports should be prepared. Also, the PAC balloon should be inflated to check for patency, and the catheter should be flushed with a heparinized solution. During PAC insertion, continuous electrocardiographic (ECG) monitoring is imperative to observe for ventricular dysrhythmias associated with catheter placement.

Once the catheter has entered the RA, the balloon is inflated to enhance flow of the catheter through the heart, and the monitor screen should be observed for the waveform (Fig. 2-5). Since the RA has a small muscle mass, a low-ampli-tude waveform will be noted. RA pressures reflect intravascular volume and compliance of the right ventricle. RA pressures, normally less than 6 to 8 mm Hg, are taken in the mean mode because there is minimal variation between systolic and diastolic pressures. Abnormally high RA pressure may denote left ventricular overload, chronic left ventricular failure, or congestive heart failure.

As the catheter enters the right ventricle (RV), a distinct change in waveform is noted. High-amplitude waveforms with definite systolic and diastolic components are apparent. The ECG monitor is observed during this time for ventricular ectopy associated with irritation of the ventricular septal wall as the PAC attempts to curve upward toward the PA. Ventricular ectopy is treated with a lidocaine hydrochloride bolus only when it contributes to further hemody-namic instability. Normal systolic RV pressures are 20 to 30 mm Hg, and nor-mal diastolic RV pressures are 0 to 8 mm Hg. The similarity in RV diastolic pressures and RA pressures is due to the open tricuspid valve during RV filling from the RA. RV systolic pressures reflect resistance to emptying. Normally, pulmonary vascular resistance is low, but abnormally high RV pressures may be seen, as in patients with pulmonary edema secondary to congestive heart failure or volume overload. Abnormally low RV pressures are seen in hypovolemia.

As the catheter floats into the PA, there is another change in waveform (Fig. 2-5). PA waveforms have distinct systolic and diastolic phases. Normal pres-sures are 20 to 30 mm Hg systolic and 8 to 12 mm Hg diastolic. Notice that the

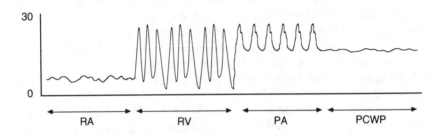

Figure 2-5 Waveform configurations during PAC insertion.

RV and PA systolic pressures are equal. As the RV contracts (systole), blood is ejected into the PA, and the distal port of the PAC measures that pressure as PA systole. During PA diastole the pulmonic valve is shut, and the mitral valve is open. Therefore, in the absence of mitral valve disease or pulmonary edema, pulmonary artery diastolic (PAD) readings reflect left ventricular preload. Abnormally high PA pressures are seen in left ventricular failure and pulmonary edema. Normally PA pressures do not change with pregnancy.[2]

Finally, the PAC floats into a "wedge" position (Fig. 2-5). The PCWP usually is recorded in the mean mode to reflect a timed average of systolic and diastolic phases. The inflated balloon obstructs right-sided heart pressures, and the distal port reads pressure from the left atrium and left ventricle across the lungs. During diastole, PCWP measures left atrial filling pressures (preload); when the mitral valve is open, the PCWP measures left ventricular preload. Normal PCWPs are 4 to 12 mm Hg, and optimum stretch PCWPs are 12 to 18 mm Hg, based on the Frank-Starling curve. PCWPs greater than 20 mm Hg usually denote some abnormal left ventricular performance (left ventricular failure, mitral valve stenosis or regurgitation, or volume overload), and PCWPs greater than 30 mm Hg usually coincide with fulminant pulmonary edema.[8] Low pressures are seen in hypovolemia. Normally pregnancy does not affect PCWPs.[2]

Once the PCWP is recorded, deflate the balloon immediately. Complications associated with prolonged wedging (greater than 10 seconds) include pulmonary infarction and pulmonary rupture. To avoid these complications during balloon inflation, a maximum of 1.5 cc of air should be injected, with careful attention being paid to the monitor screen. Inflation should stop once the wedge waveform configuration occurs.

After PAC insertion, a chest radiograph is ordered to confirm proper line placement. The nursing flowsheet documentation should include a strip recording of PA and PCWP readings and description of (1) application of an occlusive dressing, (2) transducer zeroing and calibration, and (3) types, ports, and rates of intravenous infusion.

Before the advent of PACs, RA or CVP lines were exclusively used to gauge intravascular volume as an indirect measure of left ventricular preload. There are two disadvantages to the older method: (1) It assumes normal right and left ventricular function, and (2) CVP changes are late events in left ventricular dysfunction. Critically ill patients with left ventricular failure and pulmonary edema need the additional information a PAC conveys—measurement of RA and PA pressures, PCWPs, and cardiac output measurements.

ARTERIAL LINES

An intra-arterial line permits continuous measurement of three blood pressure components: systolic, diastolic, and mean pressure. Systolic pressure represents the highest pressure occurring in an artery following contraction of the left ventricle. Systolic pressure reflects large-artery compliance, SVR, and left ventricular function. Conversely, diastolic pressure represents the lowest pressure in an artery during relaxation of the ventricle. Diastolic pressure reflects rapidity of blood flow, vessel elasticity, and SVR. Mean arterial pressures reflect average perfusion pressure over the majority of the cardiac cycle.

The intra-arterial waveform should include (1) a rapid upstroke to systole, (2) a clear dicrotic notch, which signifies closing of the aortic valve, and (3) a definite end-diastole (Fig. 2-6). Normally systolic blood pressure ranges between 90 and 140 mm Hg, diastolic between 60 and 90 mm Hg, and the mean between 65 and 85 mm Hg.

Generally, an artery suitable for an intra-arterial line has the following characteristics: (1) a diameter large enough to permit accurate measurement of pressure without the catheter's occluding the artery, (2) adequate collateral circulation should occlusion of the vessel occur, (3) ease of access to the site for nursing care, and (4) a site not prone to infection. In the adult population, the most common insertion site is the radial artery, when there is adequate collateral circulation. Other insertion sites include the femoral, brachial, dorsalis pedis, and axillary arteries.

The major complications associated with intra-arterial catheters are ischemia and necrosis, which occur because of inadequate collateral circulation. The radial artery is tested for collateral circulation by manually occluding the patient's radial and ulnar arteries at the wrist for about 1 minute. Ask the patient to clench and unclench her fist to encourage the palm to blanch, and then release the pressure on the ulnar artery and observe the palm for capillary refill. The

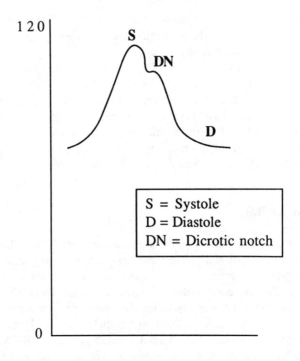

Figure 2-6 Arterial waveform.

palm should turn pink within 5 seconds. If blood return is slow, collateral circulation may be inadequate. Repeat the procedure, known as the Allen test,[6] on the patient's other wrist and compare results to determine the best insertion site. Slow blood return does not always indicate arterial occlusion; it may indicate inadequate cardiac output or poor capillary refill secondary to shock. In any case, the physician may choose an alternate site when collateral circulation is questionable.

Intra-arterial thrombus formation and embolization are controlled by continuous flushing devices on the pressure monitoring tubing and keeping stopcocks covered and free of particulate matter. The use of 20-gauge nontapered Teflon catheters produces the lowest incidence of thrombosis in the adult population.[9]

The most obvious risk factor of intra-arterial monitoring, infection, is avoided with routine dressing changes and maintenance of stopcock sterility. Certainly, the length of time the catheter is in place affects the risk of infection. Percutaneous insertions have lower infection rates when compared to cutdown techniques. Suturing intra-arterial lines in place reduces catheter movement, which contributes to infection from skin contaminants.

Nursing documentation should include an intra-arterial strip recording and descriptions of (1) dressing changes, (2) zeroing and calibrating the transducer, and (3) circulation to the affected extremity.

CONCLUSION

Hemodynamic monitoring provides valuable data for assessing the condition and planning and evaluating the treatment of critically ill patients. Knowledge and understanding of the highly technical equipment is essential for quality patient care delivery. Importantly, high technology cannot replace good physical assessment skills. The patient's level of consciousness, hourly urine output, vital signs, and breath sounds are valuable information in complete assessment. Finally, always treat the patient, never treat the monitor.

Helpful Tips

1. Note that there is respiratory variation associated with most PCWP readings, related to the changes in intrathoracic pressures. PCWP readings should be taken at end-expiration, when the respiratory cycle is most stable.[10]
2. Positive end-expiratory pressure (PEEP) will abnormally raise PA and PCWP readings because of the increase in intrathoracic pressure. Likewise, cardiac output may fall because of the increased resistance.
3. Evaluate PA, PCWP, and arterial pressures in terms of trends, not by one isolated reading that may be affected by the patient's emotional status, activity, or labor contractions.
4. Periodically monitor the pressure tubing setup. The heparinized flush bag should be under 300 mm Hg pressure so that the flushing device continuously delivers 3 mL of heparinized solution through the tubing per hour.
5. Protect the pressure tubing stopcocks with occlusive covers to maintain sterility of equipment and prevent infection.
6. The PAC does not remain stationary within the PA; it floats with the blood flow.

DEFINITION OF HEMODYNAMIC TERMS

Afterload—Afterload deals with pressure. Left ventricular afterload reflects the resistance the left ventricle has to overcome to pump blood around the systemic circuit, also known as systemic vascular resistance. Right ventricular afterload is the resistance the right ventricle has to overcome to eject blood into the lungs, also known as pulmonary vascular resistance.

Left ventricular compliance—A measure of the ability of the left ventricular muscle wall to stretch, in order to fill. Decreased compliance, perhaps related to cardiomyopathy, would indicate a degree of inelasticity in the muscle wall that would inhibit filling.

Preload—Preload deals with blood volume or venous return. Left ventricular preload is the amount of blood in the left ventricle just prior to systole. Pulmonary capillary wedge pressure clinically measures left ventricular preload.

Pressure transducer—Electronic device that converts physiologic pressure changes in an artery or vein to an electrical signal that is displayed on a monitor screen as a pressure wave in terms of millimeters of mercury. The pressure changes are transmitted from the patient to the diaphragm of the transducer via fluid-filled rigid tubing.

Myocardial contractility—Inherent ability of the myocardium to pump.

Stroke volume—Amount of blood pumped with each heartbeat.

REFERENCES

1. Benedetti TJ, Cotton DB, Read JC, Miller FC. Hemodynamic observations in severe preeclampsia with a flow-directed pulmonary artery catheter. *Am J Obstet Gynecol.* 1980;136:465-470.
2. Kirshon B, Cotton DB. Invasive hemodynamic monitoring in the obstetric patient. *Clin Obstet Gynecol.* 1987;30:579-590.
3. Clark SL, Cotton DB. Clinical indications for pulmonary artery catheterization in the patient with severe preeclampsia. *Am J Obstet Gynecol.* 1988;158:453-458.
4. Cotton DB, Lee W, Huhta JC, Dorman KF. Hemodynamic profile of severe pregnancy-induced hypertension. *Am J Obstet Gynecol.* 1988;158:523-529.
5. Hankins GDV. Invasive cardiovascular monitoring: an update. *Contemp OB/GYN.* 1985;26:ll4-131.
6. Lough ME. Introduction to hemodynamic monitoring. *Nurs Clin North Am.* 1987;22:89-ll0.
7. Berkowitz RL, Rafferty TD. Invasive hemodynamic monitoring in critically ill pregnant patients: role of Swan-Ganz catheterization. *Am J Obstet Gynecol.* 1980;137:127-134.
8. Cotton DB, Benedetti TJ. Use of the Swan-Ganz catheter in obstetrics and gynecology. *Obstet Gynecol.* 1980;56:641-645.
9. Kaye W. Invasive monitoring techniques: arterial cannulation, bedside pulmonary artery catheterization, and arterial puncture. *Heart Lung.* 1983;12:395-427.
10. Riedinger MS, Shellock FG, Swan HJC. Reading pulmonary artery and pulmonary capillary wedge pressure waveforms with respiratory variations. *Heart Lung.* 1981;l0:675-678.

SUGGESTED READING

Noone J. Troubleshooting thermodilution pulmonary artery catheters. *Crit Care Nurse.* 1985;8:68-76.

O'Quin R, Marini JJ. Pulmonary artery occlusion pressure: clinical physiology. Measurement, and interpretation. *Am Rev Respir Dis.* 1983;128:3l9-326.

Chapter 3

Hypertension in Pregnancy

Mary Ellen Burke and L. Kay Medford

Hypertension in pregnancy is an abnormal finding and a poor prognostic indicator. Hypertensive disorders in pregnancy affect 5% to 7% of all pregnancies[1,2] and present a management challenge to the obstetric care provider. These disorders include mild hypertension that may only require astute observation and assessment and severe hypertensive disorders with vascular, renal, hepatic, pulmonary, and central nervous system (CNS) damage and maternal death. Potential fetal outcomes range from normal to intrauterine growth retardation (IUGR) to intrauterine fetal demise (IUFD). Hypertension may exist prior to pregnancy, develop during pregnancy, or be complicated by pregnancy. Hypertension constitutes one of the most frequently occurring and potentially life-threatening complications of pregnancy.

Hypertension in pregnancy is a well-documented disease state, and one that requires intensive nursing care. Second only to hemorrhagic disorders in terms of maternal mortality, hypertension appears in a variety of forms. This complicates medical and nursing diagnosis and may critically delay proper management. Nursing management of the critically ill hypertensive patient requires assessment skills, in-depth knowledge of the potential pathophysiologic changes of the disease, and knowledge of high-risk and critical care nursing skills to prevent maternal and/or fetal compromise and to implement nursing actions when compromise has occurred.

TERMINOLOGY

The Committee on Terminology of the American College of Obstetricians and Gynecologists (ACOG) has established specific definitions for hypertension in pregnancy that relate to the specific time period in which it occurs (Table 3-1).[2]

49

Table 3-1 Synopsis of ACOG Definitions

1. pregnancy-induced hypertension
    a. preeclampsia
       1) mild
       2) severe
    b. eclampsia
2. chronic hypertension antedating pregnancy (any etiology)
3. chronic hypertension (any etiology) with superimposed PIH
    a. superimposed preeclampsia
    b. superimposed eclampsia

Pregnancy-Induced Hypertension

Pregnancy-induced hypertension (PIH) refers to any hypertension that develops during pregnancy. The term is frequently used as a synonym for preeclampsia and eclampsia. Both of these disease states involve hypertension that develops during pregnancy, although preeclampsia and eclampsia also have additional signs and symptoms distinct from those of simple hypertension during pregnancy.

PIH describes the patient in whom an elevation of blood pressure is the only manifestation of hypertensive disease noted, and in whom no previous hypertensive disorder has been identified. PIH is defined as a blood pressure of ≥ 140 mm Hg systolic or ≥ 90 mm Hg diastolic after the 20th week of gestation, or a rise of 30 mm Hg systolic or 15 mm Hg diastolic from prepregnant or second trimester measurements of blood pressure. This is important to note in the population of women who normally have low blood pressure, that is, those who have a blood pressure of 90/60. In such women, a blood pressure of 120/78 would signify a hypertensive state. The elevated blood pressures of PIH must be noted on two occasions at least 6 hours apart. Pregnant women who are not chronically hypertensive start their pregnancy with a blood pressure equivalent to their prepregnant blood pressure. The blood pressure decreases during the second trimester of pregnancy, returning again to the blood pressure equivalent to the prepregnant state in the third trimester. PIH occurs after the 20th week of pregnancy and may be diagnosed during the antepartum, intrapartum, or postpartum period.

Preeclampsia is defined as the presence of hypertension accompanied by proteinuria, edema, or both. A rise in the blood pressure of 30 mm Hg systolic or 15 mm Hg diastolic, accompanied by proteinuria or edema, is also preeclampsia. Proteinuria is defined as the presence of 300 mg or more of protein in a 24-hour urine collection, or 2+ or greater proteinuria on urine dipstick on two samples collected at least 6 hours apart. Edema is defined as a weight gain of 5 pounds or greater in 1 week, or an accumulation of fluid resulting in greater than 1+ pitting edema after 12 hours of bed rest. The nursing assessment should focus on the development of edema in addition to the location of the edema. The majority of pregnant women develop some pedal and leg edema. Assessment should include questioning the patient about any edema and noting any edema that develops in the face, hands, or sacral region and is present upon rising. A dietary history may distinguish weight gain caused by edema from that which is due to increased calorie intake.

Severe preeclampsia is defined as a blood pressure of 160/110 mm Hg or greater at bed rest on two occasions at least 6 hours apart (any two readings of 160/110 or greater should be reported to the physician, irrespective of timing) in the presence of proteinuria and/or edema. Proteinuria in severe preeclampsia is defined as 5 g or greater in a 24-hour collection of urine, or 3+ to 4+ proteinuria measured on a dipstick. Other signs and symptoms of severe preeclampsia include oliguria (less than 30 mL/h of urine output), blurry vision, spiderwebs or spots in front of the eyes, headache (especially pounding headache), and right upper quadrant epigastric pain (Table 3-2). The patient may have thrombocytopenia, impaired liver or renal function, a concentrated hemoglobin level or hematocrit, evidence of altered or destroyed red blood cells, or anemia. The patient may also present with pulmonary edema, a severe and potentially life-threatening finding in the woman with severe preeclampsia.

Table 3-2 Signs and Symptoms of Severe PIH

1. systolic blood pressure of 160 mm Hg or > on two occasions 6 hours apart
2. diastolic blood pressure of 110 mm Hg or > on two occasions 6 hours apart
3. 5 g of protein in a 24-hour urine specimen
4. 3+ to 4+ proteinuria on a dipstick (should be followed with a 24-urine collection)
5. oliguria, urine output less than 30 mL/h or 400 to 500 mL in 24 hours
6. CNS disturbances
   a. headache
   b. blurred vision
   c. scotomata
   d. altered consciousness
   e. seeing spots or spiderwebs in front of eyes
7. epigastric pain
8. thrombocytopenia
9. rising serum glutamic-oxaloacetic transaminase (SGOT)
10. pulmonary edema or cyanosis

Eclampsia

Eclampsia, derived from the Greek word for "sudden flash," is defined as the onset of maternal seizures or coma unrelated to any underlying neurologic condition, in the presence of hypertension, proteinuria, and/or edema. The term "sudden flash" is an apt description of the seizures, which occur with frightening rapidity and are associated with severe maternal and fetal morbidity and mortality. A severe headache may be a precursor of the seizures. The seizures are typically clonic and tonic in nature. The postictal phase may be characterized by any one or a combination of the following: respiratory arrest followed by spontaneous respiration, coma, maternal acidosis, fetal stress as evidenced by abnormal fetal heart rate patterns on the fetal heart monitor, and/or fetal demise. The incidence of eclampsia may be divided into antenatal, intrapartum, and postpartum periods, with a 25% incidence occurring antenatally, 50% intrapartum, and 25% postpartum.[3] Many antenatal seizures occur at home and are unwitnessed, which necessitates a thorough history when patients present in an unresponsive or comatose state.

Etiology

PIH has no known etiology. The disease has been well documented since 1743,[4] and a review of medical texts from 1895 to 1985 documents the exact signs, symptoms, and disease patterns of PIH, although the theories regarding its etiology and treatment have differed.[4-12] Blood banking, antibiotics, the use of magnesium sulfate to treat and prevent eclamptic seizures, hospitalization of patients with mild to moderate PIH, continuous assessment of patients with severe preeclampsia, pharmacologic agents to treat hypertension, maternal-fetal intensive care units, and invasive hemodynamic monitoring have all contributed to decreased maternal morbidity and mortality from this condition. Neonatal mortality (i.e., death the first 28 days of life) has improved with the advent of neonatal intensive care units.

There have been and are numerous theories regarding the cause of PIH. PIH was referred to as toxemia for many years, based on an underlying theory that toxins were released during the pregnancy that caused the increased blood pressure. That the placenta plays an important role in the development of PIH is rarely questioned. There is an increased incidence of PIH with molar pregnancy and multiple gestation pregnancy,[8,10,12,13] which supports the theories of placental involvement. This disease has been referred to as the "disease of theories," a term attributed to a Dr. Zweifel in the fifth edition of *Williams Obstetrics* in 1923.[8(p 609)] Early in the 20th century, the disease was split into 12 separate toxemias; gradually clinicians and researchers recognized that it was one disease that could affect any or all organ systems. This recognition was further assisted by the realization that the disease could present in a variety of forms.

The knowledge that PIH is a multisystem disease spurred researchers to find the answer to the riddle of the underlying cause of PIH. A great deal of scientific attention was placed on the theory that preeclampsia relates to the renin-angiotensin-aldosterone changes associated with pregnancy. The combined action of angiotensin II and aldosterone should produce an increase in blood pressure by increasing plasma volume via the retention of sodium and water.[14] Hypertension in pregnancy appears to produce the opposite result. Women who subsequently develop preeclampsia exhibit an increased diastolic pressure in response to administration of angiotensin.[15] While angiotensin levels are lowered in the hypertension-complicated pregnancy, there is evidence to suggest increased pressor sensitivity to the hormone.[16,17] During the past 10 years theories ranging from parasitic infections, to immune system deficiency, to genetic causation, to a socioeconomic status effect, to prostaglandin involvement have been suggested.

One of the most recent etiologic models is based on the theory that preeclampsia is a disease of elevated cardiac output.[18] This model suggests that patients who ultimately develop preeclampsia have a higher than average cardiac output as early as the first trimester. The theory suggests that preeclampsia is a hemodynamic continuum beginning with high cardiac output–low systemic vascular resistance in the early stages and progressing to low cardiac output–high systemic vascular resistance in the end stages of the disease. Theorists postulate that the damage to the organs is initially produced by vasodilation of terminal arterioles, which leaves the capillaries vulnerable to the pressures of increased cardiac output, and that vasospasms are a late, and potentially protective, response to the turbulent flow state.

Irrespective of the proposed etiology, PIH is a multiorgan disease state. The disease probably starts weeks or months before it becomes evident in the patient. PIH is a highly complex disease that may have one cause or be multifactorial in origin.

Chronic Hypertensive Disease

Chronic hypertensive disease is defined as a persistent elevation of the blood pressure ≥140/90 mm Hg prior to pregnancy, or prior to the 20th week of pregnancy in the absence of hydatidiform molar pregnancy. The patient may or may not have been identified or treated for chronic hypertension prior to pregnancy. Chronic hypertension may be complicated by superimposed preeclampsia/eclampsia. Any patient with an elevated blood pressure prior to the 20th week of pregnancy should be evaluated for chronic hypertension, and possibly molar pregnancy. Assessment of patients with an elevation of blood pressure prior to the 20th week of gestation should include a complete blood count (CBC), platelet count, and blood urea nitrogen (BUN), creatinine, uric acid, and serum glutamic-oxaloacetic transaminase (SGOT) levels. A 24-hour creatinine clearance test may also assist in differentiating the presence of chronic hypertension from PIH.

PATHOPHYSIOLOGY

Pregnancy-Induced Hypertension

PIH is a disease characterized by vasospasm of the arterial and venous blood vessels. In this vasospastic disease, arterial and venous circulation become disrupted by alternating segments of constriction and dilatation in the affected blood vessel.[2,12] The vasospasm can be identified by examining the retinal arterioles, which clearly exhibit it. In patients with severe PIH, vasospasm may be seen in the nail beds and produces prolonged capillary refill times. Nurses and physicians may be unable to successfully start an intravenous line. The vasospasm impedes the flow of blood through the arterial system, resulting in hypertension. These vasospasms occur in all of the major organs, the CNS, the uterus, and the placenta.

In PIH there is damage to the blood vessels by turbulent flow, direct epithelial changes, and/or vasospasm. The blood supply to the actual blood vessels is decreased when vasospasm occurs. The blood vessels are acutely stretched in the areas where the segmental dilatation takes place. These vasospastic actions injure the endothelium with the result that platelets, fibrinogen, and other blood components leak out into the interendothelium.[2,12,18] There may be a decrease in the level of platelets and fibrinogen because of the damage to the blood vessels. The first response of a damaged blood vessel is to contract (an additional source of vasospasm). Platelets and fibrinogen are then deposited and form a clot to prevent further escape of blood components; this further narrows the lumen of the blood vessel. Microangiopathic hemolytic anemia may result as the red blood cells are torn or destroyed in trying to pass through these narrow segments. Red blood cell destruction can be seen on a peripheral blood smear in the form of burr cells, abnormal red blood cells characterized by spiny projections, and schistocytes, fragments of red blood cells. In severe cases, the patient with microangiopathic hemolytic anemia may have a drop in hemoglobin level and hematocrit. This is usually seen in severe vasospastic disease and in the hemolysis, elevated liver enzyme levels, and low platelet count (HELLP) syndrome. Anemia may first be detected in the severely preeclamptic patient after an initial administration of intravenous fluid.

Chronic Hypertension

Chronic hypertension may be caused by vascular disease, renal disease, vascular changes secondary to diabetes mellitus, immune disorders such as lupus or scleroderma, and a variety of other underlying causes. Chronic hypertension is frequently diagnosed during pregnancy, as many women may present for initial health care during a pregnancy. Women who seek care in the second trimester present a special problem in the assessment of possible chronic hypertension, since blood pressure normally decreases in the second trimester. Any woman who has a diastolic blood pressure of 80 mm Hg or greater in the second trimester should be evaluated for chronic hypertension.[19] Mean arterial blood pressure (MAP) may be an effective method to determine chronic hypertension, especially in the second trimester.[20] MAP is determined by using a formula:

$$MAP = \frac{\text{Systolic blood pressure} + 2\left(\text{diastolic blood pressure}\right)}{3}$$

An increase in mean arterial pressure in the second trimester is associated with an increase in perinatal mortality. The increase becomes significant when the pressure exceeds 90 mm Hg.[20]

Chronic hypertension, whatever the cause, places the patient at risk for vascular and organ damage. Pregnancy increases the risk that the hypertension may become worse, especially when superimposed PIH develops. Patients with chronic hypertension alone are also at risk for having abruptio placentae, with 5% to 10% of these women having an abruption.[12]

Superimposed Pregnancy-Induced Hypertension

PIH superimposed on chronic hypertension is associated with increased maternal and fetal compromise. Approximately 25% of patients with chronic hypertension develop superimposed PIH.[2,21] The hemodynamic and vasoactive alterations of PIH added to a previously compromised system of chronic hypertension create a profound narrowing of the vessel lumens. Superimposed PIH may further constrict the blood vessels, which results in damage to the vessels and vulnerable organs. Chronic hypertension patients who develop superimposed PIH are treated similarly to patients who develop severe preeclampsia.[2,19,21] The nurse working with these patients should regard them as very high risk and know that their condition can exacerbate and they can become critically ill in an extremely short period of time.[19,21]

Pathophysiologic Changes in Organ Systems

PIH and superimposed PIH disrupt the maternal system, with a secondary effect on the fetus. PIH may cause damage in any or all of the following systems: renal, uteroplacental, pulmonary, hepatic, CNS. PIH also alters the amount of circulating volume and is responsible for hematologic changes, as well as changes in cardiac function. The following discussion reviews the changes in the maternal system and discusses potential effects on the fetus. It is important to note that the laboratory values presented are based on normal values for the pregnant patient (Table 3-3).

The Renal System

Pregnancy produces an increase in renal function relating to an increase in the plasma blood volume of 40% to 50% by approximately the 30th week of pregnancy.[22] Renal plasma blood flow and the glomerular filtration rate increase by 30% to 50% in the first trimester of pregnancy.[22-24] In preeclampsia, proteinuria develops and may be associated with a glomerular lesion, known as capillary endotheliosis, that causes a partial obstruction of the lumen and may cause ischemia of the lumen. The lesion was reported in the early scientific literature of PIH, and its underlying pathophysiology is now understood. It is hypothesized to develop secondary to hypercoagulability, which may precipitate the formation of fibrin-fibrinogen immunoglobulins,[25] which cause ischemic damage to the lumen.

The plasma volume, the renal plasma flow, and the glomerular filtration rate are decreased in PIH. They may be dramatically decreased in cases of severe

---

Table 3-3 Normal Laboratory Values in Pregnancy

Hemoglobin	10–12 g/dL
Hematocrit	32%–40%
Plasma blood volume	Up by 40% to 50%
Glomerular filtration rate	Up by 30% to 50%
Uric acid	4.5 mg/dL
BUN	12 mg/dL
Creatinine	0.8 mg/dL
Creatinine clearance	150–200 mL/min
SGOT	35 mg/dL (may vary between labs)
Colloid oncotic pressure	23 mm Hg

PIH and superimposed PIH. They may also be decreased in chronic hypertension, especially in those patients whose hypertension is secondary to renal disease. Uric acid, creatinine, and BUN blood levels rise. Serum uric acid levels may be used as a marker for the development of PIH in those patients without underlying renal disease. A uric acid level of 4.5 mg/dL or greater is considered to be a marker for PIH.[15] Creatinine clearance may decrease. In severe cases, oliguria develops, which may reflect volume depletion (secondary to the movement of intracellular fluid to the extracellular space) or severe renal vasospasm.[26,27] Severe proteinuria (greater than 3+ on dipstick or 5 g in a 24-hour collection) is associated with an increase in perinatal mortality.[2,12] The amount of proteinuria may vary secondary to the amount of vasospasm occurring. Hematuria may reflect an increase in red blood cell destruction. The urine may start out clear, then become blood tinged, then darker, finally ending up looking like cranberry juice. This is not caused by "traumatic insertion" of a Foley catheter, on which the blame for bloody urine is often placed. Acute tubular necrosis with short-term renal failure may also be seen in cases of severe PIH. The renal effects of PIH are typically reversed following delivery, unless there has been marked renal cortical necrosis, resulting in permanent renal damage.

The Uteroplacental System

Uteroplacental perfusion is disrupted and decreased in the presence of the vasospasm and decreased circulating volume associated with PIH. IUGR, oligohydramnios, and IUFD have an increased chance of developing with PIH and chronic hypertension; the incidence may rise even more with chronic hypertension complicated by superimposed PIH. The maternal circulation joins the placental circulation at the spiral arteries in the intervillous space. The spiral arteries are constricted in women with PIH.[28] Normally, the spiral arteries are dilated and provide a passive channel for blood flow. In women with PIH, the spiral arteries constrict on the maternal side, thereby decreasing perfusion. Uteroplacental circulation may be further impeded by the development of lesions that result from damage to the endothelium of uteroplacental blood vessels.

Women with chronic hypertension are at increased risk for a decrease in perfusion prior to the development of superimposed PIH. Chronically hypertensive patients often have atherosclerotic changes associated with the underlying disease process. The development of superimposed PIH complicates placental perfusion by decreasing the dilation of the spiral artery to an even greater degree. The severity of the decrease in size of the spiral arteries and the increase in the number of lesions present in the artery are probably related to the severity of the hypertension.[19] The greater the amount of spiral artery contraction and the greater the number of lesions in the artery, the less the amount of blood that will be able to reach the placenta and the fetus.

Patients with chronic hypertension are also at increased risk for IUGR and IUFD associated with an inability to increase plasma blood volume in pregnancy.[19] The lack of an increase in plasma blood volume becomes most significant with the development of superimposed PIH. PIH causes fluid to shift from the intravascular space to the extracellular space. A normal pregnant woman experiences an increase in plasma fluid volume of 40% to 50% by the 30th week of gestation. If PIH develops, large amounts of fluid shift to the extravascular space before placental perfusion becomes seriously disrupted. Women with severe preeclampsia may end up with all of their pregnancy fluid gain, as well as additional fluid, in the extracellular space, resulting in fetal stress and massive edema. The woman who is chronically hypertensive has little fluid in the intravascular space and is profoundly affected by the edema of PIH. Because of this decreased intravascular volume, diuretics are not used in the management of PIH unless the patient has pulmonary edema. Diuretics decrease the amount of volume circulating in the intravascular system, thereby decreasing placental perfusion even more. In contrast, intravenous fluid administration may not alleviate the decreased intravascular volume.

The Pulmonary System

Colloid oncotic pressure (COP) is the gradient controlling whether fluid remains in the capillary or moves into the interstitial space. Colloids are protein molecules. The most important plasma colloid proteins, in descending order of importance, are albumin, globulin, and fibrinogen.[3] Colloids are also found in the intracellular space. As large molecules, colloids cannot cross an uninjured semipermeable membrane. When there is no injury to such a membrane (e.g., the wall of a blood vessel), fluid moves from the area of the lowest concentration of colloids to the area of highest concentration. COP is the pressure gradient caused by the plasma colloid proteins that keeps fluid inside the capillary, preventing loss of fluid to the extracellular space.[3] Colloids differ from crystalloids, which can move through undamaged semipermeable membranes. Ringer's lactate and 5% dextrose and water are examples of crystalloid solutions, while blood products (any type), Plasmanate, and albumin are colloid solutions. Colloid solutions are used to bring fluid into the intravascular space, in the absence of damaged vascular endothelium. They are used with great care when PIH is present, because colloids can escape through damaged vascular endothelium into the intravascular space, resulting in further escape of fluid to the extravascular space, worsening both generalized and pulmonary edema.

The role of colloids in fluid balance was first documented by Starling in 1896, when he described what is now known as Starling's law of the capillary: Fluid moves in or out of a capillary bed in response to an imbalance of colloid and fluid. Every capillary bed has its own unique level of permeability. COP is one of the few oncotic pressures that can be measured.[29] However, the measurement of COP may be falsely increased by venous stasis, hemolysis, or a tourniquet left in place for an extended period of time.[3]

Pregnancy normally causes a decrease in COP secondary to hormonally induced changes. Normal COP values in pregnancy are listed in Table 3-4. COP decreases during pregnancy as the plasma blood volume increases. COP reaches a nadir at 35 to 36 weeks of pregnancy.[3] COP decreases even more during the intrapartum period and bottoms out in the first 24 hours postpartum.[30]

Patients with PIH, and especially those with severe PIH, also experience a further reduction in COP during the intrapartum and postpartum periods.[31] COP may drop to extremely low levels (Table 3-4). COP may be further decreased by the infusion of large volumes of crystalloid solutions, mobilization of fluid from the extravascular space to the intravascular space, supine position of the mother during labor, or blood loss at delivery.[3] The administration of a single liter of crystalloid solution has been demonstrated to cause a 12% decrease in COP. This change may persist for 2 to 5 days after the administration of the fluid.[32] Patients with PIH should be monitored for fluid overload and should be placed on strict intake and output measurements. An indwelling urinary catheter with a urimeter may assist in the measurement of hourly urine output. To avoid inadvertent fluid administration and to accurately administer intravenous fluid, controlled infusion devices should be used.

Patients with PIH or superimposed PIH are at increased risk for developing pulmonary edema.[3,29,30,33–35] The underlying hypothesis is that the lower COP associated with pregnancy is complicated by damage to the capillaries secondary to PIH. Colloids leak out into the extravascular space, or into the urine.[3] Pulmonary edema must be recognized as an ever-present risk in a pregnancy

---

Table 3-4 Colloid Oncotic Pressure Values in Pregnancy

Nonpregnant	28 mm Hg
Antepartum	22–23 mm Hg
Intrapartum	19–23 mm Hg
Postpartum	13–17 mm Hg
PIH (antepartum)	17–18.5 mm Hg
PIH (postpartum)	13–14 mm Hg

complicated by PIH. All patients with PIH should have their breath sounds checked in their initial assessment, and repeated checks should be done if there are any clinical signs or symptoms of pulmonary edema, or in the event of fluid challenges. The signs and symptoms of pulmonary edema include coughing, difficulty breathing, chest pain, increased heart and respiratory rate, cyanosis, and pink, frothy sputum.

The Hepatic System

Hepatic damage is thought to be related to the vasospasm associated with PIH, which may result in ischemia and necrosis of liver tissue. Vascular changes may be so great that there is hemorrhagic necrosis in the liver; if this occurs along the edge of the liver, a subcapsular hematoma will result. Subcapsular hematoma may result in rupture of the liver, since the liver is encapsulated by Glisson's capsule and cannot expand in the presence of damage. This event is associated with a high rate of maternal mortality. Rupture of the liver is a surgical emergency requiring immediate stabilization and repair. Analysis of SGOT levels may assist in identifying the patient at risk for hepatic damage. Frequently, there will be a rise in the SGOT level without concomitant changes in the patient's symptomatology. Patients with developing or present liver damage may also complain of right upper quadrant or epigastric pain or discomfort. An ultrasonogram and/or a computerized axial tomography (CAT) scan of the liver may be useful in identifying the presence of a subcapsular hematoma.

The Central Nervous System

The CNS effects of PIH produce a spectrum of complications from mild disturbances to eclamptic convulsions and cerebrovascular accidents (CVAs). Cerebrovascular resistance is increased in patients with PIH, while cerebral blood flow appears to remain unaltered.[19] The mechanism responsible for the development of cerebral edema remains undocumented. The cause may be a decrease or loss of cerebral autoregulation due to hypertension; another hypothesis is that it is secondary to eclamptic seizures.[36] Cerebral edema and cerebral hemorrhage may develop and are the major causes of maternal mortality in PIH.[31,36] The patient may complain of scotomata (blind spots or areas); visual disturbances such as seeing a spiderweb, snowflakes, or spots in the visual field; blurry or double vision; headache (often of the frontal variety); or feeling sleepy. The patient may present with hyperreflexia (easily elicited by patellar tap), clonus, or convulsions (eclampsia). Increased blood pressure is associated with increased risk of a CVA but does not appear to increase the patient's chance of eclampsia.

The Hematologic System

Plasma blood volume increases 40% to 50% in pregnancy. Patients with PIH, severe PIH, or chronic hypertension may experience a dramatically decreased amount of circulating plasma volume. As noted, patients with chronic hypertension may not be able to increase their circulating plasma volume, and those with chronic hypertension and superimposed PIH will have higher maternal and fetal mortality.[12,19] The decrease in the circulating plasma volume is not clearly understood. It may be the result of the vasospasm and vasoconstriction of PIH, or it may be secondary to the movement of intravascular fluid to the extravascular space. One hypothesis states that it is due to a combination of these factors. Regardless of etiology, there is a decrease in the amount of circulating volume (this change will reverse itself usually within 24 to 72 hours postpartum, with a return of fluid to the intravascular space). The change in circulating plasma volume means that diuretics are not used in the care of these patients, except in the treatment of pulmonary or cerebral edema, and colloid or crystalloid solutions are used only with great care due to their potential to alter fluid balance. The administration of regional anesthetics may produce vasodilation that will then produce an underfilled intravascular compartment.

The degree of hemoconcentration in the pregnant patient with PIH will vary. Hemoglobin levels and the hematocrit normally decline in pregnancy; in the woman with PIH, they may increase. This increase may be used as a marker in the progress of the disease. Hemoconcentration develops as intravascular fluid shifts to the extravascular space. This shift is usually noted prior to delivery, or with the infusion of crystalloid or colloid solutions. There may also be a dramatic decrease in the hemoglobin level and hematocrit with the infusion of intravenous solutions, or during the postpartum period as fluid returns to the intravascular space. The decrease may be very dramatic when there has been red blood cell destruction associated with the vasospasm of PIH. A peripheral blood smear should be performed when the hemoglobin level and the hematocrit drop more than 20%; the presence of burr cells and schistocytes signifies the destruction of red blood cells.

The appearance of thrombocytopenia has been identified as a complication of PIH. As platelets adhere to damaged portions of the vascular endothelium, they are consumed, and the platelet count decreases. Thrombocytopenia (a platelet count less than 100,000) increases the patient's risk of hemorrhage during delivery. The lowered platelet count may also affect the choice of anesthesia for delivery; thus this information should be communicated to the anesthesia care provider.

Patients with severe PIH are at risk for disseminated intravascular coagulation (DIC), a secondary response to the PIH disease state. The signs and symptoms of DIC include oozing of blood from intravenous injection or surgical sites, decreased fibrinogen levels, increased levels of fibrin degradation or fibrin-split products, and a prolonged partial thromboplastin time and/or prothrombin time.

The Cardiac System

Cardiac function in patients with PIH is greatly altered. This has recently been documented in a study that demonstrated that cardiac output (CO) was elevated in women who developed PIH, prior to the increase in blood pressure and other symptoms normally associated with the diagnosis.[37] Patients in the study also retained a higher than normal CO throughout their pregnancies. The authors concluded that women who develop PIH characteristically develop and maintain high CO and may have an inherent difference prior to and after pregnancy, compared to women who remain normotensive during pregnancy.[37] The authors also suggested that PIH is a condition initially characterized by high CO and decreased systemic vascular resistance (SVR).

HEMODYNAMIC MONITORING OF THE CRITICALLY ILL PIH PATIENT

Hemodynamic monitoring refers to the use of a pulmonary artery catheter to continuously measure central venous pressure (CVP) and pulmonary artery pressures. Pulmonary capillary wedge pressure (PCWP) and CO may be measured intermittently. Pulmonary artery catheterization provides assessment tools to direct the medical and nursing management of the patient with PIH. Indications for pulmonary artery catheter placement in the patient with PIH may include oliguria unresponsive to fluid bolus, hypertensive crisis, failed hydralazine therapy, pulmonary edema, cerebral edema, sepsis, DIC, the HELLP syndrome, or multisystem organ failure.

Hemodynamic findings of PIH are typically as follows:

1. CVP is low or normal.
2. CVP and pulmonary artery wedge pressure (PAWP) do not always correlate in PIH; thus CVP measurements alone may be misleading in the management of these patients.
3. Myocardial contractility is increased or unaffected in PIH.[12]
4. Heart rate may be increased.
5. Cardiac output is higher than normal.[38]

Patients who develop oliguria should not be considered as one group of patients but rather as a group divided into three specific subsets[39]:

1. patients with low PCWP, hyperdynamic ventricular function, and moderate elevation of SVR
2. patients with normal or increased PCWP and CO and normal SVR
3. patients with elevated PCWP and SVR and depressed ventricular function

Patients in subset 1 are treated with volume infusion. Patients in subset 2 are treated with pharmacologic agents designed to reduce either the preload or the afterload. Patients in subset 3 are treated with volume restriction and afterload reduction. Patients who are persistently oliguric should have a pulmonary artery catheter placed to confirm the diagnosis and monitor the effects of fluid challenges or pharmacologic treatment. Fluid administration can be monitored closely by following both PCWP and CVP values.[39-41]

HELLP SYNDROME

The HELLP syndrome was first described as such in the literature in 1982.[42] Many patients with PIH present with the symptoms of this syndrome, which may not initially suggest PIH as a diagnosis. The original paper discussing the condition sought to describe the syndrome so that all health care givers might become more aware of this presentation of PIH and not be led into misdiagnosis and delay of treatment for PIH. The HELLP syndrome is often confused with cholelithiasis, hepatitis, pyelonephritis, or other medical or neurologic disorders, especially in the absence of hypertension. Frequently, these women present at a fairly early gestational age; the mean originally described was 32.5 weeks for primiparas and 33.2 weeks for multiparas. The range was from 24 to 36.5 weeks for primiparas and 25 to 39 weeks for multiparas.[43]

The HELLP syndrome is a form of severe PIH. The patient is often critically ill and requires specific nursing care. Maternal and neonatal morbidity and mortality are increased in the HELLP syndrome.[43] The patients usually present with complaints of nausea (with or without vomiting), right upper quadrant tenderness, and malaise. A significant number (90%) of women also describe epigastric pain.[43] These patients may also present with significant hypertension (greater than 160/110 mm Hg); unfortunately, many do not exhibit this marked hypertension on admission.

Hemolysis and anemia will be detected in these patients with a routine CBC. The hemolysis is present in every patient with the diagnosis. It occurs as the red blood cell attempts to pass through the damaged small blood vessels. A peripheral blood smear should be performed. The peripheral smear will document the presence of burr cells, schistocytes, and polychromasia (variations in the color of the red blood cells).

Elevated liver enzyme levels are a distinct characteristic of the HELLP syndrome, though this finding may be noted in any patient with PIH. Hepatic changes associated with PIH have been previously described.

Low platelet count has also been described. Sequential platelet counts should be examined for a trend in decreasing numbers of platelets. The platelet count may decrease precipitously and the SGOT level may rise dramatically within a few hours.

ANTIHYPERTENSIVE TREATMENT

Hypertensive crisis is defined as an elevation of blood pressure greater than 200 mm Hg systolic and 120 mm Hg diastolic. At these pressures, vascular damage occurs rapidly, and the patient is at risk for multiple organ system damage and failure, encephalopathy, myocardial ischemia, and stroke. Antihypertensive treatment, therefore, is initiated at systolic levels of 180 mm Hg and diastolic levels of 110 mm Hg to allow therapeutic modalities to become effective before crisis levels are reached.

Antihypertensive therapy is used to decrease blood pressure and the work of the left ventricle and to increase renal and placental perfusion. One of the important forms of antihypertensive treatment is simple bed rest in a lateral position.[19,21] The lateral position decreases blood pressure, increases renal and uterine perfusion, mobilizes extravascular fluid, and causes a decrease in endogenous catecholamine production.[19,21] Many patients will respond to this therapy. Other patients will require pharmacologic therapy to achieve a decrease in blood pressure. The goal of pharmacologic therapy is to reduce both the systolic and the diastolic pressures, the end goal being to keep the diastolic pressure between 90 and 100 mm Hg. Maternal blood pressure is not reduced to normal levels because of the decreased intravascular volume. Maternal instability and fetal stress may be evident at diastolic pressures less than 90 mm Hg.

Pharmacologic Therapy

Hydralazine

Hydralazine hydrochloride is a vasodilator. It is frequently the antihypertensive agent of choice in pregnant women.[12,21,26,44-47] Hydralazine hydrochloride has proven over the years to be a safe, effective agent in refractory hypertension. It is administered in intermittent intravenous boluses or by a continuous infusion. Hydralazine hydrochloride relaxes smooth arteriolar muscle, resulting in vasodilatation. The onset of action may be variable but is typically within 15 to

20 minutes. Heart rate, cardiac output, and oxygen consumption may be increased, although individual responses to intravenous administration have been noted.[46-48] Patients with severe PIH may need to have their intravascular volume increased by the infusion of intravenous solutions prior to the administration of hydralazine. This may help decrease maternal hypotension and fetal stress.[47-50] Patients who do not respond to intravenous hydralazine should be considered for pulmonary artery catheter placement for hemodynamic monitoring.[37,40,47,51] Hydralazine is initially administered in intravenous push boluses of 5 to 10 mg every 15 to 20 minutes until the blood pressure starts to decrease.[12,26,46] If the blood pressure remains labile, a continuous infusion may be started; the usual dose is 100 mg of hydralazine in 200 mg of saline, titrated to keep the diastolic pressure between 90 and 100 mm Hg.[19] This solution should be administered via a controlled infusion device.

Labetalol

Labetalol hydrochloride was approved for use as an antihypertensive agent in 1984. It is a selective ß-blocking agent. Labetalol decreases systemic vascular resistance without altering CO. Unlike other ß-blockers, it is not associated with IUGR, fetal bradycardia, hypoglycemia, or respiratory depression.[44] Labetalol has a rapid onset of action but a variable length in its duration of action.[45] This agent may be administered via intravenous bolus or continuous infusion pump.

Ketanserin

Ketanserin is another selective ß-blocker of type 2 serotonin receptors.[21,46,52] Serotonin causes vasospasm, hypertension, oliguria, and a renal lesion similar to the glomerular lesion associated with PIH in humans in animal studies.[46] Experiments are presently being conducted to determine the safety and efficacy of ketanserin in the patient with PIH. A small number of patients were treated with ketanserin (10 mg) by intravenous push every 10 minutes in one study. The blood pressure was effectively lowered with minimal side effects for the mother and fetus. It was noted that the frequency of contractions was reduced. There were no noted effects on the fetus. Ketanserin may be useful in treating postpartum patients with PIH but may not be effective in patients with chronic hypertension with superimposed PIH.[46] Ketanserin is still considered an experimental drug in the treatment of hypertension in pregnancy.

Diazoxide

Diazoxide is a first-line drug of choice for treatment of severe hypertension in a nonpregnant patient; its use in pregnancy remains controversial, though. Diazoxide is an extremely potent vasodilator. It decreases blood pressure and vascular resistance, while increasing CO and heart rate.[53,54] Diazoxide causes a rapid drop in blood pressure, often decreasing diastolic pressures to 60 to 70 mm Hg from diastolic pressures of greater than 100 mm Hg. This may be accompanied by fetal bradycardia.[46,53] The hypotension is treated by the infusion of large volumes of crystalloid solution, which has been previously noted to be associated with a decrease in COP and a possible increase in the risk of pulmonary edema. Diazoxide also causes maternal and fetal hyperglycemia. It is associated with inhibition of labor,[53,54] which may not be a desired effect in a woman who needs to be delivered imminently. However, oxytocin does overcome the inhibitory effects of diazoxide.[46,53] There have been a few investigatory studies performed using smaller bolus doses of 30 to 60 mg every 1 to 2 minutes; this schedule was associated with fewer episodes of severe maternal hypotension and fetal effects.[46] The blood pressure must be monitored continuously with a diazoxide infusion because of its almost immediate onset of action.

Nitroglycerin

Nitroglycerin is a very potent vasodilator. It has an extremely rapid onset of action, working directly on vascular smooth muscle. Its ability to decrease blood pressure depends on the patient's intravascular volume status.[54,55] Intravenous nitroglycerin infusion is considered to be an experimental therapy in the treatment of the woman with PIH. Nitroglycerin decreases MAP and CO in those pregnant patients treated with albumin as a volume expander prior to the administration of an intravenous infusion of nitroglycerin (0.1 mg/kg/min), titrated to reduce the maternal blood pressure.[55] An MAP below 106 mm Hg during or after the infusion may be associated with the development of fetal stress. Fetal heart rate variability may be decreased secondary to a decrease in cerebral autoregulation and an increase in cerebral volume.[21,46,55] Nitroglycerin is absorbed by the typical polyvinylchloride tubing and intravenous bags, so it must be administered via special tubing.

Nitroprusside

Sodium nitroprusside is a very rapid acting, short-lived, and potent but predictable arteriolar and venous smooth muscle dilator. In nonpregnant patients, it is the drug of choice for hypertensive emergencies. The use of sodium nitroprusside in the pregnant woman remains controversial. Nitroprusside, through a series of physiologic reactions, causes the release of cyanide. Animal data have documented that fetal cyanide toxicity may occur without the mother becoming symptomatic.[46] It is recommended that nitroprusside administration be limited to those patients who are so critically ill as to require its administration and who will be delivered within 30 minutes after the initial infusion is begun.[43,46] Delivery of the fetus must be performed within that half hour after beginning the infusion. Nitroprusside is sensitive to light, and the infusion system must be wrapped in the foil protector accompanying each vial. This agent should be infused via an infusion pump, and the patient should have an arterial line in place to monitor rapidly changing arterial pressures.

NURSING CARE OF THE CRITICALLY ILL PATIENT WITH PIH

Pharmacologic Anticonvulsant Treatment

Magnesium sulfate ($MgSO_4$) is the agent of choice in the United States for prevention and control of eclamptic seizures and for control of CNS changes preceding the development of eclamptic seizures. Magnesium sulfate, as already noted, is not an antihypertensive agent. It works by reducing acetylcholine release in the CNS, interfering with and decreasing the number of impulses allowed through the ganglia.[46,55] Magnesium sulfate also decreases the excitability of muscle fibers to direct stimulation and relaxes smooth muscle. At this time, it is being used concurrently as an agent to stop preterm labor. Magnesium sulfate does cause an initial, transient decrease in blood pressure in patients with mild to severe PIH due to its effect on smooth muscle, including the smooth muscle of the vascular system. This response is of short duration and does not continue with prolonged infusion.[56,57]

To prevent eclamptic seizures, magnesium sulfate is administered first in a bolus of 6 g in 150 mL of 5% dextrose in water over a 15- to 30-minute period of time. The initial loading dose is followed by continuous infusion, via an infusion pump, of 2 to 3 g/h, the exact dose depending on the patient's renal status, patellar response, and respiratory status. A patient who is oliguric will build up magnesium since magnesium is excreted through the kidneys. The patellar or other reflex response should be assessed frequently to identify any patient at risk for magnesium toxicity. Magnesium sulfate administration should be halted if the respiratory rate drops to 14 breaths per minute or below, in the absence of a sleep pattern.

Serum magnesium levels should be monitored every 6 to 8 hours. The therapeutic range is between 4 and 7 mEq/L. Above 8 mEq/L, in the patient with PIH, a decrease in the patellar response may be seen. A magnesium level greater than 10 mEq/L is associated with a decrease in respirations, and respiratory arrest and cardiovascular collapse may occur at levels of 13 to 25 mEq/L. Calcium gluconate, an antidote to magnesium toxicity, should be available at all times to any patient receiving magnesium therapy. Ten milliliters of 10% calcium gluconate solution is administered via slow intravenous push, to treat magnesium toxicity.

In the United States magnesium sulfate has been the drug of choice to treat eclamptic seizures; phenytoin may also be used. The medication is given in a 6-g loading dose no faster than 1 g/min; this is followed by intravenous infusion of 2 to 3 g/h. Some patients may need an additional 2-g intravenous push to halt convulsions. The magnesium level must be monitored frequently, but the nurse should rely on clinical assessments such as checking the reflexes and counting respirations every 15 minutes following a seizure and administration of the loading dose to assess the patient for signs of toxicity.

Nursing Management

Nursing management of the patient who is critically ill with PIH or HELLP syndrome has been discussed throughout this chapter. This section will summarize the nursing management previously mentioned and add other facets inherent in the care of these patients.

Nursing care of the severely or critically ill patient with PIH should be given in a maternal-fetal intensive care unit (ICU), a labor/delivery area with specially trained and educated staff, or in an adult ICU with perinatal nurses acting as consultants/caregivers with the ICU team.

A priority for the nurse caring for the critically ill PIH patient is the initial nursing assessment of the patient. Taking vital signs and assessment of the fetal heart rate still remain the first steps. The initial blood pressure will be obtained by auscultation or by using an automated blood pressure cuff. In either case, the measurement should be obtained directly over the brachial artery. The patient must be placed in a lateral position. The nurse is responsible for recording which arm was used to obtain the blood pressure.[19] If the measurements are consistently acquired in one arm, it becomes easier to see the development of a trend.

The mother should have continuous fetal surveillance. An intravenous line, preferably using a 16- to 18-gauge catheter, should be established immediately. A larger gauge will permit a more rapid rate of fluid administration, especially of blood or blood products. Critically ill patients should have an arterial line for central hemodynamic monitoring. Blood should be obtained for a CBC and platelet count. If the platelet count is low, it may be necessary for the laboratory personnel to perform a manual count. Blood should also be obtained for determinations of blood type and an antibody screen; uric acid, BUN, creatinine, and SGOT levels; prothrombin time; partial thromboplastin time; fibrinogen level, and fibrin degradation products level. An indwelling urinary catheter with a urimeter should be placed. Hourly intake and output measurments should begin at this point, with a running hourly total. Urine should be evaluated each hour for the presence or absence of protein.

Medications and fluids are administered as ordered. The patient, if antepartum, may have an anesthesia consultation. Spinal and epidural anesthesia may be contraindicated in the patient with severe hypertension.[58] These methods of anesthesia may result in vasodilatation and a profound drop in blood pressure, or may be contraindicated secondary to DIC. Epidural anesthesia is used when given segmentally, using lower doses of medication over a period of time until anesthesia is established. General anesthesia may be indicated for a cesarean section; however, intubation causes a sharp rise in the blood pressure, increasing the risk of a CVA.

CONCLUSION

The care of the patient with any form of hypertension is a challenge for the nurse. Patients with PIH require expert nursing care, frequent blood pressure determinations, aggressive antihypertensive therapy, continuous monitoring of intake and output, analysis of laboratory tests, invasive hemodynamic monitoring (if indicated), and fetal surveillance. In summary, the pregnant patient with PIH is at risk for both maternal and fetal compromise. The goal of the health care team is to accurately assess the progress of the disease, reduce the impact of the disease, and prevent further organ system insult or damage.

REFERENCES

1. Anderson G, Sibai B, eds. Hypertension in pregnancy. In: *Obstetrics: Normal and Problem Pregnancies.* Toronto, Canada: Churchill Livingstone; 1986.
2. Gant N. Management of preeclampsia. *ACOG Tech Bull* 1986;91:1-5.
3. Wu PYK, Udani V, Chan L, Miller FC, Henneman CE. Colloid osmotic pressure: variations in normal pregnancy. *J Perinatol Med.* 1983;11:193-199.
4. Dieckmann W, ed. *The Toxemias of Pregnancy.* St. Louis: CV Mosby; 1941.
5. Norris R, ed. *An American Textbook of Obstetrics.* Philadelphia: WB Saunders; 1895.
6. Williams J, ed. *Williams Obstetrics.*Vol. 2. New York: D. Appleton; 1908.
7. Eden T, ed. *Practical Obstetrics.* St. Louis: CV Mosby; 1915.
8. Williams J, ed. *Williams Obstetrics.* Vol. 5. New York: D. Appleton; 1923.
9. Davis C, ed. *Gynecology and Obstetrics.* Hagerstown, MD: WF Prior; 1939.
10. Kerr J, ed. *Combined Textbook of OB-GYN.* Baltimore: Williams & Wilkins; 1946.
11. Pritchard JA, ed. *Williams Obstetrics.* 17th ed.. Norwalk, CT: Appleton-Century-Crofts; 1985.
12. Chesley L, ed. *Hypertensive Disorders in Pregnancy.* New York: Appleton-Century-Crofts; 1978.
13. Zuspan F, ed. Hypertensive disorders in pregnancy. In: *Clinical Obstetrics.* New York: John Wiley & Sons; 1987.

14. Ferris T, ed. Toxemia and hypertension. In: *Medical Complications during Pregnancy*. Philadelphia: WB Saunders; 1982.
15. Walker J, ed. *An Introduction to the Principles of Disease*. Philadelphia: WB Saunders; 1982.
16. Easterling T, Benedetti TJ, Schumker B. Maternal hemodynamics and fetal outcome in pregnancies complicated by hypertension. *Am J Obstet Gynecol*. 1991;164:272S.
17. Willis SE. Hypertension in pregnancy: pathophysiology. *Am J Nurs*. 1982;27:792-797.
18. Doany W, Brinkman CR. Antihypertensive drugs in pregnancy. *Clin Perinatol*. 1987;14:783-805.
19. Page EW, Christianson R. The impact of mean arterial pressure in the middle trimester upon the outcome of pregnancy. *Am J Obstet Gynecol*. 1976;125:740-746.
20. Burton A, ed. *Physiology and Biophysics of the Circulation*. Chicago: Year Book Medical Publishers; 1965.
21. Zuspan FP. Chronic hypertension in pregnancy. *Clin Obstet Gynecol*. 1984;27:854-873.
22. McCarthy EP, Pollack VE. Maternal renal disease: effect on the fetus. *Clin Perinatol*. 1981; 8:307-319.
23. Gabert HA, Miller JM Jr. Renal disease in pregnancy. *Obstet Gynecol Surv*. 1985;40:449-461.
24. Arias F, Mancilla-Jimenez R. Hepatic fibrinogen deposits in preeclampsia: immunofluorescent evidence. *N Engl J Med*. 1976;295:578-582.
25. Pritchard JA, Cunningham FG, Pritchard SA. The Parkland Memorial Hospital protocol for treatment of eclampsia: evaluation of 245 cases. *Am J Obstet Gynecol*. 1984;148:951-963.
26. Lee W, Gonik B, Cotton DB. Urinary diagnostic indices in preeclampsia-associated oliguria: correlation with invasive hemodynamic monitoring. *Am J Obstet Gynecol*. 1987;156:100-103.
27. Kelley M, Mongiello R. Hypertension in pregnancy: labor, delivery and postpartum. *Am J Nurs*. 1982;27:813-822.
28. Moise KJ Jr, Cotton DB. The use of colloid osmotic pressure in pregnancy. *Clin Perinatol*. 1986;13:827-842.
29. Gonik B, Cotton DB, Spillman T, Abouleish E, Zavisca F. Peripartum colloid osmotic pressure changes: effects of controlled fluid management. *Am J Obstet Gynecol*. 1985;151:812-815.
30. Benedetti TJ, Kates R, Williams V. Hemodynamic observations in severe preeclampsia complicated by pulmonary edema. *Am J Obstet Gynecol*. 1985;152:330-334.
31. Benedetti TJ, Quilligan EJ. Cerebral edema in severe pregnancy-induced hypertension. *Am J Obstet Gynecol*. 1980;137:860-862.
32. Hibbard LT. Maternal mortality due to acute toxemia. *Obstet Gynecol*. 1973;42:263-270.
33. Benedetti TJ, Carlson RW. Studies of colloid osmotic pressure in pregnancy induced hypertension. *Am J Obstet Gynecol*. 1979;135:308-311.
34. Gonik B, Cotton DB. Peripartum colloid osmotic pressure changes: influence of intravenous hydration. *Am J Obstet Gynecol*. 1984;150:99-100.
35. Haupt MT, Rackow EC. Colloid osmotic pressure and fluid resuscitation with hetastarch, albumin and saline solutions. *Crit Care Med*. 1982;10:159-162.
36. Lang RM, Borow KM. Pregnancy and heart disease. *Clin Perinatol*. 1985;12:551-569.
37. Clark SL, Cotton DB, Lee W, et al. Central hemodynamic assessment of normal term pregnancy : *Am J Obstet Gynecol*. 1989;161:1439-1442.
38. Mabie W, Ratts T, Sibai B. The central hemodynamics of severe preeclampsia. *Am J Obstet Gynecol*. 1989;161:1443-1448.
39. Clark SL, Horenstein JM, Phelan JP, Montag TW, Paul RH. Experience with the pulmonary artery catheter in obstetrics and gynecology. *Am J Obstet Gynecol*. 1985;152:374-378.
40. Weinstein L. Syndrome of hemolysis, elevated liver enzymes, and low platelet count: a severe consequence of hypertension in pregnancy. *Am J Obstet Gynecol*. 1982;142:159-167.
41. Jackson RE. Hypertension in the emergency department. *Emerg Clin North Am*. 1988;6:173-196.

42. Clark SL, Greenspoon JS, Aldahl D, Phelan JP. Severe preeclampsia with persistent oliguria: management of hemodynamic subsets. *Am J Obstet Gynecol.* 1986;154:490-494.
43. Mabie WC, Gonzalez AR, Sibia BM. A comparative trial of labetalol and hydralazine in the acute management of severe hypertension complicating pregnancy. *Obstet Gynecol.* 1987;70:328-333.
44. Berkowitz D, Coustan D, Moyoshiko T, ed. *Handbook of Drugs in Pregnancy.* 2nd ed. Toronto, Canada: Churchill Livingstone; 1986.
45. Cotton DB, Gonik B, Dorman KF. Cardiovascular alterations in severe pregnancy-induced hypertension seen with an intravenously given hydralazine bolus. *Surg Gynecol Obstet.* 1985;161:240-244.
46. Kock-Weser J. Hydralazine. *N Engl J Med.* 1976;295:320-323.
47. Shepherd A, Linm M-S, McNay J, Ludden T, Musgrave G. Determinants of response to intravenous hydralazine in hypertension. *Clin Pharmacol Ther.* 1981;30:773-781.
48. Vink GJ, Moodley J, Philpott RH. Effect of dihydralazine on the fetus in the treatment of maternal hypertension. *Obstet Gynecol.* 1980;55:519-522.
49. Hulme VA, Odendall HJ. Intrapartum treatment of preeclamptic hypertension by ketanserin. *Am J Obstet Gynecol.* 1986;155:260-263.
50. Neuman J, Weiss B, Rabello Y, Cabal A, Freeman RK. Diazoxide for the acute control of severe hypertension complicating pregnancy: a pilot study. *Obstet Gynecol.* 1979;53:50S-53S.
51. Landesman R, deSouza JA, Coutinho EM, Wilson KH, deSousa MB. The inhibitory effect of diazoxide in normal term labor. *Am J Obstet Gynecol.* 1968;103:430-433.
52. Morishima HO, Cohen H, Brown WU, Daniel S, Neimann WH, James LS. The inhibitory action of diazoxide on uterine activity in the subhuman primate: placental transfer and effect on the fetus. *J Perinatol Med.* 1973;1:13-23.
53. Cotton DB, Longmire S, Jones MM, Dorman KF, Tessem J, Joyce TH. Cardiovascular alterations in severe pregnancy-induced hypertension: effects of intravenous nitroglycerin coupled with blood volume expansion. *Am J Obstet Gynecol.* 1986;154:1053-1059.
54. Herling IM. Intravenous nitroglycerin: clinical pharmacology and therapeutic considerations. *Am Heart J.* 1984;108:141-149.
55. Cotton DB, Gonik B, Dorman KF. Cardiovascular alterations in severe pregnancy-induced hypertension: acute effects of intravenous magnesium sulfate. *Am J Obstet Gynecol.* 1984;148:162-165.
56. Young BK, Weinstein HM. Effects of magnesium sulfate on toxemic patients in labor. *Obstet Gynecol.* 1977;49:681-685.
57. Canez MS, Reed KL, Shenker L. Effect of maternal magnesium sulfate treatment on fetal heart rate variability. *Am J Perinatol.* 1987;4:167-170.
58. Pritchard JA, McDonald PC, Gant N. Analgesia and anesthesia. In: *Williams Obstetrics.* 17th ed. Norwalk, Conn.: Appleton-Century-Crofts; 1985.

Chapter 4

Acute Pulmonary Insults during Pregnancy

Karen Dorman

The physiologic alterations associated with pregnancy have a profound effect on each of the major organ systems. These alterations are critical for maintaining homeostasis in the mother as well as providing an adequate environment for the fetus during pregnancy. The respiratory system is one of the most critical to maintain during a healthy pregnancy. It is also a system from which a variety of problems can arise that affect the outcome for the mother and fetus. The obstetric nurse must be aware of the normal alterations in function and be astute regarding abnormal changes and the actions required to compensate for these changes.

RESPIRATORY ALTERATIONS

There is a 40% to 50% increase in plasma volume and cardiac output during pregnancy. To maintain adequate oxygenation of maternal and fetal tissues, respiratory function must also increase. Hyperventilation is seen as early as the first trimester of pregnancy and reaches a peak at term. Many patients complain of shortness of breath as early as the first trimester, and by the last trimester 60% experience dyspnea. Although the exact cause of the dyspnea is unknown, it is thought to be progesterone induced.[1] By 36 weeks' gestation, these changes have reached a plateau, which remains until delivery.

The enlarging uterus also produces structural changes that aggravate many physiologic functions. The diaphragm is elevated at term, but the anteroposterior and transverse diameters of the chest increase to compensate. Minute ventilation is increased by 48% at term over nonpregnant values. Although the respiratory rate does not change appreciably, tidal volume increases from 500 mL to 800 mL per breath. There is an increase in oxygen consumption of approximately 21% that is related to cardiac work and fetal metabolism. Oxygen consumption is further increased by 40% during labor and up to 100% in the second stage.

The residual volume, defined as the amount of air remaining in the lung after the tidal volume has been exhaled, decreases. Functional residual capacity is reduced by 20%, causing these patients to become hypoxic more quickly and to have less respiratory reserve than nonpregnant women.

Normal maternal blood gases reflect hyperventilation. The pH is slightly elevated (7.40 to 7.44), arterial oxygen (PaO_2) is increased to 106 mm Hg, and arterial carbon dioxide ($PaCO_2$) is decreased to 30 mm Hg. The maternal PaO_2 must remain $\geq$ 60 mm Hg for adequate fetal oxygenation, providing all other factors that influence oxygen transfer across the placenta remain optimum.[2] Fetal hemoglobin has a great affinity for oxygen, so that the relatively small increases in umbilical PvO_2 seen after maternal administration of 100% oxygen will increase fetal oxygen saturation and oxygen content significantly. The maternal to fetal transfer of oxygen is directly related to placental flow. This emphasizes the importance of uterine displacement, which decreases the pressure of the uterus on the vena cava and allows greater venous return and enhanced cardiac output. Awe and colleagues[3] also reported a significant increase in maternal PaO_2 when patients sat up in bed. Proper hydration is also important since animal studies showed that administration of oxygen to hypovolemic subjects did not prevent a decrease in fetal PvO_2 and fetal distress. Primate studies showed that maternal hyperoxygenation reduced the incidence of late decelerations but did not correct fetal acidosis, thus having more a stabilizing than a corrective effect.[4]

There are many complications of pregnancy that involve the respiratory system. Although there is a significant maternal risk related to many of these complications, the problem is exaggerated antepartum. Maternal hypoxemia not only causes fetal hypoxemia but also may be worsened by the fetal oxygen requirements. Thus antepartum patients with severe respiratory complications must be monitored carefully, as delivery may be required to save the mother and fetus. The most common respiratory complications are presented below. Although usually referred to as separate diseases, many of these conditions cause others or may actually be a progression of another.

PULMONARY EDEMA

The incidence of pulmonary edema in pregnancy is difficult to determine since it often is reported as a complication of other problems of pregnancy. Pulmonary edema is usually classified as either cardiogenic or noncardiogenic. A third mechanism related to a reduction in the colloid osmotic pressure (COP) has been postulated.[5-7] COP is defined as the pressure exerted by the protein fraction of the blood that opposes capillary hydrostatic pressure and helps to keep fluid within the vessels. Treatment differs for each of these mechanisms, so determination of the type is paramount prior to initiation of therapy.

Pathophysiology

Cardiogenic pulmonary edema occurs as a result of left ventricular failure. As the left ventricle begins to fail, it is unable to completely and efficiently empty its contents. This leads to dilation of the ventricle and an increase in the left ventricular end-diastolic pressure (LVEDP), which is reflected in the pulmonary capillary wedge pressure (PCWP). As this process continues, the left atrium is unable to empty, causing elevated pressures in the pulmonary veins and arteries. When untreated, the hydrostatic pressure of the fluid, represented by the PCWP, becomes greater than the pressure exerted by the protein fraction of the blood (COP), which holds fluid within the vessels. When the PCWP-COP gradient is greater than 4 mm Hg, fluid is forced into the interstitial spaces and alveoli, making gas exchange impossible. Hemodynamically, this patient presents with an elevated PCWP and low left ventricular stroke work index (LVSWI).

Noncardiogenic pulmonary edema is a result of increased pulmonary capillary membrane permeability. The precipitating event may be a direct injury that damages the alveolar capillary membrane, such as smoke inhalation or gastric content aspiration. Substances such as gram-negative toxins released with septic shock damage the same membrane. Once permeability is altered, fluid flows into the interstitial spaces and alveoli. The final effect is the same as in cardiogenic pulmonary edema, decreased gas exchange and hypoxemia. However, these patients present with a normal or slightly elevated LVSWI and a normal PCWP, indicating normal left ventricular function. Noncardiogenic pulmonary edema can also be diagnosed when the protein content of the serum compared with that of the pulmonary edema fluid is ≥ 0.4.[5]

The third mechanism described involves lowering of the COP.[5,6] The same components involved in cardiogenic pulmonary edema are also involved in this situation, but the mechanisms are reversed. The patient presents with normal left ventricular function (as indicated by normal LVSWI and PCWP), but the COP is lower than normal. Again, when the PCWP-COP gradient is greater than 4 mm Hg, fluid leaks into the pulmonary interstitium and alveoli.[6] Normally, pregnant patients have a lower COP because of the expansion of the plasma volume; the normal nonpregnant COP of 25 mm Hg is decreased in pregnancy to 22 mm Hg.[8] In reality, the combination of mild cardiogenic pulmonary edema and a decreased COP may cause pregnant patients to develop pulmonary edema at a lower PCWP than nonpregnant patients.

Predisposing Conditions

Pulmonary edema is frequently mentioned as a complication of pregnancy-induced hypertension (PIH). [5–11] The incidence is approximately 3%.[11] All three mechanisms are cited as a cause of pulmonary edema in PIH. Patients with cardiogenic pulmonary edema present with a greatly increased systemic vascular resistance (SVR) and frequently an elevated cardiac output. The arterial spasm associated with PIH causes the elevated SVR. The heart, already overworked in the pregnant state, fails because of the elevated SVR. The altered COP mechanism is also cited as a cause of pulmonary edema in the PIH patient whose COP is decreased to approximately 18 mm Hg antepartum because of the exaggerated protein loss associated with the disease. Postpartum, these values decrease to 15 mm Hg, probably because of blood loss and intravenous hydration[8]; thus these patients may develop pulmonary edema with a PCWP as low as 19 mm Hg. Altered pulmonary membrane permeability is cited as a cause of pulmonary edema in PIH, although the cause is unknown. These mechanisms often are seen in combination.

Betamimetic therapy for preterm labor causes pulmonary edema in approximately 5% of patients treated, and 50% of the those patients had twin gestation.[12] The exact cause is unknown, but fluid overload is thought to be a precipitating factor.[13] Patients in preterm labor often are hydrated when admitted and then are placed on betamimetic drugs, which cause sodium and water retention as well as tachycardia. Thus cardiogenic pulmonary edema may result. Wagner et al.[14] observed that patients on betamimetic therapy have normal or increased myocardial function, possibly indicating a noncardiogenic component.

Pre-existing cardiac disease is also related to the development of cardiogenic pulmonary edema. Mitral valve stenosis or prolapse resulting from rheumatic heart disease is the most frequently reported cause of pulmonary edema in patients with cardiac disease.[15] The left ventricular function is depressed slightly prior to pregnancy, such that the increased myocardial work of pregnancy and/or labor may cause left ventricular failure.

Noncardiogenic pulmonary edema is frequently the result of sepsis, gastric aspiration, smoke inhalation, and many other pulmonary insults.[7,16–18] The alteration in pulmonary capillary membrane permeability is due to an injury to the capillary endothelium.[19] Gram-negative endotoxin is the causative agent associated with sepsis, while the acidity of the gastric contents precipitates pulmonary edema when aspiration occurs. Amniotic fluid embolism is another condition that results in pulmonary edema, with probably a combination of cardiogenic and noncardiogenic properties.[18] Since amniotic fluid embolus has so many unique components, it will be discussed in depth as a separate entity.

Patient Presentation

Although the symptoms vary with the severity and progression of disease, most patients complain of acute shortness of breath, dyspnea, and tachypnea.

Auscultation of the chest may be normal or may yield coarse rales and rhonchi. Radiographically, the chest may appear normal, have patchy infiltrates, or be completely opaque, which is indicative of fluid in the interstitial spaces. In severe cases, the patient may cough up large amounts of pink frothy sputum. The majority of patients develop pulmonary edema within 72 hours postpartum, when fluid in the interstitial spaces mobilizes into the intravascular space.[9,11,15] The exceptions include preterm antepartum patients on betamimetic therapy and septic patients. Excessive fluid administration caused by hydration for regional anesthesia, massive blood transfusion, or other reasons may be another cause of pulmonary edema.[5]

Therapy

Therapy begins with the delivery of supportive care. Since pulmonary edema is frequently an acute event that threatens the life of the patient and fetus, initial efforts must be directed toward the maintenance of adequate oxygenation. In the pregnant patient, adequate oxygenation is defined as a PaO_2 of 60 mm Hg with an oxygen saturation of at least 90%.[2] This can sometimes be accomplished with oxygen by Venturi mask but may require continuous positive airway pressure (PCAP) by mask or mechanical ventilation with the addition of positive end expiratory pressure (PEEP). (See "Adult Respiratory Distress Syndrome" for a discussion of PEEP.) When the patient is stabilized, the type of pulmonary edema should be identified prior to the initiation of drug therapy. This can be done with a pulmonary artery flow-directed catheter and determination of LVSWI and PCWP. Another advantage of the pulmonary artery catheter is the ability to monitor results of therapy. Drug therapy varies with the type of pulmonary edema and the precipitating factor. Morphine sulfate is one of the few drugs that can be used with all types of pulmonary edema. It is given in small doses and titrated to patient response to decrease the anxiety that accompanies acute shortness of breath.

Therapy for noncardiogenic pulmonary edema is supportive, with occasional use of steroids to possibly decrease the endothelial response to injury and bronchodilators to control bronchial spasm.[20] There are a few reports of administration of furosemide. The use of albumin, a colloid, is usually contraindicated in noncardiogenic pulmonary edema since the protein molecules could pass through the damaged capillary membrane into the interstitium and alveoli and possibly pull with them more fluid because of the osmotic properties of protein.[21] Antibiotics are recommended for the septic patient, and betamimetic therapy should be discontinued if it was used.

Drug therapy for cardiogenic pulmonary edema should decrease the SVR, increase the cardiac output, and maintain or optimize urinary output. The agents used to accomplish these goals differ widely among authors. Strauss and colleagues[10] recommend the use of sodium nitroprusside to decrease SVR, diuretics to decrease the preload or venous return, and digitalis as an inotropic agent. The use of hydralazine as well as sodium nitroprusside is recommended by Sibai et al.[11] to decrease SVR, and dopamine may be added for cardiovascular support. Dopamine in low doses (<5 μg/kg/min) is suggested for maintenance of renal perfusion. The majority of these reports refer to postpartum patients or short-term therapy prior to imminent delivery, vaginally or surgically. Jacobs and co-workers[13] report that the use of diuretics, aminophylline, digitalis, and morphine and restriction of fluid intake to 1500 to 2000 mL/day resolve pulmonary edema caused by betamimetic therapy. They add that delivery is not necessarily indicated unless maternal oxygenation is inadequate for fetal well-being.

AMNIOTIC FLUID EMBOLUS

Amniotic fluid embolus is a rare phenomenon (1 in 20,000 to 30,000 deliveries) that is associated with a mortality rate of 86%, the majority of which occurs within the first 2 hours after the acute incident. It is responsible for 10% of maternal deaths.[18]

Predisposing Factors

The most frequently reported precipitating factors include advanced maternal age, large fetus, multiparity, and short, tumultuous labor.[18] Morgan[22] reviewed 272 cases and found that 88% were multiparous and the average age of the patient was 32 years. However, he disputes the remaining factors since the average fetal size was normal and only 28% of the patients had short, tumultuous labors. Placental abruption was present in 50% of the cases, and fetal death occurred prior to amniotic fluid embolism in 40%.[23]

It is postulated that the primary acute event is severe pulmonary hypertension that is produced as a direct effect of amniotic fluid and debris on the lung. This debris increases pulmonary pressures, which leads to right heart failure and severe hypoxia.[23] These are transient effects, lasting approximately 30 minutes in the animal model. In patients who survive, left ventricular failure with elevated PCWP and normal right ventricular function occur as secondary events. The degree of pulmonary edema is more severe than the degree of left ventricular failure, indicating there may be a component of noncardiogenic pulmonary edema as well. Clark and colleagues[24,25] report that the primary complication is left ventricular failure, followed by a decrease in LVSWI and an elevated PCWP. The left ventricular failure is the predisposing event to the elevation in pulmonary arterial pressures. Amniotic fluid embolus results in massive disseminated intravascular coagulation, which may occur because amniotic fluid activates the fibrinolytic system, but the cause remains unknown. This bleeding disorder may occur in combination with uterine atony, causing extreme blood loss.

Patient Presentation

The majority of patients have an acute onset of symptoms during or immediately post delivery. They develop acute respiratory distress, shock out of proportion to blood loss, and frequently chills, shivering, sweating, or seizures. Pulmonary edema occurs acutely in most patients, with production of pink frothy sputum. Chest pain is rare. These events are followed by acute cardiovascular collapse. The diagnosis is confirmed by aspiration of blood from the pulmonary artery and identification of fetal squamous cell, lanugo hair, vernix, and mucin on a slide. Often this diagnosis is made during autopsy.[18]

Treatment

The treatment is separated into two phases, acute and secondary.[23] First, attempts should be made to sustain oxygenation of the blood, including intubation, mechanical ventilation, and, in many cases, cardiopulmonary resuscitation. Second, a pulmonary artery catheter is recommended to determine hemodynamic management and appropriate cardiovascular support. Inotropic agents such as digitalis and vasopressors such as dopamine may be required. Another essential component of therapy is correction of the bleeding disorder by administration of blood and blood products. Low-dose heparin therapy is recommended by some when blood products are inadequate; however, this remains controversial. Other medications, such as steroids and bronchodilators, have been suggested but remain controversial.[24]

ADULT RESPIRATORY DISTRESS SYNDROME

In 1967 Ashbaugh et al.[26] described a syndrome in patients who acutely developed dyspnea, hypoxemia, decreased lung compliance, and diffuse infiltrates in the alveoli. The disease is extremely tragic in that it frequently affects young patients, such as victims of trauma, who were previously healthy. The mortality rate is usually quoted as 50% to 70%, although it can be as high as

90% when the precipitating event is sepsis.[27] This high mortality rate remains despite better knowledge of the disease process.

Pathophysiology

Adult respiratory distress syndrome (ARDS) is essentially a continuation of the disease processes associated with noncardiogenic pulmonary edema. It is caused by many separate or combined factors. The precipitating event may be a direct injury damaging the alveolar capillary membrane or damage of the same membrane via substances from the pulmonary vasculature. The end result is stiff, noncompliant lungs. The progression can be divided into four phases (Table 4-1).[27]

The initial insult is associated with minimal respiratory symptoms. There is an increase in pulmonary capillary membrane permeability and proteinacious fluid leaks from the vessels into the interstitium and alveoli. Red and white blood cells move into the interstitium as well, causing further damage to the type I alveolar cells, which are responsible for surfactant production. A hyaline membrane also begins to form. It is not until stage III that acute respiratory distress occurs, with symptoms of severe dyspnea and hypoxemia. The alveolar fluid increases, thus decreasing the lung volume. Intrapulmonary shunting, which is defined as a defect in oxygen transfer from the alveolus to the blood caused by pulmonary arterial spasm or fluid in the alveoli, begins. The compliance or elasticity of the lung decreases as fluid accumulates and the

---

Table 4-1 Phases of ARDS

	Histology	Patient Parameters
Phase I (initial)	No findings	Hyperventilation
Phase II (latent)	Progressive alveolar and interstitial edema	Auscultatory changes Pulmonary disease on radiograph
Phase III	Alveolar septum 5–10 times thicker than normal Infiltration by leukocytes, plasma cells, and histiocytes	Acute respiratory failure, dyspnea, tachypnea, hypoxemia
Phase IV (irreversible)	Intra-alveolar fibrosis and fibroblastic infiltration of the alveolar septum	Intrapulmonary shunts >30%, severe hypoxemia, metabolic and respiratory acidosis

hyaline membrane thickens, making it much more difficult to ventilate the lung. Intubation and mechanical ventilation are necessary to sustain oxygenation at this point. As the disease worsens, shunting increases, and dead space can take up as much as 60% of the tidal volume, causing severe hypoxemia. Death usually results from myocardial ischemia.

ARDS is the result of many disorders including those that cause noncardiogenic pulmonary edema. Other causes include near drowning and drug overdose. Additional obstetric causes include amniotic fluid embolus, eclampsia, septic abortion, abruptio placentae, dead fetus syndrome with disseminated intravascular coagulation, hemorrhagic shock, and pulmonary infection. The incidence of ARDS in obstetrics is difficult to determine since most of the references in the literature are isolated case reports.[28,29]

Patient Presentation

The first clinical symptoms include dyspnea, tachypnea, hypoxemia, and cyanosis. Occasionally, fine, diffuse rales, which are easily differentiated from the coarse rales found in cardiogenic pulmonary edema, are auscultated. At this early stage, the symptoms could be related to a number of diagnoses. The definitive diagnosis of ARDS is realized when the patient has moderate to severe hypoxemia (PaO_2 of $\leq$ 60 mm Hg on 40% FIO_2), bilateral infiltrates on a chest radiograph, and normal left atrial pressures (18 mm Hg).[26] Pulmonary compliance is less, making the lungs stiff, and there is an increase in dead space or unventilated lung tissue as fluid accumulates.

The hypoxemia becomes refractory to supplemental oxygen. The patient must be intubated and mechanically ventilated with higher pressure because of decreased compliance. Radiographically, the lungs have bilateral diffuse infiltrates secondary to extravascular fluid and atelectasis. The pulmonary secretions are usually thick and have a protein content slightly less than or equal to that of serum. Hemodynamically, the patient presents in the first two phases with a normal pulmonary capillary wedge pressure and a slightly elevated pulmonary artery diastolic pressure because of elevated pulmonary vascular resistance. As the disease progresses, the pulmonary arterial pressure elevates markedly, while the pulmonary artery wedge pressure (PAWP) remains normal, in the absence of left ventricular dysfunction.

Therapy

The efficacy of therapy is determined by the severity of lung injury, the success of initial treatment, and the prevention of complications. When ARDS is diagnosed, the treatment is essentially supportive in nature. Therapy is focused on correcting the underlying cause of ARDS when possible. Intubation and mechanical ventilation are usually necessary to maintain the PaO$_2$ at 60 mm Hg.[30] Prolonged exposure to an inspired O$_2$ content greater than 60% causes pulmonary injury. Thus PEEP is usually added to increase ventilation by opening collapsed alveoli. PEEP is a continuous positive pressure that remains in the lung throughout the respiratory cycle, providing a larger surface area for gas exchange and decreasing the intrapulmonary shunt.[31] Intrapulmonary shunt is defined as that portion of the cardiac output going from the right side of the heart to the left side of the heart without respiring with alveolar gas, or blood that respires but achieves a PO$_2$ less than ideal.[32] The usual amount of PEEP is 10 to 25 cm H$_2$O, but the optimal amount depends on patient response. A major complication of PEEP is decreased cardiac output since the increase in intrathoracic pressure decreases venous return. PEEP also is associated with pulmonary barotrauma by overdistention of patent alveoli, pneumothorax, and subcutaneous emphysema.[31] The optimal amount of PEEP for each patient will maximize the PaO$_2$ as well as allow adequate cardiac output. Hemodynamic monitoring with a pulmonary artery flow-directed catheter is recommended for diagnosis of ARDS as well as the determination of adequate cardiac output.

Another important point of therapy is the maintenance of adequate hemoglobin to assure the best oxygen-carrying capacity. Judicious fluid therapy is required to decrease the possibility of concomitant left ventricular failure. Support of the total patient including nutrition and proper electrolyte balance is required to provide the patient the best chance for recovery.[27]

Complications of ARDS

Several complications, other than lung injury, may occur, which increases the mortality rate. Gastrointestinal bleeding is sometimes seen in patients who are intubated, due to stress ulceration in the stomach. Maintenance of an elevated gastric pH with antacids and medications that decrease gastric acid production is important.

The decrease in cardiac output seen with PEEP may be severe enough to cause fetal distress or renal failure. Dopamine in low dosages (<5 µg/kg/min) often increases renal perfusion without affecting peripheral blood pressure.[21] Occasionally, dialysis is required for filtration and fluid balance until the kidneys recover.

Infection is always a possibility with patients who have had a massive insult and have an accumulation of secretions that encourage bacterial growth. Disseminated intravascular coagulation is also caused by many of the same mechanisms that cause ARDS, including hemorrhage, aspiration of gastric contents, and sepsis.

PULMONARY EMBOLUS

Pulmonary embolus is an acute and often fatal condition affecting young, previously healthy patients. The onset is usually sudden and terrifying for the person experiencing it.

Pathophysiology

Pulmonary embolism is caused by the migration of thrombi formed in the legs (95%); the majority are from sites above the knee.[32,33] The source is usually deep veins, not the superficial veins involved in thrombophlebitis. The clot migrates to a portion of the pulmonary circulation and eventually becomes lodged in a vessel of the same size, preventing further blood flow to an area distal to the clot. Diminished blood flow to an area of the lung results in unoxygenated blood circulating peripherally. The severity of hypoxemia relates to the size and location of the clot.

Predisposing Factors

The incidence in pregnant patients is the same as in nonpregnant patients (0.3 to 0.5 per 1000).[33,34] Intrapartum pulmonary embolus is rare. However, the risk to patients in the first month postpartum is 49% greater than for nonpregnant patients.[34] There is a 1.5 in 1000 chance during pregnancy of deep vein thrombosis, and pulmonary embolism occurs in approximately 0.4 in 1000 deliveries. The increased occurrence postpartum relates to the hypercoagulable state of pregnancy. The fibrinogen level is elevated from 300 mg/dL to 450 mg/dL, and there is also a decrease in fibrinolytic activity. There is a large amount of venous stasis associated with pregnancy that is due to pressure of the gravid uterus on the vena cava. Pelvic thrombosis is more common in patients undergoing cesarean section rather than vaginal delivery because of decreased mobility and increased chance of pelvic infection. The incidence usually increases with age, parity, obesity, and decreased ambulation.

Patient Presentation

Symptoms depend on the severity and location of the embolus. Tachypnea and dyspnea are the most frequently seen symptoms of pulmonary embolus and are usually seen prior to diagnosis of deep vein thrombosis.[35-37] Pleuritic chest pain and apprehension occur in over 60% of cases. Other symptoms frequently seen are cough, tachycardia, rales, hemoptysis, and cyanosis. Patients with over 50% obstruction may present with signs of right-sided heart failure with jugular venous distention or liver distention. Multiple small pulmonary emboli may present with the same symptoms as a massive pulmonary embolus or without any symptoms at all. A chest radiograph may reveal atelectasis, infiltrates, or effusion.

Diagnosis

The diagnosis of a pulmonary embolus is made by detection of abnormal PaO_2 (at <80 mm Hg), an abnormal ventilation scan, or pulmonary angiography.[34] The unequivocal diagnosis of pulmonary embolus must be made prior to initiation of treatment. Anticoagulant therapy carries many risks for the patient, especially if she remains pregnant; however, mortality has been reported in up to 28% of untreated cases.[34] The patient who presents with tachypnea, dyspnea, and an arterial PaO_2 of <80 mm Hg should be suspected of having a pulmonary embolus. A chest radiograph may rule out other diagnoses but seldom confirms the diagnosis of pulmonary embolus. A perfusion or ventilation lung scan consists of intravenous or bronchial administration of a radioactive substance under fluoroscopy, and it will detect areas of decreased perfusion or ventilation. A pulmonary angiogram may be done if the ventilation and perfusion scans are not diagnostic. Antepartum fetal exposure is from 50 to 500 mrads and more, in angiography.[36]

Treatment

Heparin is the drug of choice for anticoagulation antepartum and intrapartum since it does not cross the placenta, and it is also used occasionally postpartum.[34–36] The intravenous route provides a more constant level of anticoagulation than does subcutaneous injection. The dose is adjusted to maintain an activated partial thromboplastin time (aPTT) of 1.5 to 2 times the control value. The risk of heparin therapy is hemorrhage, which occurs in approximately 5% to 10% of patients. The anticoagulation effect can be reversed quickly with protamine sulfate in the event of an emergency delivery.

Warfarin is used only in postpartum patients since it crosses the placenta and is associated with a fetal malformation known as warfarin embryopathy in 15% to 25% of patients when administered in the first 6 to 9 weeks of gestation.[38] It is titrated using the partial thromboplastin time (PTT) to maintain 1.5 to 2 times the control value. The major risk seen with warfarin is hemorrhage. Many medications increase or decrease the anticoagulation effect, so care should be taken to evaluate concomitant drug therapy. Full anticoagulation is recommended for 7 to 10 days, followed by 6 weeks of subcutaneous heparin in antepartum patients or oral warfarin in postpartum patients. Antithrombus hose (TED hose), elevation of the leg, and moist heat are recommended when a clot is detected in the leg.

Oxygen therapy is administered per mask for most patients during the acute phase after a pulmonary embolus. Occasionally, in the case of a large embolus, intubation and mechanical ventilation may be required until the clot dissolves or is removed.

Surgical treatment is not frequently utilized since anticoagulant therapy is usually effective. Those patients with a pulmonary embolus large enough to require surgery often die within an hour of the event. If the patient survives the acute event and is diagnosed with a massive embolus, an embolectomy may be performed. Interruption of the vena cava using clips, ligation, or filters is occasionally used for recurring emboli despite heparinization. Thrombotic therapy using urokinase or streptokinase is also available. These agents activate the fibrinolytic system to actually dissolve the clot. This therapy cannot be used prior to delivery because of the high risk of hemorrhage.

NURSING IMPLICATIONS

The care of patients with respiratory problems is multifaceted. These patients are often critically and acutely ill, with many other organ systems being affected. Thus the nurse must be constantly watching for symptoms that may herald yet another crisis.

With a few exceptions, care of all respiratory patients is similar, regardless of the primary disease. First and foremost is the maintenance of adequate ventilatory function. Since the nurse is almost constantly with the patient, she or he is the first to notice subtle signs of increasing hypoxemia, decreasing compliance, and respiratory fatigue indicative of a worsening condition. These patients require *frequent assessment* (at least every 1 to 2 hours in acute episodes and every 4 hours otherwise) of respiratory rate, breath sounds, and general condition. Although patients are able to verbalize, their nonverbal behavior may be more indicative of their condition. Patients in respiratory distress present with tachypnea, tachycardia, restlessness, cool and clammy skin, and cyanosis, and they utilize accessory muscles to breathe. Respiratory assessment should include a detailed exam of normal and adventitious breath sounds and accurate documentation of the location of the adventitious sounds.

The primary nursing goal should be optimization of oxygen exchange. This can be facilitated by making the patient as comfortable as possible, elevating the head of the bed, and providing warm, humidified oxygen by mask or nasal cannula when the patient does not tolerate the mask. Provision of emotional and physical support is of ultimate importance since apprehension worsens the respiratory distress.

Arterial blood gases should be obtained prior to initiation of therapy and 30 minutes after changes in ventilatory support. Blood gases drawn in this manner provide an early assessment of how the patient is tolerating the alterations in therapy and aid in determining whether increased ventilatory support is required.

Monitoring the patient's response to therapy is another nursing responsibility. Oxygen saturation measures the amount of oxygen attached to hemoglobin. The reduction of oxygen in the blood prompts the dissociation of oxygen from hemoglobin, resulting in a decreased saturation. The pulse oximeter provides a continuous readout of arterial oxygen saturation, which falls acutely during a hypoxic episode, indicating the need for further assessment. Mixed venous oxygen saturation is another method to determine the adequacy of cardiopulmonary function. The source of the mixed venous blood gas is the distal port of the pulmonary artery catheter. Knowledge of the side effects of medications commonly given to patients with respiratory complications is also important, such as the increased occurrence of dysrhythmias with bronchodilators and the decrease in cardiac output following diuresis.

Patients on mechanical ventilation experience these same fears and apprehensions but are unable to verbalize. Every effort should be made to allow patients to write notes and ask questions. They often feel out of control of respiration, become agitated, and "fight" the ventilator. Use of a sedative such as morphine sulfate given intravenously in small doses relieves some of the panicky feeling. Explanation of equipment and procedures also helps allay fear. These patients must be assessed frequently for decreased breath sounds caused by secretions or movement of the endotracheal tube into one of the bronchi. The ventilator must also be assessed for proper function and correctly set alarms.

When intubated, patients are no longer able to clear their airways of secretions, so suctioning is required. However, suctioning is not a benign procedure and may cause trauma of the carina, hypoxia, and extreme apprehension. Thus suctioning should be done according to need as demonstrated by rhonchi heard on auscultation or increased pressures required to ventilate. The procedure should be explained and the patient hyperoxygenated with five breaths of 100% oxygen. When secretions are tenacious, 3 to 5 mL of normal saline may be instilled prior to oxygenation.[39] The suction catheter is then inserted without suction until resistance is met and withdrawn quickly, using a twisting motion and intermittent suction. The oxygen is quickly replaced, the patient again hyperoxygenated, and suctioning is repeated when necessary.

Patients requiring PEEP for the treatment of pulmonary edema or ARDS are even more susceptible to hypoxemia during suctioning or ventilatory tubing changes. A special PEEP valve placed on the endotracheal tube maintains PEEP during these procedures.[40]

Hemodynamic monitoring is important for the differential diagnosis of similar disease processes, but especially to determine the effects of therapy. To be effective, the readings must be accurate. Ventilated patients have falsely elevated pulmonary artery pressures when the digital readout is used because of the positive pressure generated by the ventilator. For accuracy, a graphic recording should be used and the pressures assessed at the end of expiration.[41] This correlates to the highest value with spontaneous breathing and the lowest with mechanical ventilation.

Another advantage of the pulmonary artery catheter in acute respiratory situations is the availability of continuous monitoring of mixed venous oxygen saturation, a direct indication of oxygen demand. This value changes immediately in response to hypoxia, increased oxygen demand, and decreased cardiac output.

CONCLUSION

The care of patients with respiratory problems requires a thorough knowledge of pulmonary physiology and pathophysiology as well as the effects of respiratory problems on other body systems. There is also a grave risk to the fetus when the patient remains pregnant while hypoxic. The majority of articles reviewed were written on postpartum care. If the patient is antepartum, the responsibilities of the nurse are doubled, for there will be signs of hypoxia from the fetus as well as from the mother, in the form of fetal distress. The most important goal in the care of these patients is maintenance of adequate oxygenation and perfusion, which results in a good outcome for mother and fetus.

REFERENCES

1. Lee W, Cotton DB. Cardiorespiratory changes during pregnancy. In: Clark SL, Phelan JP, Cotton DB, eds. *Critical Care Obstetrics.* Oradell, NJ: Medical Economics Books; 1987:39-70.
2. Easterling TR, Benedetti TJ. Principles of invasive hemodynamic monitoring in pregnancy. In: Clark SL, Phelan JP, Cotton DB, eds. *Critical Care Obstetrics.* Oradell, NJ: Medical Economics Books; 1987:10-23.
3. Awe RJ, Nicotra MB, Newson TD, Viles R. Arterial oxygenation and alveolar-arterial gradients in term pregnancy. *Obstet Gynecol.* 1979;53:182-186.
4. Boba A, Linkie DM, Plotz EJ. Fetal responses to maternal oxygen inhalation during hemorrhagic stress. *Am J Obstet Gynecol.* 1967;97:919-924.
5. Benedetti TJ, Kates R, Williams V. Hemodynamic observations in severe preeclampsia complicated by pulmonary edema. *Am J Obstet Gynecol.* 1985;152:330-334.
6. Puri VK, Weil MH, Michaels S, Carlson RW. Pulmonary edema associated with reduction in plasma oncotic pressure. *Surg Gynecol Obstet.* 1980;151:344-348.
7. Puri VK, Freund U, Carlson RW, Weil MH. Colloid osmotic and pulmonary wedge pressures in acute respiratory failure following hemorrhage. *Surg Gynecol Obstet.* 1978;147:537-540.

8. Benedetti TJ, Carlson RW. Studies of colloid osmotic pressure in pregnancy-induced hypertension. *Am J Obstet Gynecol.* 1979;135:308-311.
9. Clark SL, Cotton DB. Clinical indications for pulmonary artery catheterization in the patient with severe preeclampsia. *Am J Obstet Gynecol.* 1988;158:453-458.
10. Strauss RG, Keefer R, Burke T, Civetta JM. Hemodynamic monitoring of cardiogenic pulmonary edema complicating toxemia of pregnancy. *Obstet Gynecol.* 1980;55:170-174.
11. Sibai BM, Mabie BC, Harvey CJ, Gonzalez AR. Pulmonary edema in severe preeclampsia-eclampsia: analysis of thirty-seven consecutive cases. *Am J Obstet Gynecol.* 1987;156:1174-1179.
12. Katz M, Robertson PA, Creasy RK. Cardiovascular complications associated with terbutaline treatment for preterm labor. *Am J Obstet Gynecol.* 1981;139:605-608.
13. Jacobs MM, Knight AB, Arias F. Maternal pulmonary edema resulting from betamimetic and glucocorticoid therapy. *Obstet Gynecol.* 1980;56:56-59.
14. Wagner JM, Morton MJ, Johnson KA, O'Grady JP, Speroff L. Terbutaline and maternal cardiac function. *JAMA.* 1981;246:2697-2701.
15. Cunningham FG, Pritchard JA, Hankins GDV. Peripartum heart failure: idiopathic cardiomyopathy or compounding cardiovascular events? *Obstet Gynecol.* 1986;67:157-168.
16. Duff P, Gibbs RS. Maternal sepsis. In: Berkowitz RL, ed. *Critical Care of the Obstetric Patient.* New York: Churchill Livingstone; 1983:189-217.
17. Karetzky MS, Khan AU. Review of current concepts in aspiration pneumonia. *Heart Lung.* 1977;6:321-326.
18. Killam A. Amniotic fluid embolism. *Clin Obstet Gynecol.* 1985;28:32-36.
19. Tranbaugh RF, Lewis FR. Mechanisms and etiologic factors of pulmonary edema. *Surg Gynecol Obstet.* 1984;158:193-206.
20. Niederman MS, Matthay RA. Asthma and other severe respiratory diseases during pregnancy. In: Berkowitz RL, ed. *Critical Care of the Obstetric Patient.* New York: Churchill Livingstone; 1983:335-366.
21. Clark SL, Greenspoon JS, Aldahl D, Phelan JP. Severe preeclampsia with persistent oliguria: management of hemodynamic subsets. *Am J Obstet Gynecol.* 1986;154:490-494.
22. Morgan M. Amniotic fluid embolus. *Anaesthesia.* 1979;34:20-32.
23. Mulder JI. Amniotic fluid embolism: an overview and case report. *Am J Obstet Gynecol.* 1985;152:430-435.
24. Clark SL, Montz FJ, Phelan JP. Hemodynamic alterations associated with amniotic fluid embolism: a reappraisal. *Am J Obstet Gynecol.* 1985;151:617-621.
25. Clark SL, Cotton DB, Gonik B, Greenspoon J, Phelan JP. Central hemodynamic alterations in amniotic fluid embolism. *Am J Obstet Gynecol.* 1988;158:1124-1126.
26. Ashbaugh DG, Bigelow DB, Petty TL, Levine BE. Acute respiratory distress in adults. *Lancet.* 1967;2:319-323.
27. Hankins GDV. Acute pulmonary injury and respiratory failure during pregnancy. In: Clark SL, Phelan JP, Cotton DB, eds. *Critical Care Obstetrics.* Oradell, NJ: Medical Economics Books, 1987:290-314.
28. Bernard GR, Bradley RB. Adult respiratory distress syndrome: diagnosis and management. *Heart Lung.* 1986;15:250-255.
29. Elkington KW, Greb LC. Adult respiratory distress syndrome as a complication of acute pyelonephritis during pregnancy: case report and discussion. *Obstet Gynecol.* 1986;67:18S-20S.
30. Craig KC, Pierson DJ, Carrico CJ. The clinical application of positive end-expiratory pressure (PEEP) in the adult respiratory distress syndrome (ARDS). *Respir Care.* 1985;30:184-201.
31. Kirby RR, Downs JB, Civetta JM, et al. High level of positive end expiratory pressure (PEEP) in acute respiratory insufficiency. *Chest.* 1975;67:156-163.
32. Moser KM. Pulmonary embolism. *Am Rev Respir Dis.* 1977;115:829-852.

33. Richards SR, Barrows H, O'Shaughnessy R. Intrapartum pulmonary embolus: a case report. *J Reprod Med.* 1985;30:64-66.
34. Handin RI. Thromboembolic complications of pregnancy and oral contraceptives. *Prog Cardiovasc Dis.* 1974;16:395-405.
35. Bolan JC. Thromboembolic complications of pregnancy. *Clin Obstet Gynecol.* 1983;26:913-922.
36. Roberts SL. Pulmonary tissue perfusion altered: emboli. *Heart Lung.* 1987;16:128-137.
37. Rutherford SE, Phelan JP. Deep venous thrombosis and pulmonary embolus. In: Clark SL, Phelan JP, Cotton DB, eds. *Critical Care Obstetrics.* Oradell, NJ: Medical Economics Books; 1987:126-151.
38. Hall JG, Pauli RM, Wilson KM. Maternal and fetal sequelae of anticoagulation during pregnancy. *Am J Med.* 1980;68:122-140.
39. Brent-Hemman E. Management of the patient requiring ventilatory support. In: Hudak CM, Gallo BM, Lohr T, eds. *Critical Care Nursing—A Holistic Approach.* 4th ed. Philadelphia: JB Lippincott; 1986:305-317.
40. Shumann L, Parsons GH. Tracheal suctioning and ventilatory tubing changes in adult respiratory distress syndrome: use of a positive end-expiratory pressure valve. *Heart Lung.* 1985;14:362-367.
41. Darovic GO. *Hemodynamic Monitoring. Invasive and Noninvasive Clinical Application.* Philadelphia: WB Saunders; 1987.

Chapter 5

Hematologic Complications in Pregnancy

Melissa C. Sisson

SICKLE CELL ANEMIA

Despite evidence that menarche is delayed and that fertility may be adversely affected, women with sickle cell anemia do become pregnant.[1] The inherited sickle cell disorders are associated with a high incidence of maternal and perinatal morbidity and mortality and are characterized by acute, recurring vaso-occlusive episodes. Homozygous sickle cell anemia (HbS-S) is the most common of the incurable hemoglobinopathies. One in 600 black Americans is affected by the disease, which along with its more severe variants, thalassemia and hemoglobin S-C disease, is responsible for shortened life spans.[2] Prior to the 1950s, pregnant patients with HbS-S were rarely seen because they did not survive puberty or they experienced severe morbidity that precluded reproduction. The potential for numerous medical and perinatal complications, including widespread organ damage, mandates that sickle cell crisis during gestation be treated as an obstetric emergency.

Pathophysiology

The hemoglobin molecule is composed of heme surrounded by four globin chains. The structure and function of the globin chains are genetically determined. Abnormalities in hemoglobin structure are representative of deletion, inversion, or substitution of the amino acid sequence in the globin chains.[3] Substitution of a single amino acid on each of the two ß-chains differentiates sickle cell hemoglobin from normal hemoglobin and is responsible for the disruption of the oxygen-carrying capacity and survival of the affected red blood cells.[2] Hypoxia and acidosis cause the sickle cell hemoglobin to aggre-

91

gate and form polymers that coalesce into a gel that converts the red cell into a sickle shape. If the cell is reoxygenated, the sickling will reverse. However, if the process is protracted, the cell membrane is affected, and irreversible sickling occurs. Sickle cells obstruct blood flow in the microvasculature; particularly susceptible are the spleen, bone marrow, and placenta. As resistance to blood flow increases, red cell passage is delayed, and cells adhere to the vessel endothelium, resulting in stasis. Vascular stasis aggravates hypoxia and acidosis, which accelerate sickling, eventually leading to tissue ischemia and infarction. The following events may initiate a crisis: acid-base derangement, dehydration, trauma, fever, viral and bacterial infection, anesthesia, hemorrhage, extreme fatigue, drug overdose, strenuous exercise, severe stress, alcohol intoxication, exposure to cold, antivenin injections, and high-altitude, nonpressurized flights.[2]

Patient Presentation

Most women with hemoglobinopathies are diagnosed prior to pregnancy; however, it is wise to screen all black parturients. After a patient is screened as being positive, the diagnosis is confirmed by hemoglobin electrophoresis, which differentiates the type of abnormal hemoglobin present. Laboratory findings that are consistent with the diagnosis of sickle cell anemia include (1) hematocrit less than 20%, (2) hemoglobin level less than 6 g/dL, (3) reticulocyte count greater than 10%, and (4) elevation of serum bilirubin level.[2]

Several factors associated with pregnancy that may complicate HbS-S include hypercoagulability, predisposition to infection, vascular stasis in the pelvis and lower extremities, increased metabolic and hematologic demands, and increased stress.[3] Sickle cell crisis refers to a number of acute events that occur in individuals with sickle cell disease. The two major categories are hematologic and vaso-occlusive crises, the latter of the two being more likely to occur during pregnancy.

Vaso-occlusive crisis usually arises during the second half of pregnancy. It is characterized by sudden recurrent episodes of pain involving the joints, abdomen, chest, and vertebrae. Hematologic crisis, by comparison, is a rare event associated with a falling hematocrit, reticulopenia, weakness, pallor, and possibly cardiac failure.[2]

When sickle cell crisis is suspected, it must be determined whether it is (1) an uncomplicated vaso-occlusive attack, (2) a crisis associated with infection, (3) a surgical or obstetric disorder, or (4) possibly an instance of malingering.[2] Infection is the precipitating event in 25% of pregnancy-related crises, with pneumonia, urinary tract infection, osteomyelitis, and endomyometritis being among the most frequently encountered types.[2]

Conditions associated with pregnancy that may mimic a vaso-occlusive crisis include ruptured uterus, abruptio placentae, and pregnancy-induced hypertension. These, along with medical-surgical conditions such as cholecystitis, pancreatitis, cystitis, and pneumonia, should be considered carefully in the differential diagnosis.

There is no definitive laboratory assay that will detect the presence of sickle cell crisis. Both vaso-occlusive crisis and infection will cause elevations of the total segmented white blood cell counts. With significant bacterial infection, bands or nonsegmented white blood cells are increased beyond what would be expected for a simple vaso-occlusive crisis.[2] Leukocyte alkaline phosphatase activity may be greatly increased secondary to bacterial infection, in contrast to a normal range for vaso-occlusive crisis alone.[2] Serum lactate dehydrogenase levels rise significantly in proportion to the severity of the crisis and therefore are useful when the patient's baseline levels are known. The serum bilirubin level is normally elevated in the patient with HbS-S and may reach 15 to 20 mg/dL during crisis.[4]

Management and Related Nursing Interventions

Perhaps the key to a successful outcome in the pregnancy that is complicated by sickle cell disease is careful vigilance throughout gestation. The time-honored therapy of these patients is largely symptomatic and centers around alleviation of crisis.[3]

Antepartum

Early prenatal care and frequent antepartum surveillance are the rule, with more centers advocating visits every 2 weeks followed by weekly visits after 20 weeks in the patient who is asymptomatic. Laboratory studies should include a complete blood count with differential, reticulocyte count, liver function tests, rubella titer, Coombs' test, VDRL, and urinalysis. Continuity of care is essential to ensure patient compliance with the regimen of tests, recommendations, and restrictions.[5] Patient response to the pregnancy and degree of anxiety should be assessed. Nutritional counseling is of importance, and folic acid supplementation is advised to prevent megaloblastic crisis. Antepartum fetal surveillance, including weekly nonstress tests/oxytocin challenge tests beginning at 34 weeks' gestation, is recommended.

The role of prophylactic transfusion therapy during the antepartum period is controversial. Some authorities advocate partial exchange of HbS-S hemoglobin for normal HbA hemoglobin in patients with severe disease.[3] Starting at 18 to 20 weeks or at 28 weeks, levels of HbA are maintained at 20%, 30%, and 40%, and hematocrit above 25%. Others recommend more conservative management, with transfusion advised only as complications arise. Probably the most critical factor is good prenatal care, with judicious use of transfusions as indicated.[6]

When vaso-occlusive crisis occurs and the pregnancy is remote from delivery, a partial exchange transfusion of HbA red cells for HbS-S red cells is an important therapy. Erythrocytophoresis can be accomplished manually or via automation, utilizing an IBM 2997 cell separator. The manual method involves phlebotomy followed by infusion of buffy coat–poor washed red blood cells. Automated erythrocytophoresis affords several advantages over the manual method. It provides closer monitoring of withdrawal and infusion, protects the patient from overload or hypovolemia, and is less time consuming, and the pain associated with the crisis begins to abate usually within 60 minutes.[2] At the end of the exchange, the hematocrit should be 30% or greater, the HbA level greater than 50%, and the hemoglobin level greater than 9 g/dL.

Because crisis is often accompanied by dehydration and hyperosmolarity, rehydration with Ringer's lactate solution, usually 1 L over 2 hours followed by 125 mL/h, is advised.[2] When the crisis is associated with an infection, broad-spectrum antibiotic therapy is initiated after cultures are taken. Since the sickle cell patient is at risk for infection, Foley catheters and central venous lines are to be avoided. If a respiratory infection is suspected or when PaO_2 is less than 70 mm Hg, oxygen therapy is indicated.[2] Three liters per minute by nasal prongs is generally adequate.

Analgesia requirements vary from patient to patient, so treatment of pain during crisis should be individualized. Meperidine may be indicated when pain is severe; however, a non-narcotic such as acetaminophen should be substituted once the crisis begins to resolve.

Continuous electronic fetal monitoring is advised during treatment for vaso-occlusive crisis because the risk of fetal loss at this time is substantial.[2] Ominous patterns should be viewed with caution since they may be transient and resolve as the mother's condition returns to normal.

Intrapartum

Labor and delivery of the sickle cell patient present both therapeutic and diagnostic challenges to the perinatal team. For example, it may be difficult to distinguish vaso-occlusive crisis from the onset of labor, or from the development of an obstetric complication such as abruptio placentae. When vaso-occlusive crisis is diagnosed, partial exchange transfusion, or at the very least, transfusion of two to four units of buffy coat–poor washed donor red blood cells, is indicated. The laboring patient is maintained in a lateral position, and oxygen therapy is initiated. Monitoring of mother and fetus must be meticulous. Vital signs and intake and output should be assessed a minimum of every hour.

Acid-base status should be evaluated serially. Coagulation studies, including platelet counts and serum fibrinogen levels, are also assessed. Continuous electronic fetal monitoring and fetal scalp sampling assist in the assessment of fetal status.

Conduction anesthesia is avoided in the patient in crisis, but may be safe and preferred in the asymptomatic patient.[2] Blood and fluid replacement is of paramount importance to maintain circulatory volume. Because cold may precipitate crisis, hypothermia in cold delivery rooms is avoided. If maternal condition has been compromised during labor and delivery, a skilled neonatal resuscitation team should be available.

Postpartum

Significant hemodynamic events occur during the postpartum period, and this, in combination with the stress of labor, may precipitate vaso-occlusive crisis. Adherence to the principles of optimal hydration, avoidance of hyperviscosity, and maintenance by transfusion of HbA at high levels are probably most critical in the immediate postoperative and postpartum periods.[2] Additionally, it is important to observe the patient closely for signs of endomyometritis and urinary tract infection. The sickle cell patient is also at risk for congestive heart failure and pulmonary embolus during the postpartum period; therefore, early ambulation is advisable.

Two of the most important nursing interventions for the pregnant patient with severe sickle cell disease are the establishment of a supportive relationship and constant vigilance for the development of complications.[2] Emotional stress alone can precipitate vaso-occlusive crisis, so that education by a caring nurse to alleviate anxiety becomes therapeutic. Attention during all phases of pregnancy to vital signs, laboratory results, intake and output, fetal reactivity, acid-base status, and pain relief directly affect medical management and can profoundly influence the outcomes of mother and fetus.

Though prospects for future treatment modalities are hopeful, sickle cell disease remains incurable. The mainstays of current therapy will therefore continue to involve careful assessment, follow-up, and attention to medical detail.

DISSEMINATED INTRAVASCULAR COAGULATION

Disseminated intravascular coagulation (DIC) has been described extensively since the 1950s. It is not a separate clinical entity but is an intermediary of other diseases, including some that may complicate obstetric practice. Weiner[7] suggests that DIC is best viewed as a continuum along which a variety of symptoms occur and broadly defines it as excess consumption of at least the soluble plasma-clotting components.

Normal Coagulation

Hemostasis is the process by which blood is maintained in a liquid state within vessels and loss of blood from damaged vessels is prevented. Disruption of the endothelium as a result of vascular damage sets into motion the first phase of hemostasis, which is formation of a temporary platelet plug. Exposure of the basement membrane of the vessel wall causes platelets to adhere and aggregate at the damaged site. The resulting platelet plug is responsible for sealing the defect.

The second phase of hemostasis involves the formation of a fibrin clot that stabilizes and strengthens the platelet plug.[8] The formation of a fibrin clot is the end product of sequential enzymatic steps that lead to the generation of thrombin. Thrombin converts fibrinogen to fibrin clot.

Coagulation is activated by three types of injuries: trauma to tissue, trauma to vascular endothelium, and trauma to red blood cells or platelets. When one or more of these initiating injuries occur, thrombin is generated via the intrinsic pathway (via activation of factor VII) or the extrinsic pathway (via activation of factor XII or release of tissue thromboplastin). Common regulatory mechanisms work through the clotting system, and a common convergent pathway brings the intrinsic and extrinsic systems together for the final stages of clot formation.[7] This final common pathway begins with the activation of factor X, which leads to the conversion of circulating prothrombin to thrombin. Thrombin acts as a proteolytic enzyme cleaving fibrinopeptides A and B from fibrinogen to form fibrin monomers. Fibrin monomers form an insoluble network at the site of injury, and, when stabilized by factor XIII, provide hemostasis.

The fibrinolytic system breaks down fibrin clot and maintains the liquid state of blood. When a fibrin clot is formed, plasminogen is incorporated into the clot and is converted into plasmin, a potent proteolytic enzyme that lyses fibrinogen and fibrin and liberates fibrin degradation products. The degradation products are known as X, Y, D, and E fragments and act to inhibit the action of thrombin and to render platelets dysfunctional by coating their surfaces.[4]

Pregnancy is a state of hypercoagulability. Changes in the hemostatic mechanism occur to maintain the pregnancy and to protect the host from blood loss at delivery. Several coagulation parameters are altered. Levels of factors X, VIII, V, VII, IX, and XII increase during pregnancy, while levels of factors XI and XIII decrease.[9] The platelet count remains within the normal range. Changes also occur within the fibrinolytic system that effectively reduce fibrinolysis until after delivery of the placenta.[9]

Pathophysiology

DIC represents the coagulation system that has gone awry. The normal regulatory mechanisms fail, so that cascade activation is no longer confined to the area of injury. Fibrin polymerizes away from the area of collagen exposure, becomes lodged in the microvasculature, and produces tissue hypoxia and ischemic necrosis.[7] Excess free plasmin degrades fibrinogen factors V, VIII, IX, and XI; adrenocorticotropic hormone; growth hormone; insulin complement; and other plasma proteins.[7] Platelets become entrapped in fibrin networks, which leads to thrombocytopenia. The process is self-perpetuating, and the clinical picture is one of consumptive thrombosis with resultant hemorrhage.

A number of obstetric conditions predispose the patient to DIC, including pre-eclampsia, eclampsia, abruptio placentae, amniotic fluid embolism, intrauterine fetal demise, and saline abortion.[7] In the normal pregnancy, the coagulation and fibrinolytic systems appear to be in a hyperdynamic state, with both increased production and turnover of many coagulation factors.[10] It has been hypothesized that the pregnant woman is in a primed state and, therefore, when exposed to the appropriate stimulus, will develop the systemic manifestations of DIC.[10]

Diagnosis

The clinical presentation of DIC is variable. The process may be compensated, with the increase in consumption of clotting factors being met by a concomitant increase in production. A gradual progression from a compensated state to an uncompensated one with a decline in levels of fibrinogen, platelets, and coagulation factors, leads to spontaneous bleeding.[11] In many patients the onset of DIC is explosive, and the clinical picture is one of a bleeding diathesis and localized thrombosis.[11] In the obstetric patient a chronic consumptive coagulopathy is more common.[7]

Hemorrhage typically occurs at sites of trauma such as venipuncture sites, surgical incision sites, intravenous or intra-arterial line sites, and drain sites. Ecchymoses, petechiae, and purpura are common. There may also be evidence of vaginal bleeding, gingival bleeding, and blood in the stool.

Seven percent of patients have clinical signs of thrombosis.[11] This is related to ischemia, and clinical manifestations are dependent on the organ affected. Signs of thrombosis may include peripheral cyanosis; gangrene; renal impairment; drowsiness, confusion, or coma; and cardiorespiratory failure.[11]

There are a variety of laboratory tests that aid in the detection of DIC and also serve to guide therapy. The most sensitive determinant of DIC is the level of antithrombin III (AT III).[7] AT III inhibits thrombin, so when there is increased thrombin in the system, AT III is consumed, and its activity declines. The more common laboratory tests are less sensitive but are useful. Traditionally, platelet count, prothrombin time (PT), partial thromboplastin time (PTT), and serum fibrinogen level are measured. The level of fibrin split products (FSP), thrombin time, and red blood cell morphology may also be helpful.

Generally, the PT, which reflects extrinsic coagulation, is prolonged, as is the PTT, which measures intrinsic coagulation. However, 50% of patients with acute DIC will have a normal PT and PTT.[7] Fifteen percent of patients will have a normal FSP level; this test assesses fibrinolytic activity. Red blood cell morphology may indicate the presence of hemolysis caused by fragmentation of red blood cells as they pass through the fibrin-obstructed microvasculature. Thrombin time measures conversion of fibrinogen to fibrin and is prolonged in DIC.

Obstetric patients who are at high risk for consumptive coagulation abnormalities should, at the minimum, undergo screening that includes a complete blood count, platelet count, PT, PTT, and serum fibrinogen level. In the patient who is actively bleeding and has a living fetus, laboratory tests may be of limited value because of delays in receiving results. In such an instance, it is recommended that 5 to 10 mL of the patient's blood be drawn and placed in a nonheparinized tube and observed for clot formation at 37°C every 30 seconds for 5 minutes; failure of clot formation suggests overt coagulopathy.[10]

Management and Related Nursing Interventions

The elimination of the underlying cause of DIC is central to its successful management. Fortunately, in most instances of obstetric DIC, this is readily accomplished by termination of the pregnancy. Removal of the fetus and placenta results in rapid cessation of the process.[11]

Initially, the outcome for mother and fetus can be improved significantly when it is recognized that the patient is at risk for DIC and the process is detected early. Assessment is of key importance, and the alert provider who detects the subtle signs of bleeding can avert disaster.

Supportive measures are critically important in the management of DIC. Acidemia, shock, and hypoxia all interact to escalate the severity of coagulopathy and should be treated aggressively.[11] Stabilization of maternal vital signs is imperative and may require vigorous volume replacement and inotropic support. Transfusion of fresh whole blood is optimal, but its availability is limited, so more realistic alternatives are packed red blood cells and fresh frozen plasma. Clotting factors and AT III are replaced by fresh frozen plasma, and the goal of red blood cell transfusion is to restore maximal oxygen-carrying capacity by increasing the hematocrit to 30%. Cryoprecipitate contains fibrinogen and other clotting factors in a smaller volume and is an alternative to fresh frozen plasma in the volume-restricted patient. Administration of platelets should be a consideration in actively bleeding or preoperative patients with platelet counts below 50,000. Spontaneous bleeding may occur with platelet counts under 20,000. Meticulous blood banking is an essential component of care for these patients.

Volume replacement should be quantitative and is best achieved by monitoring central venous or pulmonary artery pressures. Urinary output is also a helpful index of volume and perfusion status when used in conjunction with other parameters. Generally, urine output exceeding 25 mL/h coincides with adequate circulating volume and perfusion.[11]

Heparin has been advocated in the treatment of DIC, but current consensus is that there are few indications for its use in obstetrics. Heparin exerts its effect by increasing the activity of AT III, which inhibits thrombin. However, in DIC AT III is consumed, theoretically reducing the effectiveness of heparin. Heparin is probably best reserved for cases that prove refractory to replacement therapy.

The effects of DIC have the potential to be systemic, particularly when blood loss is great. Renal failure, shock lung, and liver failure can occur in association with hypoperfusion secondary to blood loss. Serial determinations of arterial blood gases and electrolyte, blood urea nitrogen, creatinine, and liver enzyme levels assist in ascertaining compromise of major organs.

The role of the perinatal nurse is that of an astute observer. When the patient is known to be at risk for DIC, intensive surveillance is mandated, and the well-being of both mother and fetus must be guarded closely. When the patient is acutely affected, many aspects of supportive therapy fall within the scope of nursing practice. Emotional support is of particular importance to the family and patient with DIC (Table 5-1).

Table 5-1 Summary of Nursing Interventions for DIC

1. Obtain history to ascertain risk status.
2. Monitor maternal vital signs and fetal heart rate continuously.
3. Provide constant physical assessment, being alert for multiple organ involvement.
4. Monitor laboratory data for abnormality.
5. Quantitate blood loss hourly.
6. Quantitate intake and output hourly.
7. Administer blood and blood products as necessary.
8. Assess hemodynamic parameters.
9. Provide emotional support.

HELLP SYNDROME

Weinstein[12] in his 1982 report of 29 cases was the first to refer to the triad of hemolysis (H), elevated liver enzyme levels (EL), and low platelet count (LP) as HELLP syndrome. The laboratory abnormalities are associated with pregnancy-induced hypertension (PIH) and have been described by other investigators. The use of the term "HELLP syndrome" seems to be growing, as is the controversy over its incidence, significance, and management.

Incidence

PIH complicates approximately 5% to 7% of pregnancies in the United States. The number of these patients who develop HELLP is presently unknown. Sibai and coworkers[13] studied 112 patients with severe preeclampsia/eclampsia and found the incidence of HELLP to be 4% to 12%. They concluded, however, that the true incidence was unknown because of variations in diagnostic criteria.

Pathophysiology

PIH is characterized by vasospasm in the microvasculature and increased capillary permeability. HELLP can be a consequence of this process.

Microangiopathic hemolytic anemia (MAHA) occurs when red blood cells (RBCs) are fragmented as they pass through fibrin-obstructed, damaged blood vessels. Vasospasm produces both fibrin deposition and damage to the intimal lining of blood vessels. RBCs are more likely to hemolyze because of a pathologic alteration in the cell membrane, which is attributed to increased levels of free fatty acids and decreased serum albumin, both of which are associated with PIH.[14]

The diagnosis of MAHA is confirmed by the presence of schistocytes and burr cells on peripheral blood smear. Schistocytes are small, irregular fragments of RBCs, and burr cells are contracted RBCs with spiny projections along the cell membrane. A low serum haptoglobin level is indicative of MAHA.[15] Haptoglobin is a plasma protein that binds with free hemoglobin, which is increased secondary to MAHA and forms a complex that is removed by the reticuloendothelial system.

A number of histologic changes occur in the liver as a result of PIH. Patients with HELLP have demonstrated fibrin thrombi in the hepatic sinusoids, with areas of focal necrosis and subcapsular hemorrhages.[14] Abnormal elevations of serum glutamic-oxaloacetic transaminase (SGOT) and serum glutamic-pyruvic transaminase (SGPT) levels are indicative of liver dysfunction. Hyperbilirubinemia has also been described, although it is a less frequent finding.

Thrombocytopenia occurs as the vascular endothelium is disrupted by intense vasospasm. Exposure of the underlying collagen activates platelets that adhere to vessel walls and form aggregates. The thrombocytopenia is, therefore, consumptive in nature. A deprivation of prostacyclin, a potent hormone that inhibits platelet activation, has been implicated as a possible mechanism for platelet consumption.[16]

Quantitation of laboratory values for diagnosis of HELLP requires further definition. Presently, criteria for diagnosis vary institutionally. Generally, the presence of schistocytosis on peripheral blood smear, an elevation of the SGOT level to 60 IU or greater, and a platelet count of less than 100,000 seem to be the laboratory abnormalities used most often to describe HELLP.

Management and Related Nursing Interventions

The management of the patient with hemolysis, elevated liver enzyme levels, and thrombocytopenia associated with PIH is controversial. Weinstein[12] advocates expeditious delivery to obtain optimal outcome for mother and fetus. Others feel a more conservative approach is warranted, particularly when the fetus is immature.[13]

Sibai and associates[13] recommend aggressive management in the presence of true HELLP because of its association with poor maternal-fetal outcome but suggest that management will depend on such variables as gestational age and degree of laboratory abnormality.

In patients managed conservatively, a number of approaches have been reported. MacKenna et al.[17] treated 27 patients with bed rest and magnesium sulfate. Goodlin and colleagues[18] recommended plasma volume expansion with 5% albumin and reported a 10% success rate in prolonging gestation. Thiagarajah and associates[19] found that laboratory abnormalities improved when patients received prednisone or betamethasone.

The definitive treatment for PIH and consequently HELLP is delivery of the pregnancy. When mother and fetus are stable, a trial of labor is warranted.[12] If fetal distress or maternal deterioration intervene, operative delivery by cesarean section may be necessary. Intravenous infusion of magnesium sulfate is advised to prevent seizures. Hypertension should be treated aggressively with liberal use of an appropriate antihypertensive agent such as hydralazine for diastolic pressures of 110 mm Hg or greater. Volume therapy must be judicious, and the patient with oliguria that persists after cautious fluid challenge may require central hemodynamic monitoring.[12] Epidural anesthesia is not generally recommended because of the risk of bleeding into the epidural.[13] Transfusion of platelet concentrates is advocated when the platelet count is less than 50,000 and surgery is anticipated. The fetus is at particular risk for intrauterine asphyxia and should be monitored closely for signs of distress. Mothers with HELLP are at increased risk for liver rupture, DIC, abruptio placentae, and acute renal failure.[13] Serial (1) determinations of electrolyte, creatinine, and blood urea nitrogen levels and the hematologic profile; (2) liver function tests; and (3) coagulation studies are therefore an important aspect of management.

The pregnancy complicated by HELLP presents a unique challenge to the perinatal nurse. As with other hematologic complications, the potential exists for involvement of all major organ systems, and constant surveillance is of key importance. The mother should be considered critically ill, and her care is often characterized by technologies more commonly found in the intensive care unit setting. Most nursing interventions are directed toward systematic assessment of cardiovascular, renal, pulmonary, hepatic, hematologic, and central nervous system function (Table 5-2). Continuous electronic fetal monitoring is imperative for early detection of fetal compromise because of impaired perfusion. Finally, the emotional needs of the patient must also be considered in the plan of care. The level of technology must be considered in the plan of care; a high level of technology used for care can be expected to increase the level of anxiety. Support must be constant, with frequent explanation of procedures and provision of opportunities to verbalize fears.

Table 5-2 Summary of Nursing Interventions for HELLP Syndrome

1. Cardiovascular
   a. Assess blood pressure every 5 to 30 minutes via arterial line.
   b. Administer antihypertensive for blood pressure greater than 160/110.
   c. Place in lateral position.
   d. Assess central venous pressure, pulmonary artery wedge pressure; cardiac output.

2. Renal
   a. Assess hourly output; report less than 30 mL/h.
   b. Check urine for protein, blood, specific gravity.
   c. Assess fluid replacement: specific gravity, hematocrit, intake and output measurement, pulmonary artery pressures.

3. Pulmonary
   a. Administer oxygen.
   b. Auscultate breath sounds frequently.
   c. Observe for respiratory distress: tachypnea, dyspnea, cyanosis.
   d. Monitor arterial blood gases as necessary.
   e. Assess respiratory rate hourly.

4. Central Nervous System
   a. Check deep tendon reflexes hourly.
   b. Observe for altered mentation.
   c. Check serum magnesium levels.
   d. Decrease sensory stimulation.
   e. Place calcium gluconate at bedside.
   f. Monitor pulse oximeter.

Table 5-2 continued

5. Hematologic
   a. Assess for bleeding.
   b. Check laboratory values: hemoglobin and hematocrit, clotting studies, platelets.
   c. Replace blood and blood products.
   d. Avoid trauma.

6. Hepatic
   a. Monitor SGOT, SGPT, LDH, bilirubin for elevations
   b. Observe for anorexia, nausea and vomiting, right upper quadrant pain, hypoglycemia.
   c. Assess signs of hepatic rupture: shock, pain, fever, leukocytosis.

7. Fetal
   a. Ensure continuous electronic fetal monitoring.
   b. Assess for uteroplacental insufficiency: late decelerations, loss of variability, tachycardia.
   c. Assist with intermittent scalp sampling as necessary.

REFERENCES

1. Charache S, Niebyl J. Pregnancy in sickle cell disease. *Clin Hematol.* 1985;14:729-746.
2. Martin JN Jr, Morrison JC. Managing the parturient with sickle cell crisis. *Clin Obstet Gynecol.* 1984;27:39-49.
3. Morrison JC. Hemoglobinopathies and pregnancy. *Clin Obstet Gynecol.* 1979;22:821-842.
4. McKay ML, Martin JN, Morrison JC. Disseminated intravascular coagulation, idiopathic thrombocytopenia purpura, and hemoglobinopathies. In: Knuppel RA, Drukker JE. *High-Risk Pregnancy: A Team Approach.* Philadelphia: WB Saunders; 1986:440-471.
5. Luff J. Pregnancy and sickle cell disease. *Nurs Clin North Am.* 1984;18:164-171.
6. Greenwalt TJ, Zelenski KR. Transfusion support for hemoglobinopathies. *Clin Hematol.* 1984;13:151-165.
7. Weiner CP. The obstetric patient and disseminated intravascular coagulation. *Clin Perinatol.* 1986;13:705-717.
8. Brandt JT. Current concepts in coagulation. *Clin Obstet Gynecol.* 1985;28:3-14.
9. Rutherford SE, Phelan JP. Thromboembolic disease in pregnancy. *Clin Perinatol.* 1986;13:719-739.
10. Sher G, Statland B. Abruptio placentae with coagulopathy: a rational basis for management. *Clin Obstet Gynecol.* 1985;28:15-23.
11. Hewitt PE, Davies SC. The current state of DIC. *Intensive Care Med.* 1983;9:249-252.
12. Weinstein L. Syndrome of hemolysis, elevated liver enzymes, and low platelet count: a severe consequence of hypertension in pregnancy. *Am J Obstet Gynecol.* 1982;142:159-167.
13. Sibai BM, Taslimi MM, El-Nazar A, Amon E, Mabie BC, Ryan GM. Maternal-perinatal outcome associated with syndrome of hemolysis, elevated liver enzymes and low platelets in severe preeclampsia/eclampsia. *Am J Obstet Gynecol.* 1986;155:501-509.
14. Shannon D. HELLP syndrome: a severe consequence of pregnancy-induced hypertension. *J Obstet Gynecol Neonatal Nurs.* 1987;16(6):395-402.

15. Poldre P. Haptoglobin helps diagnose HELLP syndrome. *Am J Obstet Gynecol.* 1987;157:1267.
16. O'Brien W, Saba HI, Knuppel RA, Scerbo JC, Cohen GR. Alterations in platelet concentration and aggregation in normal pregnancy and preeclampsia. *Am J Obstet Gynecol.* 1986;155:486-490.
17. MacKenna J, Daver NL, Brame RG. Preeclampsia associated with hemolysis, elevated liver enzymes, and low platelets—an obstetric emergency? *Obstet Gynecol.* 1983;62:751.
18. Goodlin RC, Cotton DB, Haesslein HC. Severe edema-proteinuria-hypertension gestosis. *Am J Obstet Gynecol.* 1978;132:595-598.
19. Thiagarajah S, Bourgeosis J, Harbert GM Jr, Caudle MR. Thrombocytopenia in preeclampsia: associated abnormalities and management principles. *Am J Obstet Gynecol.* 1984;150:1-7.

Chapter 6

Shock in the Pregnant Patient

Kitty Cashion

Shock is a state of reduced tissue perfusion that results in cellular hypoxia.[1] Shock should not be thought of as a static disease state but rather as the body's dynamic response to reduced tissue perfusion, in its attempt to maintain homeostasis. Much has been written about the management of the several different types of shock that occur in children and adults. This chapter will discuss only the three types of shock that most commonly occur during pregnancy: hypovolemic, septic, and cardiogenic.

Management of shock during pregnancy differs in two important respects from its management in other adults. First, normal physiologic changes occur during pregnancy in most body organ systems. Therefore, the laboratory values and ranges for vital signs that are considered normal for adults often do not apply to pregnant women. (See Chapter 1 for more information.) Also, during the antepartum and intrapartum stages of pregnancy, the clinician essentially manages two patients, the mother and the fetus. Advances in technology within the past 2 decades have made it possible to assess and treat the fetus and to evaluate the effects of treatment on it just as we do for the mother. Therefore, the risks and benefits to both patients must be considered in planning care.

PATHOPHYSIOLOGY

The most common type of shock occurring during pregnancy is hypovolemic, resulting from hemorrhage. In early pregnancy, the most common cause of severe hemorrhage is ruptured ectopic pregnancy. During the latter stages of pregnancy, hemorrhage is usually caused by placenta previa or abruptio placentae. Major causes of postpartum hemorrhage include uterine atony, genital tract lacerations, and uterine prolapse.[2]

Regardless of the cause, obstetric hemorrhage can result in the rapid loss of large amounts of blood, leading to hypovolemia. Classically, signs and symptoms of hypovolemic shock include tachycardia; hypotension; cool, clammy, pale, or cyanotic skin; and restlessness, confusion, and a feeling of impending doom.[1–3]

Hypovolemia results in decreased cardiac output and arterial blood pressure, which stimulates baroreceptors in the aortic and carotid arteries. Stimulation of these baroreceptors activates the sympathetic portion of the autonomic nervous system and results in the release of powerful hormones, epinephrine and norepinephrine. Epinephrine and norepinephrine stimulate α and ß receptors located throughout the body. Epinephrine stimulates both ß$_1$ receptors, located in the heart, and ß$_2$ receptors, found in blood vessels. The stimulation of these ß receptors results in a stronger, more rapid heart rate and dilatation of coronary and cerebral blood vessels. Norepinephrine stimulates α receptors, which causes peripheral vasoconstriction. This sympathetic response to hypovolemia occurs quickly, as the body enters the early, or compensated, stage of shock. The sympathetic response is indeed life saving, for it assures blood flow to the heart and brain at the expense of other organs.[1,4]

A slower hormonal response, mediated through the kidneys, also occurs during the early stage of shock. Increased amounts of aldosterone are produced, which causes retention of sodium and hence water in the body. This water retention increases blood volume and thus blood pressure, which results in oliguria, one of the cardinal signs of shock.[3,4]

As time passes, the vasoconstriction of the microcirculation causes cells to become anoxic and to begin anaerobic metabolism. Anaerobic metabolism is a very inefficient means of producing energy. Large amounts of lactic acid accumulate, resulting in metabolic acidosis. Eventually, individual cells are destroyed, leading to organ failure. The acidotic environment surrounding the cells leads to a change in the microcirculation. The arterioles dilate, while the venules remain constricted. As a result, blood enters the microcirculation but cannot get out. Large amounts of acidotic blood are trapped in the microcirculation, where disseminated intravascular coagulation may occur. At the same time, circulating blood volume and cardiac output are markedly decreased, causing a drop in blood pressure. At this point, the patient is in late or irreversible shock, and death is inevitable.[1,4]

Septic shock may occur during pregnancy as a result of overwhelming infection caused by gram-positive bacteria, viruses, fungi, and rickettsiae. The majority of cases of septic shock, however, are caused by gram-negative bacteria, particularly *Escherichia coli, Klebsiella* species, *Pseudomonas aeruginosa*, and *Serratia*.[5–7] It is also common to find mixed polymicrobial infections in obstetric patients.[8] Septic shock is caused primarily by toxins liberated by these micro-organisms into the bloodstream, particularly endotoxins. These endotoxins activate the complement system and also cause the release of kinins, which results in vasodilatation, a decrease in vascular resistance, and a corresponding drop in blood pressure. Just as in hypovolemic shock, the body attempts to restore blood pressure through increased cardiac output and vasoconstriction. This mixture of vasodilatation and vasoconstriction results in a condition where some body organs receive an overabundance of blood flow, while others do not receive enough.[5] Ultimately, just as in hypovolemic shock, poor tissue perfusion will result in cellular damage, multiorgan failure, and death.[1]

The kinins released into the bloodstream during septic shock cause inflammatory responses that result in epithelial damage and increased capillary permeability, in addition to vasodilatation.[8] Although these effects occur throughout the body, nowhere is their impact more powerful than in the lungs. Increased capillary permeability allows leakage of intravascular fluid into the pulmonary interstitial spaces and causes noncardiac pulmonary edema. In addition, damage to pulmonary epithelial tissue and destruction of type 2 pneumocytes impairs the production of surfactant, the substance that prevents alveoli from collapsing. The alveoli, therefore, either collapse or are fluid filled, and the lungs become stiff and noncompliant. Increased hypoxemia, despite the administration of oxygen, becomes inevitable. This condition, sometimes described as shock lung, white lung, or Da Nang lung, is best known as adult respiratory distress syndrome (ARDS).[3,4]

Obstetric patients who experience septic abortion, chorioamnionitis, postpartum infection, and/or pyelonephritis are at risk for developing septic shock.[7] Since abortion was legalized in the United States in 1973, fewer women undergoing this procedure become septic. The incidence of death from septic shock is much lower in obstetric patients than in others, 0% to 3% compared to 10% to 81%; however, septic shock remains one of the major causes of death for obstetric patients.[8]

Because of the vasodilatation that occurs in the early (warm) stage of septic shock, patients often present with chills, fever, hypotension, mental confusion, tachycardia, tachypnea, and flushed skin. As septic shock progresses, they develop cool, clammy skin, bradycardia, and cyanosis.[9]

A third type of shock that may be seen during pregnancy is cardiogenic. In pregnant women, the major cause of cardiogenic shock is severe valvular disease. As more women with cardiac problems live into adulthood and desire to bear children, this form of shock will, unfortunately, probably occur more frequently. In cardiogenic shock, the heart becomes unable to pump blood efficiently throughout the body. Initially the heart attempts to compensate for its low output by increasing its rate. Eventually, however, this tachycardia further weakens the heart, forcing it to work for longer periods of time and increasing its need for oxygen and other nutrients. The inability of the heart to efficiently pump blood throughout the body leads to hypervolemia of the heart itself and of the pulmonary venous circulation. The remainder of the body, however, is in a hypovolemic state.[3,7] Again, just as in hypovolemic and septic shock, poor tissue perfusion eventually results in cellular damage, multiorgan failure, and death. Classic signs of cardiogenic shock include distended neck veins, dyspnea, and hypoxia.[3]

MEDICAL MANAGEMENT

The primary goal of medical management is to treat the underlying cause of shock.[1] When the underlying problem is corrected quickly, while the patient is still in the compensatory stage of shock, the prognosis often is good. In the antepartum and intrapartum stages of pregnancy, treatment of hypovolemic shock caused by hemorrhage requires immediate delivery, either vaginally or by cesarean section. Postpartum hemorrhage may be managed either medically or surgically. Treatment of the underlying causes of hypovolemic shock is discussed in Chapter 7.

Treatment of the underlying cause of septic shock first requires identification of the site of infection. Urine, blood, and sputum samples for culture and sensitivity are routinely collected. Ultrasonography or computerized axial tomography (CAT) scanning may be employed to isolate the site of infection. If material can be isolated from sites of infection, it should also be cultured. Cultures are obtained prior to beginning antibiotic therapy.[6,9]

A combination of antibiotics in massive doses is given intravenously, since coverage for both gram-negative and gram-positive bacteria must be provided. Penicillin, an aminoglycoside such as tobramycin, and clindamycin are frequently used in combination to treat septic shock.[7,8] Once begun, antibiotic therapy should not be altered unless the patient's response is poor or cultures indicate an organism that cannot be effectively treated by the medications being administered.[7]

The second major goal of treatment is to restore and maintain tissue perfusion. This requires both adequate oxygenation and maintenance of circulating blood volume.[1] Patients in shock may develop ARDS, with resulting respiratory failure and hypoxemia. Both oxygen therapy and mechanical ventilation are required at times to ensure adequate tissue oxygenation.[10]

Cardinal signs and symptoms of acute respiratory failure include tachypnea, labored breathing, use of accessory muscles for breathing, cyanosis, anxiety, and exhaustion.

In the presence of these signs and symptoms, arterial blood gas values should be obtained.[10,11] Increased $PaCO_2$ and decreased pH and PaO_2 values indicate that the patient is not ventilating adequately and confirm the diagnosis of respiratory failure.[12] Mechanical ventilation should be instituted at this point to restore the pH to a normal range, to reduce the work of breathing, and to ensure alveolar ventilation.[11]

Patients with ARDS who require mechanical ventilation are generally managed on volume-controlled ventilators. Assist-control and intermittent mandatory ventilation are the most frequently used ventilatory patterns. This allows the patient spontaneous breaths but ensures that a predetermined number of breaths each minute will contain a full tidal volume. Low levels of positive end-expiratory pressure (PEEP) often are used to re-expand the alveoli, which otherwise might collapse because of the loss of surfactant that occurs during ARDS. PEEP, therefore, reduces hypoxemia and allows patients to be ventilated using lower FIO_2. The use of even low levels of PEEP is associated with decreased cardiac output, pneumomediastinum, and pneumothorax, but its advantages are generally thought to outweigh its disadvantages.[10]

Generally, restoration of adequate circulating blood volume is first attempted through vigorous fluid resuscitation. In hypovolemic shock secondary to obstetric hemorrhage, fluid resuscitation involves infusion of either whole blood or blood products and crystalloid solutions to increase both the circulating blood volume and the oxygen-carrying capacity of the blood. Until recently, the success of fluid resuscitation was usually measured by serial hematocrits and urine output. The goal of fluid replacement was to keep the hematocrit at approximately 30% and to maintain an hourly urine output of approximately 30 mL.[13]

Currently, invasive hemodynamic monitoring provides an excellent means of evaluating fluid resuscitation in patients with hypovolemic shock. The Swan-Ganz pulmonary artery catheter, which is flow directed and balloon tipped, is inserted usually through the jugular or subclavian vein and threaded through the right atrium, tricuspid valve, and right ventricle and into the pulmonary artery. By measuring pulmonary artery pressure (PAP), the catheter evaluates right-sided function of the heart. The balloon can be inflated at the catheter's tip, which seals off the right side of the heart, and the pulmonary artery wedge pressure (PAWP), which indicates left-sided heart function, can be measured. The Swan-Ganz catheter can also measure central venous pressure (CVP) and calculate cardiac output. Chapter 2 contains a more thorough description of the pulmonary artery catheter. The use of this catheter is recommended to manage shock when an infusion of greater than five units of blood or blood products is used to stabilize the patient's condition. A thorough evaluation of the patient's hemodynamic status allows the clinician to adequately replenish the circulating blood volume without overloading the cardiovascular system.[1,4] Normal hemodynamic values in pregnancy have only recently become available.

Medical antishock trousers (MAST) are occasionally used to stabilize hypovolemic shock in pregnant patients. MAST suits are made of strong, waterproof, radiolucent nylon and consist of three chambers, one for each leg and one for the abdomen, which can be inflated separately.[14] A MAST suit helps to stabilize blood pressure by causing increased systemic vascular resistance. The tamponade effect produced by inflating the abdominal compartment can help control abdominal bleeding in early pregnancy and postpartum.[14,15] During mid- or late pregnancy, however, inflation of the abdominal compartment should be avoided. The goal of treatment is to inflate the suit until adequate blood pressure is obtained, without producing complications. MAST suits generally should not remain inflated longer than 48 hours. Deflation should begin with the abdominal compartment and must be accomplished slowly with frequent monitoring of the patient's condition.[14] See Chapter 8 for more information about the use of MAST in pregnant patients.

Occasionally, vasoactive drugs are used in addition to fluid resuscitation to restore cardiovascular function. Such drugs should be used with extreme caution prior to delivery. They maintain cardiac output at the expense of significant vasoconstriction, which further jeopardizes the fetus.[8,15] Dopamine in low doses causes an increase in cardiac output along with increased blood flow through the mesenteric and renal arteries. As the dosage is increased, however, the resultant vasoconstriction causes a decrease in tissue perfusion.[7,8] These drugs, despite their inherent dangers, should be used in patients who fail to respond to other forms of treatment.

NURSING CARE

Care of the pregnant patient who experiences any type of shock requires that the nurse possess expertise both in critical care and in obstetrics. Continuous assessment of the patient is crucial. Although the basic pathophysiology in shock occurs at the cellular level, current assessment tools can only measure conditions at this level indirectly. It is also important to remember that all body organs and organ systems are involved in shock. Basic principles of nursing care are listed below in approximate order of priority. Because the pregnant patient in shock is critically ill, multiple nursing actions often need to be carried out simultaneously.

A brief assessment to evaluate the patient's cardiovascular, respiratory, and neurologic systems should be the first priority. The blood pressure, character and rate of pulse and respirations, skin color and temperature, and mental status must be assessed rapidly. Also look for obvious sites of bleeding or infection. This assessment must be repeated at frequent intervals during the initial period of treatment and stabilization.

Next, since immediate fluid replacement will be necessary, two peripheral intravenous lines should be established with large-bore (14- or 16-gauge) catheters. A crystalloid solution such as Ringer's lactate should be infused immediately while waiting to obtain whole blood or packed red blood cells. Blood samples for typing and cross-matching and an initial hematocrit, as well as for other laboratory tests, should be drawn at the time of insertion of the intravenous line.

If the patient is obviously dyspneic, determining arterial blood gases to evaluate her ventilatory status is the next priority. Oxygen administration by face mask at 6 to 8 L/min may be sufficient to correct hypoxemia. Should oxygen alone fail to correct the problem, intubation and mechanical ventilation may be initiated to increase PaO_2 or to decrease the work of breathing for the patient. When mechanical ventilation is instituted, the patient will probably have an arterial line inserted to facilitate frequent arterial blood gas evaluation.

Patients on mechanical ventilation frequently require antianxiety drugs such as diazepam. Occasionally, patients remain hypoxic despite mechanical ventilation and hyperventilate, or "buck the respirator," to compensate for the hypoxia. In some cases, it may be necessary to paralyze all skeletal muscle function with pancuronium bromide to overcome this reflexive hyperventilation.[10] Because anxiety can exacerbate the problem, patients need to be told why they are receiving ventilatory therapy and should be given a simple explanation about how the machine works. In particular, they need to be told that they cannot speak as long as the endotracheal tube is in place. Patients can communicate using sign/body language, paper and pencil, flash cards, or a magic writing slate.[10,12]

Routine nursing care for ventilator-dependent patients includes frequent (every 1 to 2 hours) auscultation of the chest to assess for secretions and to verify that the endotracheal tube remains in the correct position.[11] Suctioning should be performed as often as necessary, and should be preceded by hyperoxygenating the patient with 100% oxygen by bag or ventilator to prevent a severe drop in arterial blood oxygenation during the procedure.[10]

Since urine output is a valuable indicator of hemodynamic status, a Foley catheter should next be inserted. Fluid intake and output must be strictly recorded every hour. Because urine output in the initial treatment stage will likely be minimal, the catheter should be connected to a collection device that can measure small amounts.

Pregnant patients in shock should receive continuous electronic fetal monitoring. Since the uterus does not receive preferential blood flow, the appearance of increasing fetal stress or distress on the monitor may well be the first indication of maternal deterioration. Decrease in fetal heart rate variability is a major cause for concern, since it indicates that the fetus is losing its ability to handle the stress placed upon it. Often, the loss of variability will be accompanied by late decelerations of fetal heart rate. The patient should be kept in a lateral position or a hip wedge should be used, to maximize blood flow to the uterus. Trendelenburg positioning should be avoided, since it causes supine hypotension. The patient should be given oxygen at 8 to 10 L/min by mask, to increase the amount of oxygen available for the fetus. As a general rule, however, concern for the mother's safety always takes precedence over the needs of the fetus.[15]

Once the initial stabilization measures described above have been accomplished, the next step will likely be insertion of a pulmonary artery catheter for hemodynamic monitoring. The nurse prepares the lines and assists the physician with insertion. Aseptic technique in this and all other invasive procedures is mandatory, since patients in shock are at high risk for infection. The patient's hemodynamic status will be assessed frequently by utilizing the indwelling Swan-Ganz catheter to measure CVP, pulmonary artery pressure, PAWP, and cardiac output. The patient in shock usually has falling CVP, PAP, and PAWP values, reflecting loss of vascular tone and/or decreasing circulating volume. Cardiac output will initially remain in the normal range as the heart increases its rate and struggles to deliver blood to vital organs. Eventually, however, the myocardium will no longer pump blood effectively, and cardiac output will decrease. Maternal death can occur from this lethal drop in cardiac output and subsequent intravascular collapse.

The room should be kept at a comfortable temperature. Even though the patient's skin feels cool and clammy because of vasoconstriction, heat should not be applied. If peripheral vasodilation occurs, blood will be shunted away from vital organs. Heat also increases the body's metabolism and thus further strains the heart to provide increased amounts of oxygen and other nutrients.[3] Excessive coolness, however, causes the microcirculation to be even more sluggish and increases the potential for disseminated intravascular coagulation and cellular anoxia.[4]

The patient and her family also have psychosocial needs that must be considered. In the United States today, childbirth is considered a normal, natural process that always results in a healthy mother and baby. The patient will likely be extremely frightened and upset to find herself in a critical care environment, surrounded by unfamiliar people and equipment. She may well be concerned about the possibility of her own death, as well as that of her fetus. Short, simple explanations about her status, the procedures to be done, and the equipment in use should be repeated as often as necessary. Family members or significant others should be allowed to stay with her, if at all possible. Remember, too, that patients often hear and remember events and conversations that occur during periods of critical illness, even though they may not be able to respond at the time.

REFERENCES

1. Beyers M, Dudas S, eds. *The Clinical Practice of Medical-Surgical Nursing.* Boston: Little, Brown & Co; 1986:221.
2. Neeson JD, May KA, eds. *Comprehensive Maternity Nursing, Nursing Process and the Childbearing Family.* Philadelphia: JB Lippincott;1986.
3. Luckmann J, Sorensen KC, eds. *Medical Surgical Nursing: A Psychophysiologic Approach.* Philadelphia: WB Saunders; 1987.
4. Osterfield G. Shock. In: Phipps WJ, Long BC, Woods NF, eds. *Medical-Surgical Nursing: Concepts and Clinical Practice.* St. Louis: CV Mosby; 1987.
5. Rice V. Septic shock: nursing implications of current medical research. *J Intravenous Nurs.* 1987;10:326-333.
6. Septic shock: a threat to the threatened. *Emerg Med.* 1987;19:25-33.
7. Knuppel RA, Rao PS, Cavanagh D. Septic shock in obstetrics. *Clin Obstet Gynecol.* 1984;27:3-10.
8. Gonik B. Septic shock in obstetrics. *Clin Perinatol.* 1986;13:741-754.
9. Calia FM, Conrad SA, Spivey WH. Septic shock. *Patient Care.* 1987;21:50-54, 64-65, 69, 73-75, 78.
10. Bradley RB. Adult respiratory distress syndrome. *Focus Crit Care.* 1987;14:48-59.
11. Winters C. Monitoring ventilator patients for complications. *Nursing.* 1988;18:38-41.
12. Mayo JM, Hamner JB. A nurse's guide to mechanical ventilation. *RN.* 1987;50:18-24.
13. Rice V. Shock management,I: fluid volume replacement. *Crit Care Nurse.* 1984;4:69-82.
14. Erceg CF. Medical anti-shock trousers: nursing implications. *AORN J.* 1986;43:1116-1121.
15. Hayashi RH. Hemorrhagic shock in obstetrics. *Clin Perinatol.* 1986;13:755-763.

Chapter 7

Hemorrhagic Complications in Pregnancy

Susan Pozaic

In the United States in 1985 and 1986, the annual maternal mortality rate from hemorrhage in pregnancy, intrapartum and postpartum, exclusive of abortion, was 0.7[1] to 1.06[2] per 100,000 live births. Though the incidence of obstetric hemorrhage is much higher, most patients do not die when appropriately managed. Hemorrhage of sufficient severity to lower maternal cardiac output impairs placental blood flow and jeopardizes fetal health and life.[3]

Third trimester hemorrhage, which occurs in 3% of all pregnancies, is defined as bright red bleeding not mixed with mucus, as in bloody show, in an amount equivalent to a menstrual period. Postpartum hemorrhage, which complicates 4% to 5% of deliveries, is defined as blood loss in excess of 500 mL occurring between delivery and 31 days postpartum.[4] Much has been written about the various causes of obstetric hemorrhage. This chapter will focus on

1. the two most common causes of late pregnancy bleeding, placenta previa and abruptio placentae
2. uterine rupture as a cause of antepartum and intrapartum hemorrhage
3. postpartum hemorrhage due to uterine atony, lacerations of the birth canal, hematomas, retained placenta, and uterine inversion

BLOOD LOSS IN PREGNANCY

The normal physiologic changes of pregnancy prepare the woman for the increased intravascular space of pregnancy and the subsequent blood loss of parturition. This is accomplished by a blood volume increase of 40% by 30 weeks' gestation in the gravida without complications. Women frequently lose 500 mL of blood at the time of vaginal delivery, and 1000 mL of blood at the time of cesarean section, without untoward effects.

The normal physiologic response to rapid loss of 1000 mL of blood includes vasoconstriction in both arterial and venous compartments and, within 4 hours, movement of extravascular fluids into the intravascular compartment, which can replace up to 30% of lost volume.[5] The increase in pregnancy-induced blood volume along with the normal physiologic response to hemorrhage prevents exhibition of early signs of hemorrhage in pregnant patients; therefore, signs and symptoms are not evident early in the hemorrhage. Lack of symptoms may allow the hemorrhage to progress unnoticed.

Classification

Hemorrhage is classified as one of four types depending on volume lost. Symptoms are based on volume deficit that, because of the normal physiologic response to hemorrhage, may not be the same as volume lost.

Class 1 reflects a 15% volume deficit. There are usually no signs or symptoms of class 1 hemorrhage.

Class 2 reflects a volume deficit of 20% to 25%. The first sign is a rise in pulse rate of 10 to 20 beats per minute and an increase in respiratory rate. Orthostatic blood pressure changes are frequently observed, with a narrowing in pulse pressure. Perfusion of the extremities may be decreased, resulting in cool, diaphoretic skin.

Class 3 reflects a volume deficit of 30% to 35%. This loss is sufficient to cause overt hypotension. Marked tachycardia of 120 to 160 beats per minute and tachypnea of 30 to 50 breaths per minute is typically present. Skin is cold and diaphoretic.

Class 4 reflects a volume deficit of 40%. Profound shock is evident in the inability to obtain a blood pressure. Pulses in the extremities are absent. Oliguria or anuria is present. Circulatory collapse and cardiac arrest will ensue if volume replacement is not immediately begun.[5]

Blood loss can be estimated by measurement of the hematocrit. Acute hemorrhage will not be manifested in the hematocrit for at least 4 hours, and complete compensation by the physiologic responses to hemorrhage requires 48 hours.[5] Intravenous fluids can produce a lowered hematocrit by dilution.

Stabilization: Assessment and Intervention

Evaluation of obstetric hemorrhage begins with a quick estimation of blood loss. The patient is asked about events preceding hemorrhage and the amount of blood lost. Clinical observation includes inspection of clothing and frank vaginal bleeding. Subsequent blood loss can be accurately determined by counting and weighing disposable pads, which are maintained beneath the patient's hips (1 g approximates 1 mL of blood). Cardiovascular and respiratory assessments include blood pressure, pulse, respirations, skin color and condition, and level of consciousness. Blood pressure and pulse are determined in the supine and, if possible, the upright positions. These vital signs may be deceptively within the normal range because large amounts of blood must be lost before signs of shock appear, which is due to the normal physiologic increase of blood volume in pregnancy and the physiologic response to hemorrhage. Postural changes may be more sensitive to a smaller loss of blood and therefore may precede hypotension and tachycardia. Cool, diaphoretic, pale, or cyanotic skin reflects a decreased cardiac output. Hemoglobin levels, hematocrit, and arterial blood gases should be rapidly assessed (Table 7-1).

Initial assessment of fetal well-being is achieved by auscultation of fetal heart tones with a fetoscope or doppler. The electronic fetal monitor is then applied and the heart rate assessed every 15 minutes thereafter. A more comprehensive noninvasive assessment by nonstress testing or biophysical profile is conducted following stabilization. Ultrasound evaluation may be necessary to confirm fetal cardiac activity. Location of the placenta is noted. Use of electronic fetal monitoring includes the tocodynamometer to ascertain the presence of uterine contractions. Assessment of uterine contractility and rigidity is also accomplished by frequent palpation of the uterus (Table 7-1).

Table 7-1 Stabilization of the Hemorrhaging Obstetric Patient

Assessments	Interventions
Maternal condition	14- to 16-gauge intravenous line
Amount of blood loss	Oxygen
Inspection	Balanced electrolyte solution
Pad count and weight	Blood (administer ordered)
Blood studies including clot observations	Foley catheter with urimeter
Cardiovascular and respiratory status	Hemodynamic monitoring
Blood pressure (postural)	
Pulse	
Respirations	
Skin color and condition	
Arterial blood gases	
Uterine assessment	
Palpation	
Tocodynamometer	
Fetal condition	
Heart tones	
Gestational age	
Well-being	

Life support interventions and operative delivery may be the only hope for patients experiencing severe bleeding, since exsanguination can occur quickly. The patient must never be left alone. She is assisted to a semi-Fowler's or a lateral position to improve maternal oxygenation and placental circulation. Blood is drawn for a complete blood count (CBC); type and cross-match of four units of packed red blood cells; Rh factor determination; electrolyte, glucose, creatinine, blood urea nitrogen (BUN) levels; and coagulation studies (prothrombin time [PT], partial thromboplastin time [PTT], platelet count, fibrinogen and fibrin split products [FSP] levels). A bedside assessment of the hemostatic system, the clot observation test, is conducted by placing 5 to 10 mL of blood in a red-topped tube. A coagulation defect is suspected when the blood in the tube does not clot within 5 minutes. If the blood clots, it should continue to be observed for 60 minutes to assess the presence of excessive fibrinolysis.[6(p 283)] Because of the risks of fetal hypoxia and the ability to increase umbilical vein oxygen content by maternal administration of oxygen, arterial blood gases are obtained in any mother with a respiratory complaint or signs of respiratory compromise prior to initiating oxygen therapy. Blood gases are determined serially to titrate oxygen flow and maintain a maternal oxygen tension greater than 60 mm Hg.[7] A pulse oximeter should be placed to provide immediate information on capillary hemoglobin saturation. Metabolic acidosis is manifested with major uncorrected hemorrhage. In the presence of a normal PaO_2 and a decreased $PaCO_2$, oxygen is administered at 12 L/min by Venturi mask.[8] If the PaO_2 drops, ventilatory support may be necessary to maintain PaO_2 above 70 mm Hg. Severe respiratory insufficiency requires continuous positive airway pressure (CPAP) or positive end expiratory pressure (PEEP) to force alveoli open.[8]

Two intravenous lines are initiated with 14-or 16-gauge catheters. A balanced electrolyte solution, such as Ringer's lactate, is rapidly administered in a volume at least three times the estimated blood loss.[8] Initially, type O, Rh-negative packed red blood cells or, preferably, type-specific blood may be administered until additional units are cross-matched. This blood will not have been completely cross-matched since that process requires 45 to 60 minutes; therefore, transfusion reactions occur with increased frequency.

Renal function can be impaired as a result of hypoxia to the tissue, which causes long-term complications, including acute tubular and cortical necrosis.[6] Since urine output reflects renal perfusion, an indwelling urinary catheter is inserted and hourly recordings of output are made. Initial therapy is directed at increasing intravascular status to maintain a urine output of at least 30 mL/h.

Invasive hemodynamic technology is used to assess intravascular status in the obstetric hemorrhage patient who requires greater than five to six units of blood products, or in the woman whose vital signs fail to stabilize. A central venous pressure catheter or, preferably, a pulmonary artery pressure catheter (Swan-

Ganz) is used to evaluate right and left atrial filling pressures (central venous pressure [CVP], pulmonary artery wedge pressure [PAWP]) and cardiac output. Fluid and blood replacement should be aggressive enough to maintain the CVP at 8 to 12 mm Hg and the PAWP at 4 to 12 mm Hg. Cardiac output should be 6 to 8 L/min in the antepartum patient after 24 weeks of pregnancy.

In preparation for delivery, ultrasound examination is conducted to assess placental location and fetal gestational age. A speculum examination is conducted to determine the source of bleeding and the most expedient and safest route of delivery. When placenta previa is suspected, speculum examination is conducted in a double setup procedure so that, should massive hemorrhage be provoked by the examination, immediate delivery by cesarean section may be accomplished. Vaginal blood is assessed for the presence of fetal red blood cells to detect fetal hemorrhage, using the Apt or Kleihauer-Betke test.

BLOOD REPLACEMENT THERAPY

The most common reasons for blood replacement therapy in the pregnant patient are hypovolemia, anemia, and the need to replace coagulation components.[9] The nurse must be aware of the various contents, indications, and risks of each preparation (Table 7-2). See Table 7-3 for a blood administration procedure.

Major Transfusion Reactions

Immediate transfusion reactions are generally either hemolytic (involving red blood cells) or nonhemolytic (caused by a reaction to the white cells, platelets, and plasma proteins).[10] Hemolytic reactions result from ABO mismatches. An antigen-antibody reaction causes rupture of the red blood cell membrane, usually of the donor blood. Intravascular hemolysis causes the release of hemoglobin, which becomes bound to haptoglobin. Once haptoglobin has been saturated, hemoglobinuria occurs, followed by hyperbilirubinemia. Clinical symptoms range from death to shortened life span of the transfused cells. The most frequent complaints are chills, fever, and body aches. Oliguria or anuria may follow or precede these complaints when there is acute renal failure.

When a transfusion reaction is suspected, the blood is stopped, further testing of the patient's blood (including typing and cross-matching, blood count, and coagulation studies) is performed, and the remaining blood and the infusion tubing are sent to the blood bank. The accuracy of clerical records is assessed, a urine specimen is obtained to assess hematuria, and the physician is notified immediately. Intake and output are monitored hourly, and diuretics may be used to improve output. Hyperkalemia is assessed by serial monitoring of serum

Table 7-2 Blood Components

	Contents	Volume	Storage	Effect
Fresh whole blood	Red blood cells Plasma coagulation factors Platelets	500 mL	Administered within 6 to 24 hours of collection	Increases volume mL to mL Increases hematocrit by 3% per unit
Stored whole blood	Red blood cells Plasma	500 mL	4°C for up to 35 days	Increases volume mL to mL Increases hematocrit by 3% per unit
Packed red blood cells	Packed red blood cells	240 mL	1–6°C for 3 years	Increases hematocrit by 3% per unit Less risk than with whole blood for transfusion reaction Only source of factors V, XI, XII
Fresh frozen plasma	Coagulation factors	200–250 mL	–18°C for 1 year	Increases fibrinogen by 10 mg/dL per unit
Cryoprecipitate	Fibrinogen coagulation factors	15–25 mL	–20°C for up to 1 year	Increases fibrinogen by 10 mg/dL per unit
Platelets	Platelets	30–50 mL	Room temperature for up to 72 hours	Increases platelet count by 5,000–10,000 µL per unit

Source: Based on information contained in:
American Association of Blood Banks. *Blood Transfusion Therapy: A Physician's Handbook*. Arlington, VA: American Association of Blood Banks;1983.
Benedetti TJ. Obstetric hemorrhage. In: Gabbe SG, Neibyl JR, Simpson JL, eds. *Obstetrics: Normal and Problem Pregnancies*. New York: Churchill Livingstone; 1986:485.
Considine T. Principles of blood replacement. In: Sciarra JJ, ed. *Gynecology and Obstetrics*. Philadelphia, PA: JB Lippincott; 1985:3:1–10.
Romero R. The management of acquired hemostasic failure during pregnancy. In: Berkowitz RL, ed. *Critical Care of the Obstetric Patient*. New York: Churchill Livingstone; 1983:219–284.

Table 7-2 continued

Advantages	Disadvantages	Administration	Uses/Special Interest
Minimal microaggregation Minimal loss of clotting factors Less expensive than component therapy	Insufficient time for screening increases risk of hepatitis and AIDS† Possibly circulatory overload if administered when component therapy is indicated	ABO-Rh compatible* Administer as rapidly as patient can tolerate	Rarely available Replaces volume and all components
Is properly screened for hepatitis and AIDS	Platelets and coagulation factors are ineffective	ABO-Rh compatible* Administer as rapidly as patient can tolerate	Replaces volume and oxygen-carrying capacity
Nonhemolytic transfusion reactions occur less than with whole blood		ABO-Rh compatible* Infuse with normal saline within 2 hours as quickly as patient can tolerate	Increase oxygen-carrying capacity without significantly increasing volume Can be given in conjunction with crystalloid for management of blood loss less than 2000 mL
	Coagulation factors are not concentrated Circulatory overload can occur	ABO-Rh specific Administer 10 mL/min	Used to replace coagulation factors and volume
Concentrated source of fibrinogen factors VIII and XIII	Need to administer more than one unit Increased risk of AIDS† and hepatitis	ABO-Rh specific Administer 10 mL/min 16–24 units administered at one time	Used to replace fibrinogen
		ABO-Rh specific Administer rapidly over 10 minutes 6–10 units administered at one time	Prophylaxis or treatment of excessive bleeding due to thrombocytopenia and platelet dysfunction

* Massive transfusion: Massive transfusions of cold blood may cause hypothermia and ventricular fibrillation; therefore, a blood warmer set at 100–110°F should be used. For every 10 units infused, 2 units of fresh frozen plasma are administered. Serum potassium is monitored following the administration of 4–6 units. Continuous cardiac monitoring is recommended.
† AIDS = acquired immunodeficiency syndrome.

Table 7-3 Blood Administration Procedure

1. Obtain baseline vital signs.
2. Check and double-check blood type and Rh, labels, numbers, and expiration date.
3. Gently invert the container to suspend components and repeat every 30 minutes.
4. Insert an 18-gauge intravenous catheter, and initiate a normal saline infusion.
5. Use appropriate infusion equipment.
    a. Whole blood, packed red cells, white cells, and plasma require a Y-blood administration set with filter. Normal saline is connected to one side of the Y-connection and is used to prime the tubing. The blood component is connected to the other side of the Y-connection. This set is connected as a piggyback into the main intravenous line. It should be connected with an 18-gauge needle into the port closest to the insertion site.
    b. Platelets require a platelet administration set. The platelet unit is connected to the single-spike administration set. Prime the tubing with the platelets and connect to main line at the flash bulb with an 18-gauge needle.
6. Remain with patient and monitor vital signs and adverse effects every 5 minutes for the first 15 minutes. During this time, blood is administered slowly at 35 to 40 drops per minute.
7. If no adverse effects are noted, increase the infusion rate (see Table 7-2), and assess the patient every 15 to 60 minutes.
8. If a transfusion reaction occurs:
    a. Stop transfusion but keep vein open with normal saline infusion.
    b. Monitor vital signs.
    c. Monitor intake and urinary output and characteristics.
    d. Monitor for signs of hyperkalemia: ECG changes, nausea, muscle weakness, diarrhea, slow or irregular heart beat, paresthesias of hands, face, and tongue.
    e. Return blood and infusion set to blood bank.
    f. Obtain urine and blood samples.
9. Continue monitoring post transfusion for delayed reactions.
10. Document time of initiation, blood component and volume administered, and patient tolerance.

electrolyte levels, electrocardiograms (ECGs), and patient signs and symptoms, including nausea, muscle weakness, diarrhea, slow or irregular heart beat, and paresthesias of the hands, face, and tongue. If it occurs, acute renal failure is self-limiting.[11]

Nonhemolytic transfusion reactions are those that occur in response to white blood cells, platelets, and plasma proteins. These reactions occur primarily in multiparous women and in patients who have received multiple blood transfusions. Nonhemolytic transfusion reactions cause a fever that may be accompanied by chills, vomiting, and, in severe cases, collapse. The fever usually resolves within 12 hours and is unlikely to cause morbidity or mortality.[11]

Noncardiac pulmonary edema is a rare complication that begins with sudden dyspnea and radiographic evidence of opacities in the lungs. It is due, in many cases, to donor antibodies reacting to the leukocytes of the recipient.[11]

Anaphylaxis may also occur when donor antibodies react with recipient leukocytes. It is very rare and is characterized by urticaria, tachycardia, flushing, wheezing, dyspnea, hypotension, and loss of consciousness.[11] The fetus is protected from anaphylaxis because maternal IgE antibodies (the immunoglobulin that mediates anaphylaxis) cross the placenta poorly; however, anaphylaxis produces maternal hypotension and asphyxia, which indirectly threaten the fetus.[12]

General treatment includes observation and early recognition of the reaction, close assessment of involved organ systems, immediate notification of the physician, and pharmacologic and supportive measures. For a mild reaction, which consists of pruritis and urticaria, 1:1000 epinephrine, 0.2 to 0.5 mL, is given subcutaneously (Table 7-4). Alternatively, diphenhydramine 50 to 80 mg intramuscularly or intravenously may be given. When a severe reaction occurs, the initial dose of epinephrine may be repeated every 3 minutes with careful monitoring of the cardiac rhythm. The systolic blood pressure is maintained above 90 mm Hg to ensure placental circulation. Intravenous Ringer's lactate or normal saline is administered for this purpose.[12]

If epinephrine has not improved respiratory distress after two or three doses, airway obstruction must be considered. Oxygen administered by nasal cannula or intermittent positive pressure breathing with 1:200 isoproterenol inhalation solution (0.5 mL) may be sufficient to improve respiratory distress. Maternal arterial PO_2 is kept above 60 mm Hg. Intubation is indicated when these measures are ineffective or when laryngeal edema is present. Aminophylline 0.25 to 0.5 g given intravenously over 15 to 30 minutes is used to treat bronchospasm that is not relieved by epinephrine. Corticosteroids may be considered in cases of persistent bronchospasm or hypotension but are of no benefit for acute anaphylaxis.[12]

PLACENTA PREVIA

Placenta previa is defined as the presence of placental tissue that partially or totally covers the internal cervical os. Placentation near the cervical os is likely when the fertilized egg implants low in the uterine cavity. This placenta may abort, it may relocate, or it may remain as a placenta previa. The occurrence of abortion and placental relocation may account for the decrease in reported incidence of term versus second trimester placenta previa. The incidence of placenta previa diagnosed in the second trimester ranges from 5% to 6.2%, [13,14]

Table 7-4 Phamacologic Treatment of Anaphylaxis

	Dose	Route	Repeat	Special Precautions
Epinephrine 1:1000	0.2–0.5 mL	Subcutaneous	Every 3 minutes	Repeat doses require continuous ECG assessment
Diphenhydramine	50–80 mg	Intramuscular/intravenous		
Isoproterenol 1:200	0.5 mL	Intermittent positive pressure breathing		
Aminophylline	0.25–0.5 g	Intravenous		Administer over 15–20 minutes

Source: Based on information contained in Witter FR, Neibyl JR. Drug intoxication and anaphylactic shock in the obstetric patient. In: Berkowitz RL, ed. *Critical Care of the Obstetric Patient.* New York: Churchill Livingstone; 1983:527–543.

while the incidence at term ranges from 0.3% to 1.8%.[13,14] In general, perinatal mortality is 8.1%.[15] Table 7-5 lists predisposing factors for placenta previa.

Classification

The most common classification system for placenta previa is based on placental location at the time of diagnosis, since the relationship between the cervical os and placental location changes with progressive dilatation of the cervix. Total or complete placenta previa occurs when the placenta completely covers the internal cervical os. Partial placenta previa occurs when the placenta covers only part of the cervical os. In marginal placenta previa, the edge of the placenta reaches the edge of the os. A low-lying placenta is one in which the placental edge approaches but does not encroach on the cervical os. In both total and partial placenta previa, some degree of placental separation is inevitable as the lower uterine segment thins and the cervix dilates, thus producing varying degrees of hemorrhage.[16]

Pathophysiology

The cause of placenta previa is not completely understood. It has been theorized that uterine scarring plays a role in the development of placenta previa, since its incidence increases with a history of uterine surgery or trauma, and multiple deliveries.[17]

Another possible mechanism for the development of placenta previa is delayed development and implantation of the fertilized ovum. A recent study noted that with increasing parity among women with placenta previa, there is an

Table 7-5 Predisposing Factors for Placenta Previa

Positive Risk Factors	Possible Risk Factors
Previous cesarean section	Previous therapeutic abortion*,†
Previous spontaneous abortion	Cigarette smoking‡
Previous dilation and curettage	Increased parity
Previous placenta previa	Increased gravidity
Repeated uterine instrumentation	Advanced maternal age

* Barrett JM, Boehm FH, Killiam AP. Induced abortion: a risk factor for placenta previa. *Am J Obstet Gynecol*. 1981;141:769–772.
† Grimes DA. Legal abortion and placenta previa. *Am J Obstet Gynecol*. 1984;149:501–504.
‡ Naeye RL. Abruptio placentae and placentae previa: frequency, perinatal mortality, and cigarette smoking. *Obstet Gynecol*. 1980;55:701–704.

increase in the ratio of male to female infants born. This is in contrast to the decrease in the ratio of male to female infants born with increasing parity among women without placenta previa.[18] This finding may be attributed to fertilization occurring early or late in a cycle, which is associated with an increase in male offspring.[19] Similarly, the development of the embryo from an over-ripe sperm or ovum may be impaired, thereby causing delayed and low implantation, which is responsible for placenta previa.[18]

The role of placental migration in the development of placenta previa is being investigated. One study reports that 72% of patients diagnosed as having a placenta previa in midtrimester did not have this condition at term.[14] It is thought that placental migration may account for a small number of these. The term "placental migration" suggests three separate mechanisms. The first involves active disruption and reattachment of the placenta. This theory is not widely supported.[14] The second proposed mechanism is that there is differential growth of the placental tissue in normal gestation, as described in human embryologic development.[20] The third mechanism is that of different rates of growth between the placenta and lower uterine segment. The lower uterine segment grows more rapidly than does the placenta.[21]

Another theory evolves from the fact that there is an increase in the number of patients with both placenta previa and placenta accreta.[17] This occurrence may represent evidence of abnormal placental implantation or may represent the characteristics of placentation at a site less optimal for placental support.

Other factors thought to play a role in the development of placenta previa include defective vascularization of the decidua, possibly because of inflammatory changes, and a large placenta, which occurs with multiple gestations and fetal erythroblastosis.[16]

Patient Presentation

The most characteristic event of placenta previa, noted in 80% of cases, is painless bright red vaginal bleeding not associated with uterine contractions that occurs after 28 weeks' gestation.[3] In the remaining 20%, 10% of patients will have bleeding and uterine contractions, and the remaining 10% will be diagnosed prior to the onset of symptoms.[22] Placenta previas that are diagnosed by ultrasonography in the second trimester frequently migrate and are not considered to be placenta previas at term.

Clinical Course

The majority of patients will have an initial bleeding episode that stops spontaneously prior to the onset of labor. The first bleeding episode is usually not associated with a maternal death, but the earlier in pregnancy the bleeding occurs, the less likely the pregnancy is to reach term.[6] In some cases, especially those with low-lying placentas, bleeding does not occur until the onset of labor and may range from slight to profuse. Bleeding originates with cervical dilation, which causes a disruption in placental site integrity. Bleeding is further augmented by the inability of the muscle fibers of the thinned lower uterine segment to contract effectively.[16]

Several reports have indicated that placenta previa may be responsible for intrauterine growth retardation. In one such study, 17.5% of neonates were so affected. Another risk is fetal anemia, which has been reported in women who required blood transfusions.[23] Intrauterine growth retardation and fetal anemia occur most often in the presence of chronic blood loss, as is sometimes encountered with the conservative management of placenta previa.[17] The greatest risk for the fetus, however, is prematurity. Delivery should be postponed until maturity effects a marked reduction in neonatal morbidity and mortality.[24]

Diagnosis

A presumptive diagnosis of placenta previa should be made in any patient who presents with painless third trimester vaginal bleeding. Other causes of vaginal bleeding, such as cervical or vaginal lesions, vasa praevia, and abruptio placentae, should be ruled out. Ultrasound evaluation is 95% accurate in diagnosing placenta previa[3]; however, as previously stated, many patients diagnosed in midtrimester via ultrasonography have no evidence of placenta previa at term. Absolute diagnosis can only be made by actual palpation of the previa during double setup examination, or at vaginal or cesarean delivery.[3]

Management

Patients with third trimester bleeding who are suspected of having a placenta previa should initially be hospitalized and placed on bed rest. Three components must be quickly assessed: (1) maternal condition related to the amount of blood lost, (2) fetal well-being, and (3) fetal gestational age. A massive, life-threatening maternal hemorrhage must be terminated, however, without regard for gestational age. The patient is stabilized as described previously in this chapter.

Management of Severe Bleeding

After stabilization, the pregnancy is terminated. Delivery is usually accomplished by cesarean section with general anesthesia since the effects of hemorrhage augment the hypotension associated with regional anesthesia.[25]

Management of Moderate Bleeding

The patient with moderate bleeding is stabilized as previously described. Once stabilized, assessment of fetal lung maturity becomes essential. Pregnancy is rarely continued in the presence of fetal lung maturity (assessed after 28 to 32 weeks using amniotic fluid) or gestational age greater than 36 weeks. Amniotic fluid is obtained by amniocentesis for evaluation of the lecithin/sphingomyelin (L/S) ratio and determination of the phosphatidylglycerol (PG) value.

If the fetal lungs are immature, the patient is placed on complete bed rest and observed in the labor and delivery area until stable. Vital signs and intake and output, including pad count and weight, are assessed hourly. Fetal monitoring and at least one intravenous line with a 16- to 18-gauge catheter are maintained. A hemoglobin level of 10 g/dL is maintained by transfusion. At least two units of packed red cells should be available at all times. Tocolytic agents may be used to minimize uterine irritability, and steroids may be administered to induce fetal lung maturity.

If the patient continues to bleed or requires more than two units of blood in 24 hours, if labor is present and progresses despite attempted tocolysis, if the fetus shows signs of distress, or if significant fetal hemorrhage has occurred, delivery is accomplished despite fetal immaturity.[17] If the patient remains stable for 24 to 48 hours, she can be managed expectantly.

Management of Mild Bleeding

The patient with mild bleeding is placed on bed rest and observed in the labor and delivery area until stable. As with moderate bleeding, fetal lung maturity dictates treatment. The mature fetus is delivered immediately. The woman with an immature fetus is a candidate for expectant management.

Expectant Management

Expectant management or chronic care is based on the principle that prematurity is the main cause of perinatal loss in pregnancies that are complicated by placenta previa, and that women rarely die of bleeding unless they have a vaginal exam, are anemic, or are in active labor.[22] The goal of expectant management is to delay delivery until the fetus is mature without incurring significant risk to the mother. Studies suggest that 66% to 75% of women with placenta previa are candidates for expectant management.[24,26]

Expectant management is usually carried out in the hospital. The patient is initially maintained on bed rest and may advance to bathroom privileges. Nursing assessments include

1. vital signs and fetal heart tones every 4 hours
2. pad count and intake and output every 8 hours
3. complete blood count and type and cross-match for two units of packed red blood cells on hold every other day
4. cardiovascular, respiratory, and abdominal assessments every 8 hours

Medical management includes nonstress testing (NST) and a biophysical profile (BPP) biweekly and with bleeding episodes, ultrasonographic assessment of fetal growth weekly and assessment of fetal lung maturity every 7 to 10 days after 32 weeks' gestation.

Prevention of hemorrhage is attempted by limiting physical activity and avoiding vaginal and rectal trauma. A sign is placed over the patient's bed stating, "No vaginal exams!" The patient is cautioned against bearing down to void or defecate. Constipation is avoided by attention to diet and the use of a stool softener. Nipple stimulation, masturbation, and coitus are prohibited.

Some institutions are allowing expectant management on an outpatient basis. Criteria for outpatient management include (1) a premature fetus, (2) no recent bleeding, (3) no anemia, and (4) a reliable patient who lives within 20 minutes of the hospital and has continuous access to transportation.[22] The patient must understand her condition, remain on bed rest, and avoid coitus. An ultrasonogram is taken and NST/BPP is conducted weekly. One study reports no difference in outcome between inpatient and outpatient management.[26] Another study, however, reports a significantly better outcome and less expense for patients managed on an inpatient basis. Neonatal morbidity was reported as 24% for inpatients versus 74% for outpatients.[27]

Expectant management is terminated when the patient begins active labor, the fetus has documented lung maturity or gestational age reaches 37 weeks, the fetus expires or has anomalies incompatible with life, excessive bleeding occurs, or another obstetric condition such as rupture of membranes or intrauterine infection develops.[22]

Route of Delivery

Patients with complete placenta previa are delivered by cesarean section. A low transverse incision is used most frequently, as long as the presenting part is accessible and the lower uterine segment is sufficiently developed to permit a generous incision. Delivery of the placenta first or delivery through the placenta has not been associated with fetal exsanguination.[6] A low vertical incision may also be helpful, especially with a transverse lie or a preterm infant.

Some institutions attempt vaginal delivery when partial placenta previa is present and there are no signs of fetal distress or intrauterine growth retardation

(IUGR). An ultrasonogram will rule out total placenta previa and abnormal presentation. During a double setup examination the type of placenta previa is diagnosed. If bleeding occurs, immediate cesarean section is necessary.

Nursing care of the patient who is in labor and who presents with partial or low-lying placenta previa includes continuous electronic fetal monitoring by internal scalp electrode, when possible, following artificial rupture of membranes to allow the fetal head to tamponade the placenta. Vital signs are monitored every 15 to 30 minutes. A baseline blood count is performed, and blood is secured for immediate transfusion. A large-bore intravenous line is es-tablished, and a cesarean section suite should be readily available. Cesarean section is performed in the presence of fetal distress, when there are other obstetric indications for abdominal delivery, and when there is significant hem-orrhage (i.e., causing hemodynamic instability, when rate of blood loss is rapid, or when total blood loss exceeds 500 mL and delivery is not imminent).[28] When labor is allowed to continue in the presence of vaginal bleeding, the blood is screened for fetal cells using the Apt or Kleihauer-Betke test. If either test is positive, an immediate cesarean delivery is performed. All vaginal exams are performed under double setup. If labor is inadequate, as documented by intrauterine pressure catheter, oxytocin may be judiciously used. When an intrauterine pressure catheter cannot be safely introduced, cesarean section may be indicated.[28]

Postpartum

Postpartum, women with placenta previa are at risk for hemorrhage. The placental site in the poorly contractile lower uterine segment may not be suf-ficiently contracted. Ecbolic agents may be used (Table 7-6). In some instances uterine artery ligation and possibly hysterectomy may be necessary. An appropriate amount of Rh immunoglobulin must be given to Rh-negative mothers of Rh-positive newborns. To determine the appropriate amount of Rh immunoglobulin to be administered, a Kleihauer-Betke test is used in addition to the Rh screen.

ABRUPTIO PLACENTAE

Abruptio placentae is premature separation of the normally implanted placenta that causes retroplacental bleeding and occurs after 20 weeks of gestation and prior to delivery of the fetus. The incidence of abruptio placentae ranges from 0.44%[29] to 2.7%[30] of all pregnancies. Perinatal mortality is greater than 50%. Overall maternal mortality is 1%.[3] Predisposing factors are listed in Table 7-7.

Table 7-6 Progression of Pharmacologic Agents Used in the Treatment of Postpartum Uterine Atony

	Action	Route and Dose	Absorption	Precautions	Side Effect
Oxytocin	Phamacologically identical to the hormone. Direct action on myofibrils causes phasic uterine contraction.	IV: 10–40 units added to 1000 mL of appropriate fluid. Run at 200–300 mL/h.	IM: effect in 3–7 minutes. Duration 30–60 minutes. IV: effect in 1 minute. Shorter duration.	Cautious use with cyclopropane anesthesia or vasoconstrictive drugs	Hypotension with rapid administration Water intoxication with prolonged administration
Ergotrate	Ergot alkaloid Produces prolonged nonphasic uterine contractions	IV/IM: 0.2 mg every 2–4 hours up to five doses.* PO: 0.2–0.4 mg every 6–12 hours. Duration 3 hours.	IV: effect immediate. Duration 45 minutes. PO: effect in 5–15 minutes. Duration 3+ hours. IM: effect in 2–5 minutes.	Hypertension	Hypertensive episodes
Methergine	Ergot alkaloid Produces sustained tetanic uterine contractions	IV: 0.2 mg injected over 60 seconds. IM: 0.2 mg every 2–4 hours as necessary. PO: 0.2 mg 3–4 times daily for up to 1 week.	Same	Hypertension	Hypertensive episodes
15-methyl PGF$_{2\alpha}$	Induces strong uterine contractions and increases tone of uterine muscles	IM: 250 µg, may repeat every 15 minutes for a maximum dose of 2 mg.	Variable. Peak effect usually in 15–30 minutes.	Cautious use in preeclamptic/eclamptic patients since this drug may cause transient diastolic hypertension, which is more pronounced in these patients. Used alone, not with other prostaglandins or oxytocin.	Nausea, vomiting, diarrhea, headache, transient pyrexia, chills, transient diastolic hypertension

*IV use only if essential as life-saving measure

Note: IV = intravenous; IM = intramuscular; PO = oral; PGF$_{2\alpha}$ = prostaglandin F$_{2\alpha}$.

Table 7-7 Predisposing Factors for Abruptio Placentae

Medical	Pregnancy
Chronic hypertension	Preeclampsia/eclampsia
Congenital hypofibrinogenemia[*]	Preterm premature rupture of membranes (PROM)
Low levels of vitamins A, E, and β-carotene[†]	Twin gestation
Diabetes	Chronic *Ureaplasma urealyticum* infection[‖]
Life Style	Supine hypotension syndrome
Unmarried	Short umbilical cord
Cigarette smoker	Lack of prenatal care[¶]
Coitus within 48 hours	Increased parity
Cocaine use[‡]	Maternal age <20 years
Snakebite[§]	Previous abruptio placentae
Trauma	
	Fetal
	Male gender
	Small for gestational age
	Congenital anomalies[#]

[*] Ness PM, Budzynski AZ, Olexa SA, Rodvien R. Congenital hypofibrinogenemia and recurrent placental abruption. *Obstet Gynecol.* 1983;61:519-523.
[†] Sharma SC, Bonnar J, Dostalova L. Comparison of blood levels of vitamin A, β-carotene and vitamin E in abruptio placentae with normal pregnancy. *Int J Vitam Nutr Res.* 1986;56:3–9.
[‡] Acker D, Sachs BP, Tracey KJ, Wise WE. Abruptio placentae associated with cocaine use. *Am J Obstet Gynecol.* 1983;146:220–221.
[§] Zugaib M, de Barros ACSD, Bittar RE, Burdmann EA, Neme B. Abruptio placentae following snake bite. *Am J Obstet Gynecol.* 1985;151:754–755.
[‖] Foulon W, Naessens A, Dewaele M, Lauwers S, Amy JJ. Chronic ureaplasma urealyticum amnionitis associated with abruptio placentae. *Obstet Gynecol.* 1986;68:280–282.
[¶] Brink AL, Odendaal HJ. Risk factors for abruptio placentae. *S Afr Med J.* 1987;72:250–252.
[#] Krohn M, Voigt L, McKnight B, Daling JR, Starzyk P, Benedetti TJ. Correlates of placental abruption. *Br J Obstet Gynaecol.* 1987;94:333-340.

Physiology/Pathophysiology

Abruptio placentae is initiated by retroplacental hemorrhage. This hemorrhage occurs in the decidua basalis and originates from degenerative changes in the small arteries that supply the intervillous space. Bleeding leads to hematoma formation that causes progressive separation of the placenta from the uterus and compression of the placental tissue, leading to local destruction.[31] Placental surface area decreases, thereby decreasing oxygen and nutrient availability to the fetus.

In most patients, bleeding extends to the edge of the placenta, at which point it may enter the amniotic fluid by passing through the fetal membranes; more commonly, it continues to pass between the membranes and the decidua vera until it reaches the internal cervical os and presents as vaginal bleeding. Depending on the time elapsed since the initial bleeding and the distance of the placenta from the cervical os, the hemorrhage may remain concealed. Therefore, the lower the implantation of the placenta, the more likely will there be early presentation of vaginal bleeding. Irritation of the myometrium by the blood causes uterine contraction, which assists the blood in reaching the cervical os.[31] Occasionally, blood infiltrates throughout the myometrium and extends into the peritoneum, resulting in a Couvelaire uterus.

Classification

The two major types of abruptio placentae are those with concealed (20%) and those with revealed (80%) hemorrhage.[3] The concealed type of hemorrhage is more dangerous since bleeding is confined to the uterine cavity. The revealed type of hemorrhage is associated with fever and has less severe complications.

Placental abruptions are classified according to severity from grades 0 to 3. Grade 0 includes rupture of a marginal sinus and is usually asymptomatic. It is diagnosed after delivery when a small retroplacental clot is discovered. Grade 1 is associated with vaginal bleeding, and possibly uterine tenderness and tetany. There are no signs of maternal shock or fetal distress. The maternal fibrinogen level is normal. Grade 2 may be associated with vaginal bleeding, or the bleeding may be concealed. Maternal blood pressure is maintained though postural deficits may be noted, and the maternal pulse may be elevated. The fibrinogen level may be decreased to a range of 150 to 250 mg/dL. Uterine tenderness and tetany are present and often are accompanied by signs of fetal distress. In grade 3 abruption, bleeding may be concealed or revealed, with signs of maternal shock and fetal demise. Coagulopathy may become evident in 30% of these patients. The uterus is tetanic and boardlike, causing persistent abdominal pain (Table 7-8).

Patient Presentation

Less than one third of all cases of third trimester bleeding are diagnosed as abruptio placentae. Many of these cases are diagnosed retrospectively, upon postpartum examination of the placenta. The classic triad of symptoms, vaginal bleeding, abdominal pain, and a hypertonic uterus, does not occur in every patient. In one report, the incidence of vaginal bleeding in patients with a live

Table 7-8 Presence of Symptoms According to Grading of Placental Abruption

	Grade 1	Grade 2	Grade 3
Vaginal bleeding	X	O	O
Concealed bleeding		O	O
Uterine tetany and tenderness	O	X	X
Maternal shock			X
Fetal distress		X	
Fetal demise		X	
Coagulopathy			O

Note: X = yes; O = possibility.

fetus was 78%. Bleeding may be dark old blood or bright red blood. Uterine tenderness or back pain occurred in 66% of patients. High-frequency uterine contractions and/or uterine tenderness occurred in only 17% of women. Fetal distress occurred in 60% of patients admitted with a live fetus, and fetal demise occurred in 15.2% of cases prior to admission.[32]

The initiation of symptoms often occurs while the woman is involved in some activity. Sudden sharp and severe pain may occur, which persists or becomes a poorly localized dull ache in the sacrum or lower abdomen. It may progress to intermittent or continuous crampy pain. Tocographic patterns demonstrate an increase in uterine resting tone from a normal of 5 to 12 mm Hg to a mean of 26.3 mm Hg.[33] Uterine contractions occur more frequently than in normal labor, at a mean of 8.4 times in 10 minutes.[34] This frequency does not change as labor progresses. Contraction amplitude is reported as less than in normal labor, at a mean of 27.6 mm Hg.[34] The woman may complain of nausea, vomiting, or dizziness. Depending on the amount of blood lost, hypovolemic shock may be present.

In more severe cases, part or all of the uterus may become rigid and boardlike. Palpation may evoke excruciating pain. While not always fatal, a major placental abruption is almost always accompanied by signs of increasing fetal stress or distress, such as meconium-stained amniotic fluid, late decelerations, alterations in variability and baseline, and sinusoidal patterns.[35] Separation of greater than 50% of the placenta is usually incompatible with fetal life.

Coagulation defects manifested by a decrease in platelet and fibrinogen levels and an elevation of PT and levels of FSP occur in 30% of patients with grade 3 placental abruptions.[3]

Complications

Maternal complications associated with premature separation of the placenta are related to blood loss and massive clotting and include hypovolemic shock, coagulopathy, and ischemic necrosis of distant organs.

Profound hypovolemia may occur as a result of brisk bleeding revealed and underestimated, or concealed. Shock is often out of proportion to the observed blood loss. Hemorrhagic shock produces the highest maternal morbidity and mortality in severe cases of abruptio placentae (see Chapter 6 for greater detail on shock).

Disseminated intravascular coagulation (DIC) occurs in approximately 10%[36] to 30%[37] of all cases of placental abruption. It occurs most often in cases of sufficient severity to cause fetal death. This complication presents clinically as generalized bleeding from mucous membranes and skin puncture sites, or as profuse uterine hemorrhage. It is thought that damage to the placental vessels allows decidual debris to enter the maternal circulation. The extrinsic pathway of clotting is thus activated, causing fibrin deposition in the microvasculature that then stimulates the fibrinolytic system. The net result is continued bleeding and tissue necrosis in organs where fibrin has been deposited. In most cases of abruptio placentae, the process of DIC is self-limited and is reversed within a few hours after delivery.[36]

Ischemic necrosis of distant organs may occur as a result of either hemorrhagic shock or DIC or both. Organs that may be involved are the kidneys, liver, adrenal gland, and pituitary gland (Sheehan's syndrome). Effects on the kidneys include acute tubular necrosis and acute cortical necrosis. These can only be distinguished on pathologic examination. Acute tubular necrosis, the most common cause of anuria in obstetric insults, may lead to acute renal failure late in the abruption process but is reversible. Acute cortical necrosis presents early in the abruption process and, when untreated, progresses to death from uremia in 7 to 12 days.[31]

Perinatal mortality for fetuses that are alive at the time of the mother's hospital admission is reported to be 18%.[32] Mortality occurs for a number of reasons. Fetal anemia may occur with blood loss from the fetal compartment. Hypoxia may occur secondary to fetal anemia or because of the decrease in placental surface nutrient exchange area. These events are of sufficient severity to cause fetal death in approximately 20% of fetuses prior to hospital admission.[6] When the fetus is alive on admission, delivery is accomplished in the best interest of mother and baby, but the newborn may face the problem of prematurity. Respiratory distress syndrome was reported as the most frequent neonatal complication, occurring in 53% of all deliveries.[32]

Another fetal consideration is that the incidence of infants who are small for gestational age is increased with abruptio placentae. One report states that 81%

of infants born secondary to severe abruption prior to 36 weeks of gestation had low birth weight for age.[38] This suggests a long-standing pathologic process. As with other forms of obstetric hemorrhage, the incidence of congenital anomalies is increased two to five times in cases with abruptio placentae.[6]

Management

Stabilization should occur as described previously in this chapter. In addition, to assess intrauterine accumulation of blood, a pen mark should be made on the abdomen at the level of the fundus and evaluation of fundal rise made with every bleeding check. Ultrasonographic examination infrequently detects cases of abruptio placentae but is essential in ruling out placenta previa. In one study, ultrasonography was helpful in detecting only 16% of abruptions.[39] Abruptio placentae presents various ultrasonographic images. A retroplacental clot, if visualized, is helpful in diagnosing abruptio placentae. Oftentimes, however, blood escapes, and no retroplacental clot is visualized.

Generally, the longer the interval between diagnosis and delivery, the poorer the neonatal outcome and the greater the risk of maternal complications. Cesarean delivery is performed in the presence of (1) fetal gestation greater than 32 weeks, (2) fetal distress, (3) heavy bleeding that places the mother and fetus in jeopardy, (4) failure to progress rapidly in labor, or (5) any contraindication to labor.[22,40] Okonofua and Olatunbosun[41] found an increased perinatal mortality in infants greater than 36 weeks of gestation who were delivered vaginally (52.2%) rather than by cesarean section (18.7%).

Vaginal delivery may be attempted using oxytocin stimulation with an immature fetus or after intrauterine fetal demise, once maternal hemodynamic stability has been achieved. Amniotomy is performed to facilitate internal monitoring of the fetus and to assess uterine tonus and the presence and frequency of uterine contractions. The loss of amniotic fluid decreases intrauterine volume, thereby allowing more efficient hemostasis at the placental site. Presence of intra-amniotic hemorrhage, a hallmark of abruptio placentae, may be detected.

In addition to stabilization, nursing management includes assessment of vital signs and vaginal bleeding every 15 minutes, intake and output including pad count and weight, and CVP/pulmonary artery pressure readings hourly. The woman is maintained in a lateral position to facilitate optimal uteroplacental perfusion. Blood is available at all times. The presence of DIC is determined by monitoring the platelet count, PT, PTT, and fibrinogen and FSP levels and by clot observation every 2 to 4 hours. Cesarean section is performed when indications as stated above develop, once coagulopathy has been corrected.

Expectant management may be attempted in patients with mild, stable abruptions when the fetus is immature. A recent study reported use of serial ultrasonograms to determine the volume of the retroplacental clot and correlated this measurement with biweekly NST and maternal symptoms. Three fetuses were managed in this way; one developed fetal distress, was delivered by emergency cesarean section, was transfused, and was discharged home on the fifth day.[42]

Expectant management is carried out in the hospital. The patient is maintained on limited activity. Nursing assessment includes assessment of the abdomen for rigidity, tenderness, and presence of contractions and of vaginal bleeding and intake and output measurement every 8 hours. Uterine irritability may be controlled with tocolytic agents. Vital signs including fetal heart tones are monitored every 4 hours. The complete blood count or hemoglobin level and hematocrit are monitored daily. At least two units of packed red blood cells are continuously available. Steroids may be administered to enhance fetal lung maturity. Assessment and facilitation of psychosocial adaptation of the patient and family must be considered.

Postpartum

In addition to routine postpartum assessments, hemodynamic status is carefully monitored by the nurse. Vital signs and vaginal bleeding are initially assessed every 15 minutes times four, then every half hour times two, and hourly thereafter until stable. Vital signs are assessed every 4 hours, while vaginal bleeding is assessed every 8 hours for the first 48 hours. Thereafter, vital signs and vaginal bleeding are assessed every 8 hours. CVP, pulmonary artery pressure, and PAWP may initially be monitored along with the hematocrit, and transfusion or diuretics implemented as needed. The hematocrit may again be assessed 24 to 48 hours after delivery. Intake and output are monitored every 8 hours. Coagulation defects generally are rapidly corrected, but occasionally administration of clotting components is necessary. Pulmonary assessments, including auscultation of all lung fields, are conducted every 2 to 4 hours, especially in patients who have had general anesthesia. Early ambulation is encouraged. A Kleihauer-Betke assay is performed on the blood of Rh immune globulin candidates to ensure that Rh-negative women receive the proper amount of Rh immune globulin.

RUPTURE OF THE UTERUS

Rupture of the gravid uterus remains one of the most dangerous complications of the antepartum and intrapartum periods. The incidence varies from one institution to another, with a range of 0.3 per 1000 deliveries[43] to 1 per 93 deliveries.[44] Maternal mortality is 5.2%, while perinatal mortality is 75%.[45]

Classification and Etiology

Uterine rupture is classified on an anatomic or etiologic basis. Anatomically, the two types of rupture that can occur are occult (incomplete) and true (complete). The incomplete rupture does not extend through the entire thickness of the uterus and the peritoneal covering. The occurrence is generally gradual. The complete rupture extends through the uterus and peritoneal covering, allowing communication between the peritoneal and intrauterine cavities.

The etiologic classification consists of three main types: (1) traumatic rupture, including instrumental, violent, or obstetric causes; (2) spontaneous rupture occurring either prior to or during labor in the presence or absence of previous uterine surgery; and (3) combinations of these.[46]

The etiologic factor most commonly referred to is the presence of a scarred uterus, usually caused by a previous cesarean section. One study reports a 30 times increase in the incidence of uterine rupture in women with a scarred uterus versus women without a scarred uterus.[47] Other etiologic factors include

1. the use of oxytocin or prostaglandins for labor induction
2. placental pathology
3. uterine trauma, including difficult forceps delivery or excessive fundal pressure
4. precipitous or long, obstructed labor
5. increased parity
6. increasing maternal age
7. anteflexion of the uterus for the purpose of epidural placement in the sitting position

Patient Presentation

The classic signs of uterine rupture are abdominal pain that may abate, cessation of uterine contractions, vaginal bleeding, and shock. One study, however, reports that less than 25% of patients who had a ruptured uterus presented with these signs.[48] Symptoms are variable and depend on the time, site, and extent of the rupture. Rupture of a previous surgical scar is less violent and dramatic than spontaneous or traumatic rupture since the scar is less vascular. In one study, 44.6% of uterine ruptures in the scarred uterus group were diagnosed by vaginal examination after delivery. Diagnosis was made in the unscarred group by the presence of shock (33.3%), vaginal bleeding (30.9%), severe abdominal pain (23.8%), or easily palpated fetal parts (16.6%).[49] Symptoms reported by patients include a sensation of tearing, diaphragmatic or suprapubic pain, anxiety, restlessness, weakness, and dizziness.

Management

Management is best directed at prevention. Patient selection for a trial of labor following previous cesarean section should be carefully conducted.

Ruptures secondary to trauma are decreasing. More liberal use of cesarean sections has decreased difficult breech and some mid- and high forceps deliveries. Fundal pressure is discouraged. Because of the wide variety of symptoms and their likeness to other causes of third trimester bleeding, uterine rupture is difficult to diagnose and, indeed, is not diagnosed until after delivery in many cases. Uterine rupture should be suspected when a woman in the third trimester or in labor suddenly develops abdominal pain with nausea, vomiting, and shock. The presence of predisposing factors such as previous cesarean section or use of oxytocin with lack of labor progress should increase suspicion.

Uterine exploration may be indicated following vaginal birth after

1. cesarean or other uterine surgery
2. breech delivery
3. cervical laceration
4. forceps delivery other than outlet
5. delivery assisted by fundal pressure
6. heavy postpartum bleeding
7. any delivery of any overly distended uterus[46]

Nursing management of a patient in labor who is at risk for uterine rupture includes careful assessment of vital signs, labor progress, and maternal symptoms. An intrauterine pressure catheter is helpful in assessing the presence and adequacy of resting tone as well as the presence of or change in contractions. A sudden loss of fetal signal using external fetal monitoring in a previously stable fetus may be a sign that the fetus has been extruded from the uterus.[49] Oxytocics must be used conscientiously according to protocols that reflect the current standard of care. When a uterine rupture is suspected, the nurse implements stabilization assessments and interventions, as previously described, notifies the physician, and prepares the patient for immediate delivery by cesarean section.

The hemoglobin level and the hematocrit may be normal and therefore are of little diagnostic value. A radiograph of the abdomen and pelvis may demonstrate extended fetal extremities, abnormal position, or intraperitoneal air.[46] Ultrasonographic evaluation assists in the diagnosis of uterine rupture by demonstrating the tear[50] or the presence of intra-amniotic and subchorionic blood.[51] Culdocentesis may assist in the differential diagnosis, but time seldom permits such evaluation. Exploratory laparotomy provides the definitive diagnosis and allows treatment. Hemodynamic stability may not be achieved until arterial bleeding is surgically corrected; therefore, blood should be rapidly infused as laparotomy is begun. Manual aortic compression helps reduce bleeding. Intravenous oxytocin may cause myometrial contraction and vessel constriction, thereby conserving blood. The ovarian vessels should be clamped immediately to further control blood loss.

The surgical correction performed is based on the type, extent, and location of the rupture as well as the patient's condition and desire for future fertility. When a previous uterine scar has ruptured, suturing the defect is the procedure of choice. Suturing of the defect may be used in patients who do not desire future fertility, but the risk of repeat rupture is undefined. Therefore, tubal ligation may be additionally recommended.[52] In the case of catastrophic blood loss, the most expedient procedure is essential, and most agree that hysterectomy is the procedure of choice.

POSTPARTUM HEMORRHAGE

Postpartum hemorrhage is defined as blood loss in excess of 500 mL following delivery. Hemorrhage occurring within 24 hours of delivery is termed acute postpartum hemorrhage, while hemorrhage occurring up to 31 days after that time is termed delayed postpartum hemorrhage.

Physiology/Pathophysiology

Hemorrhage most frequently occurs immediately before or after delivery of the placenta. Placental separation occurs when there is a discrepancy between the decreased intrauterine size and the constant placental surface area. Placental blood flow at term is approximately 600 mL/min; therefore, when myometrial contraction does not occur, severed vessels are not compressed, and blood loss can be massive.

The three most common causes of postpartum hemorrhage are uterine atony, lacerations of the birth canal, and retained placenta.[53] Other causes include hematoma formation and uterine inversion. Predisposing factors for postpartum hemorrhage are listed in Table 7-9.

Specific Mechanisms of Postpartum Hemorrhage

Uterine Atony

Uterine atony is the most common cause of postpartum hemorrhage. It occurs when the uterine corpus fails to contract, thereby allowing continued blood loss from the placental site. The nurse suspects uterine atony when excessive vaginal

Table 7-9 Predisposing Factors for Postpartum Hemorrhage

General Factors	Pregnancy Factors	Labor Factors
Low-cost housing*	Primipara†	Dystocia
Malnutrition	Uterine overdistention	Prolonged first stage of
Coagulation defect	(multiple pregnancy,	labor
	hydraminios)	Second stage labor >1
	Intrauterine fetal demise	hour
	Placenta previa	Precipitous delivery
	Placenta accreta	Induced labor
	Abruptio placentae	Forceps delivery
	Previous postpartum	Magnesium sulfate use in
	hemorrhage	labor§
	Grand multipara‡	Retained placenta
		β-Hemolytic streptococ-
		cal colonization‖

* Watson AJS, Phillips K. Poat-partum haemorrhage is associated with poor housing, not multiparity, in Botswana. *Lancet.* 1986;2:1462–1463.
† Gilbert L, Porter W, Brown VA. Postpartum haemorrhage—a continuing problem. *Br J Obstet Gynaecol.* 1987;94:67–71.
‡ Lucas WE. Postpartum hemorrhage. *Clin Obstet Gynecol.* 1980;23:637–646.
§ Herbert WNP, Cefalo RC. Management of postpartum hemorrhage. *Clin Obstet Gynecol.* 1984;27:139-147.
‖ Crowley J. Post-delivery bleeding due to group B beta-haemolytic streptococcal infection. *N Z Med J.* 1984;97:377.

bleeding occurs in the presence of a soft and boggy uterus. It is often associated with retained placenta or ruptured uterus.

Initial management consists of uterine massage and assessment of bladder distention. The uterus will frequently respond to uterine massage but may again become atonic. The use of external counterpressure may be implemented by pushing upward on the uterus through the abdomen. The bladder is quickly assessed for the presence of overdistention that does not allow adequate uterine contraction. If the bladder is overdistended, it should be emptied by an indwelling catheter. Bimanual uterine massage is attempted next. This is accomplished by massaging the fundus through the abdomen with one hand while simultaneously massaging the uterus in an upward manner through the vagina, using the other hand. Exploration of the uterine cavity can, at this time, be carried out by the physician to identify the presence of retained placenta or ruptured uterus. Other manipulative techniques that have been used include uterine packing, intrauterine lavage,[54] and medical antishock trousers (MAST), which may allow hemostasis to occur by circumferential pneumatic compression.[55] Pharmacologic measures include administering ecbolic agents (Table 7-6).

When manipulative and pharmacologic measures are insufficient to control hemorrhage, interventions listed for stabilization of the bleeding obstetric patient are instituted.

Surgical treatment is implemented next. Hysterectomy is the definitive treatment, but in an attempt to maintain fertility, ligation or embolization of the hypogastric or uterine arteries that supply the uterus may be carried out first. Regional intrauterine infusion of vasoconstrictive agents may also be attempted.[53]

Lacerations of the Birth Canal

The nurse suspects lacerations of the birth canal when excessive bright red vaginal bleeding is associated with a well-contracted uterine fundus. Lacerations may occur with a spontaneous delivery but occur more frequently with an instrumented, manipulated delivery. The perineum is inspected and the physician notified. Medical management includes careful inspection of the lower genital tract. Any laceration that is bleeding and is longer than 2 cm is repaired. If bleeding continues, extension of the laceration into the lower uterine segment or the broad ligament should be suspected. Stabilization measures are initiated, and surgical intervention including artery ligation or hysterectomy may be necessary, depending on the area lacerated and the amount of blood lost.

Hematomas

Hematomas may develop because of pressure by the fetus, forceps, anesthesia needles, or improper repair of a laceration. They occur either early or late in the postpartum period. Bleeding is hidden, and hematoma development is usually gradual; therefore, they may not be detected until significant blood loss has occurred.

The diagnosis of pelvic hematoma is made after delivery when local pain and tenderness, secondary bleeding, and possibly anemia and shock develop. The nurse suspects a perineal hematoma when the perineal skin becomes ecchymotic, distended, firm, and painful. The physician is notified. Hematomas of the vulva and perineum are treated initially with ice and are monitored frequently for increase in size and signs of infection. Often, the pressure inside the hematoma acts to tamponade further blood loss. If this does not occur and hematoma formation is excessive and causes distortion of the perineum, the hematoma is excised, the blood clot removed, and the vessel ligated or blocked by tamponade. Continued treatment consists of observation of the hematoma site for healing and signs of infection; warm sitz baths and dry heat are instituted to encourage resorption of remaining blood.

Paravaginal hematomas may occur following difficult operative deliveries. If these are large, micturition and defecation may be affected by local pressure.

Those that cause shock are vigorously treated with blood transfusion. Excision, clot evacuation, and bleeding vessel ligation are carried out under general anesthesia. If bleeding is not controlled, packing may be necessary; this is removed gradually over a few days.

Supralevator hematomas may be due to uterine rupture, broad ligament varicosities, or ovarian vessel aneurysms. Symptoms include pressure on the urinary bladder and rectum, causing micturition and defecation urgency, and increasing abdominal distention with pelvic and abdominal organ displacement. This requires laparotomy and blood replacement. The hematoma is incised and the bleeding vessels are ligated. If hemostasis is not accomplished, ligation or embolization of the uterine, ovarian, or hypogastric arteries may be necessary. A careful examination of the abdominal cavity is conducted to rule out such causes as uterine rupture. Hysterectomy is necessary in extreme cases.

Retained Placenta

In 75% of deliveries, expulsion of the placenta occurs within 10 minutes of delivery.[56] In some cases, when the third stage exceeds 30 minutes or vaginal bleeding is excessive, manual removal of the placenta is attempted. Regardless of the means of delivery of the placenta, all placentas are thoroughly examined to establish that all tissue has been removed.

Hemorrhage may occur either early or late in the postpartum course. The presence of placental fragments in the uterus prevents effective uterine contraction, thereby allowing excessive blood loss from the placental site. Retained placental tissue is removed manually or with a curette. General anesthesia and/or tocolytic drugs may be necessary to relax the uterus for placenta removal. Oxytocin is given intravenously following placenta removal. Involution and bleeding are monitored afterward.

Inversion of the Uterus

Inversion of the uterus is a very rare cause of postpartum hemorrhage, occurring in 1 per 20,000 deliveries in the United States.[57] Uterine inversion is classified as complete when the fundus extends beyond the cervix and as incomplete when the fundus does not extend past the cervix. It is further classified as acute when the cervix is not contracted and as subacute when the cervix is contracted. Inversion of the uterus occurs most often during the third stage of labor as a result of uterine atony, sudden decompression of a distended uterus, strong expulsive efforts, fundal pressure, or traction on the umbilical cord.

The patient will have acute abdominal pain, and sudden and profuse hemorrhage, and approximately one third of the patients will develop shock that may be out of proportion to blood loss. The fundus may be difficult or impossible to palpate through the abdomen.

Maternal mortality is rare when immediate treatment directed at managing shock, replacing the uterus, and removing the placenta is instituted. Stabilization measures are first initiated. If the placenta is partially detached, it is removed. If it has not begun to detach, it is left in place until the uterus is repositioned.

The uterus is repositioned by applying pressure to the center of the protruding uterus while applying lateral cervical traction. When the cervix is contracted, replacement is facilitated by administering a general anesthetic such as halothane or a tocolytic agent such as terbutaline.[58] The hand remains inside the uterus until a firm contraction occurs following administration of intravenous oxytocin and intramuscular ergots. Packing may be used to prevent recurrence. The placenta is allowed to detach spontaneously. In rare cases, laparotomy is required to reposition the uterus. Hydraulic pressure secured by infusion of intravenous fluids into the posterior fornix while occluding the introitus has been effective in repositioning the uterus.[57] Sepsis may follow uterine inversion; patients, therefore, receive prophylactic antibiotics.

REFERENCES

1. National Center for Health Statistics. Advance Report of Final Mortality Statistics. *Monthly Vital Statistics Report.* 1986;37(suppl):42.
2. National Center for Health Statistics. *Vital Statistics of the United States—1985.* 1988;64.
3. Hayashi RH, Castillo MS. Bleeding in pregnancy. In: Knuppel RA, Drukker JE, eds. *High-Risk Pregnancy: A Team Approach.* Philadelphia: WB Saunders; 1986:419-439.
4. Vorherr H. Puerperium: maternal involutional changes— management of puerperal problems and complications. In: Sciarra JJ, ed. *Gynecology and Obstetrics.* Philadelphia: JB Lippincott; 1985;2:1-44.
5. Benedetti TJ. Obstetric hemorrhage. In: Gabbe SG, Neibyl JR, Simpson JL, eds. *Obstetrics: Normal and Problem Pregnancies.* New York: Churchill Livingstone; 1986:485.
6. Knight AB, Arias F. Third trimester bleeding. In: Arias F, ed. *High Risk Pregnancy and Delivery.* St. Louis: CV Mosby; 1984:278-300.
7. Niederman MS, Matthay RA. Asthma and other severe respiratory diseases during pregnancy. In: Berkowitz RL, ed. *Critical Care of the Obstetric Patient.* New York: Churchill Livingstone; 1983:335-366.
8. Lucas WE. Postpartum hemorrhage. *Clin Obstet Gynecol.* 1980;23:637-646.
9. Romero R. The management of acquired hemostasic failure during pregnancy. In: Berkowitz RL, ed. *Critical Care of the Obstetric Patient.* New York: Churchill Livingstone; 1983:219-284.
10. Rafferty TD, Keefer JR, Barash PG. Fluid management in the massively bleeding obstetric patient. In: Berkowitz RL, ed. *Critical Care of the Obstetric Patient.* New York: Churchill Livingstone; 1983:47-61.
11. Perkins HA. Blood transfusion. In: Wyngaarden JB, Smith LH, eds. *Cecil Textbook of Medicine* 17th ed. Philadelphia: WB Saunders; 1985:936-940.
12. Witter FR, Neibyl JR. Drug intoxication and anaphylactic shock in the obstetric patient. In: Berkowitz RL. *Critical Care of the Obstetric Patient.* New York: Churchill Livingstone; 1983:527-543.
13. Gallagher P, Fagan CJ, Bedi DG,Winsett MZ, Reyes RN. Potential placenta previa: definition, frequency, and significance. *AJR.* 1987;149:1013-1015.

14. Townsend RR, Laing FC, Nyberg DA, Jeffrey RB, Wing VW. Technical factors responsible for "placental migration": sonographic assessment. *Radiology.* 1986;160:105-108.

15. McShane PM, Heyl PS, Epstein MF. Maternal and perinatal morbidity resulting from placenta previa. *Obstet Gynecol.* 1985;65:176-182.

16. Pritchard JA, MacDonald PC, Gant NF, eds. Obstetric hemorrhage. In: *Williams Obstetrics.* Norwalk, CT: Appleton-Century-Crofts; 1985:389-342.

17. Musick SC, Cotton DB. Placenta previa. In: Sciarra JJ, ed. *Gynecology and Obstetrics.* Philadelphia: JB Lippincott; 1987;2:1-6.

18. MacGillivray I, Davey D, Isaacs S. Placenta praevia and sex ratio at birth. *Br Med J Clin Res.* 1986;292:371-372.

19. Harlap S. Gender of infants conceived on different days of the menstrual cycle. *N Engl J Med.* 1979;300:1445-1448.

20. Clark SL, Koonings PP, Phelan JP. Placenta previa/accreta and prior cesarean section. *Obstet Gynecol.* 1985;66:89-92.

21. King DL. Placental migration demonstrated by ultrasonography. *Radiology.* 1973;109:167-170.

22. Huff RW. How to handle third-trimester bleeding. *Contemp Ob/Gyn.* 1982;20:39-50.

23. Dommisse J. Placenta praevia and intra-uterine growth retardation. *S Afr Med J.* 1985;67:291-292.

24. Cotton DB, Read JA, Paul RH, Quilligan EJ. The conservative aggressive management of placenta previa. *Am J Obstet Gynecol.* 1980;137:687-695.

25. Gibbs CP. Anesthetic management of the high-risk mother. In: Sciarra JJ, ed. *Gynecology and Obstetrics.* Philadelphia: JB Lippincott; 1980;3:1-11.

26. Silver R, Depp R, Sabbagha RE, Dooley SL, Socol ML, Tamura RK. Placenta previa: aggressive expectant management. *Am J Obstet Gynecol.* 1984;150:15-22.

27. D'Angelo LJ, Irwin LF. Conservative management of placenta previa: a cost-benefit analysis. *Am J Obstet Gynecol.* 1984;149:320-326.

28. Chervenak FA, Lee Y, Hendler MA, Monoson RF, Berkowitz RL. Role of attempted vaginal delivery in the management of placenta previa. *Obstet Gynecol.* 1984;64:798-801.

29. Karegard M, Gennser G. Incidence and recurrence rate of abruptio placentae in Sweden. *Obstet Gynecol.* 1986;67:523-528.

30. Vintzileos AM, Campbell WA, Nochimson DJ, Weinbaum PJ. Preterm premature rupture of the membranes: a risk factor for the development of abruptio placentae. *Am J Obstet Gynecol.* 1987;156:1235-1238.

31. Weinbaum PJ, Preucel RW, Gabbe SG. Placental abruption. In: Sciarra JJ, ed. *Gynecology and Obstetrics.* Philadelphia: JB Lippincott; 1985;2:1-11.

32. Hurd WW, Miodovnik M, Hertzberg V, Lavin JP. Selective management of abruptio placentae: a prospective study. *Obstet Gynecol.* 1983;61:467-473.

33. Burchell HJ, Odendaal HJ, deWet JI, Badenhorst PN. Uterine contraction patterns in abruptio placentae. *S Afr Med J.* 1985;67:48-50.

34. Odendaal HJ, Burchell H. Raised uterine resting tone in patients with abruptio placentae. *Int J Gynaecol Obstet.* 1985;23:121-124.

35. Heinonen PK, Kajan M, Saarikoski S. Cardiotocographic findings in abruptio placentae. *Eur J Obstet Gynecol Reprod Biol.* 1986;23:75-78.

36. Long CA, Jelovsek FA, Quirk JG. Abruptio placenta. *J Arkansas Med Soc.* 1987;83:475-478.

37. Rivlin ME, Morrison JC, Bates GW, eds. Hemorrhage in pregnancy. In: *Manual of Clinical Problems in Obstetrics and Gynecology.* Boston: Little Brown & Co; 1982:22.

38. Hibbard BM, Jeffcoate TNA. Abruptio placentae. *Obstet Gynecol.* 1966;27:155-167.

39. Nyberg DA, Cyr DR, Mack LA, Wilson DA, Shuman WP. Sonographic spectrum of placental abruption. *AJR.* 1987;148:161-164.

40. Metzger DA, Bowie JD, Killam AP. Expectant management of partial placental abruption in previable pregnancies. A report of two cases. *J Reprod Med.* 1987;32:789-792.
41. Okonofua FE, Olatunbosun OA. Cesarean versus vaginal delivery in abruptio placentae associated with live fetuses. *Int J Gynaecol Obstet.* 1985;23:471-474.
42. Rivera-Alsina ME, Saldana LR, Maklad N, Korp S. The use of ultrasound in the expectant management of abruptio placentae. *Am J Obstet Gynecol.* 1983; 146: 924-927.
43. Fedorkow DM, Nimrod CA, Taylor PJ. Ruptured uterus in pregnancy: a Canadian hospital's experience. *Can Med Assoc J.* 1987;137:27-29.
44. Elkins T, Onwuka E, Stovall T, Hagood M, Osborn D. Uterine rupture in Nigeria. *J Reprod Med.* 1985;30:195-199.
45. Rahman J, Al-Sibai MH, Rahman MS. Rupture of the uterus in labor: a review of 96 cases. *Acta Obstet Gynecol Scand.* 1985;64:311-315.
46. Schrinsky DC, Benson RC. Rupture of the pregnant uterus. A review. *Obstet Gynecol Surv.* 1978;33:217-232.
47. Lao TT, Leung BF. Rupture of the gravid uterus. *Eur J Obstet Gynecol Reprod Biol.* 1987;25:175-180.
48. Van der Merwe JV Jr, Ombelet WUAM. Rupture of the uterus: a changing picture. *Arch Gynecol.* 1987;240:159-171.
49. Zuidema LJ, Goldkrand JW, Work BA Jr. Uterine contractility after rupture of the gravid uterus: a case report. *Am J Obstet Gynecol.* 1984;50:783-784.
50. Suonio S, Saarikoski S, Kaariainen J, Virtanen R. Intrapartum rupture of uterus diagnosed by ultrasound: a case report. *Int J Gynaecol Obstet.* 1984;22:411-413.
51. Gale JT, Mahony BS, Bowie JD. Sonographic features of rupture of the pregnant uterus. *J Ultrasound Med.* 1986;5:713-714.
52. Plauche WC, Von Almen W, Muller R. Catastrophic uterine rupture. *Obstet Gynecol.* 1984;64:792-797.
53. Lucas WE. Postpartum hemorrhage. *Clin Obstet Gynecol.* 1980;23:637-646.
54. Fribourg SRC, Rothman LA, Rovinsky JJ. Intrauterine lavage for control of uterine atony. *Obstet Gynecol.* 1973;41:876-883.
55. Pearse CS, Magrina JF, Finley BE. Use of MAST suit in obstetrics and gynecology. *Obstet Gynecol Surv.* 1984;39: 417-418.
56. Herbert WNP, Cefalo RC. Management of postpartum hemorrhage. *Clin Obstet Gynecol.* 1984;27:139-147.
57. Andersen HF, Hopkins M. Postpartum hemorrhage. In: Sciarra JJ, ed. *Gynecology and Obstetrics.* New York; JB Lippincott; 1989;2:1-10.
58. Kovacs BW, DeVore GR. Management of acute and subacute puerperal uterine inversion with terbutaline sulfate. *Am J Obstet Gynecol.* 1984;150:784-786.

Chapter 8

Trauma during Pregnancy

Nan H. Troiano

It is not uncommon for women to remain participants in a wide variety of activities throughout pregnancy, with subsequent exposure to the risk of accidents at least equal to that of the general population. Several factors may be identified that contribute to the increased incidence of injury during pregnancy:

1. trend toward active employment
2. participation in sports and recreational activities
3. increased violent behavior of society
4. increased mobility of society

Statistics tend to support recognition of accidental injury as a significant complication during pregnancy. Trauma is the leading cause of death in women of childbearing age, and vehicular accidents represent the leading cause of maternal injury.[1] Though difficult to determine accurately, it is estimated that 7% of pregnant women will seek medical assistance as a result of accidental injury.[2] The actual figure may be higher, as pregnancy is not always known or acknowledged at the time attention is sought. In addition, care may be administered in a variety of settings outside traditional emergency departments, including obstetric units, trauma services, and outpatient facilities, thereby making data collection more difficult. The frequency with which pregnant women sustain injury also increases with each trimester. Approximately 10% of injuries occur during the first trimester, about 40% during the second trimester, and 50% during the third trimester.[3]

GENERAL NURSING ISSUES

Care of the obstetric trauma patient represents yet another challenge for nurses. Assessment and stabilization measures may begin in a variety of settings

147

and involve a number of health care providers, depending upon the nature of the injury and associated circumstances. Usually care will be initiated either on-site or in an emergency or trauma department. In such cases, paramedics or emergency transport personnel and emergency department nurses will be the initial care providers. Occasionally, however, such patients will be admitted directly to the obstetric department with initial care provided by labor and delivery nurses.

Optimal maternal and fetal outcome after obstetric trauma is facilitated when the primary nurse, irrespective of the location where initial care is rendered, possesses a working knowledge of

1. priorities in emergency stabilization
2. mechanisms of trauma
3. physiologic alterations during pregnancy
4. techniques of maternal and fetal assessment

It is readily apparent that emergency department and obstetric nurses each bring a unique expertise to such a patient care situation, based on education and clinical experience in one or more of these areas. Yet in this age of rapid health care advancements, it is increasingly difficult to maintain proficiency in all areas. Therefore, consultation and collaboration between these two nursing specialties represent important strategies to improve care.

PHYSIOLOGIC CHANGES OF PREGNANCY AND TRAUMA

Physiologic changes normally associated with pregnancy may affect significantly both the nature of maternal or fetal injury and the outcome. Several specific responses to trauma are particularly unique to the pregnant patient. It is imperative, therefore, that the nurse incorporate these principles into care of the obstetric trauma patient. A summary of these changes and their relationship to trauma is presented in Table 8-1.

Cardiovascular

Pregnancy most dramatically affects the cardiovascular system. As previously discussed in Chapter 1, blood and plasma volume as well as maternal heart rate increase by the 10th week of gestation, thereby significantly increasing cardiac output. Systemic vascular resistance is lowered secondary to the effect of progesterone and the perfusion of the uteroplacental bed, thereby decreasing the arterial blood pressure. The subsequent hemodilution is evidenced by a reduction in hematocrit.

Table 8-1 Physiologic Changes of Pregnancy and Relationship to Trauma

System	Change	Significance
Cardiovascular	⇑ Volume	No clinical signs of shock until 30% loss of circulating volume
	⇑ Heart rate	
	⇑ Cardiac output	
	⇓ Systemic vascular resistance	
	⇓ Arterial blood pressure Vena caval compression	⇓ Uteroplacental perfusion with supine position
Respiratory	⇑ Tidal volume	Chronic compensatory alkalosis
	⇑ Oxygen consumption	
	⇓ Functional residual capacity	⇓ Blood buffering capacity
	⇓ Arterial P_{CO_2}	
	⇓ Serum bicarbonate	Risk of acidosis when normal nonpregnant blood gas values used to guide ventilation
Gastrointestinal	⇓ Gastric motility	Bowel sounds less audible
	⇓ Gastroesophageal sphincter competency	Delayed emptying time ⇑ Risk of aspiration
Renal	⇑ Blood flow	⇑ Risk of stasis and infection
	Dilation or ureters and urethra	
	Bladder displaced	⇑ Susceptibility to injury
Musculoskeletal	Displacement of abdominal viscera	Altered probability of injury Altered pain referral patterns
	Pelvic venous congestion	⇑ Risk of hemorrhage with injury
Reproductive	⇑ Uterine enlargement	⇑ Vulnerability to injury
	⇑ Pelvic vascularity	Potential for significant blood loss with uterine injury

This hypervolemia during pregnancy may enable the patient to maintain adequate perfusion and exhibit no clinical signs of hypovolemic shock until there has been approximately a 30% loss of circulating volume.[4] With such acute blood loss, though other systems may continue to receive perfusion, the uterus is treated as a nonessential organ, with a concomitant decrease in blood flow and reduction in fetal oxygenation.

Vena caval compression by the gravid uterus, as occurs when the patient is in the supine position, may further reduce cardiac output by inhibition of venous return to the heart. This supine hypotension syndrome, when coupled with traumatic blood loss, may cause severe shock in the pregnant patient.[5]

Respiratory

The diaphragm is displaced by the gravid uterus, with a subsequent broadening of the chest wall and compensatory flaring of the ribs. This permits intrathoracic volume to remain constant. Tidal volume increases, and respiratory rate increases slightly.

These alterations, in light of increased oxygen consumption during pregnancy and decreased functional residual capacity, create a chronic compensated respiratory alkalosis.[6] Arterial PCO_2 and serum bicarbonate levels are decreased, which may impede blood buffering capacity. Hypoxic tissue damage, therefore, occurs more rapidly when the pulmonary system is compromised by trauma.[7] Maternal acidosis may also occur in the patient who requires assisted ventilation when normal nonpregnant values are used to guide diagnosis and therapy of acid-base disturbances.[8]

Gastrointestinal

Gastric motility is reduced because of displacement of the stomach and colon by the uterus. In addition, there is a decrease in gastroesophageal sphincter competency.[9] For these reasons, the risk of aspiration increases. The time of the patient's last meal may not be a reliable indicator of whether the stomach has emptied, and bowel sounds may be less audible. Therefore, severe trauma or need for general anesthesia usually necessitates placement of a nasogastric tube.

Renal

Renal blood flow increases significantly during pregnancy, with dilation of the ureters and urethra. This alteration of the urinary collecting system results in increased risk of stasis and infection. The bladder, displaced anteriorly by the uterus, gradually becomes more susceptible to injury.

Musculoskeletal

Abdominal viscera are displaced upward, which results in altered pain referral patterns and probabilities of injury. The usual response to peritoneal irritation is altered by this stretching of the abdominal wall. Therefore, muscle guarding and rebound, which otherwise would be expected, may be absent despite significant intra-abdominal organ injury.[10]

Secondary to a widening of the symphysis pubis and abdominal protuberance, gait instability contributes to the incidence of falls. Also, by the third trimester, marked venous congestion in the pelvis increases the potential for hemorrhage with both bony and soft tissue pelvic injuries.[7]

Reproductive

As pregnancy progresses, the uterus becomes the largest intra-abdominal structure and thereby becomes more vulnerable to injury. Due to the increased vascularity of the pelvis, what at first may appear to be a minor abdominal injury could result in major hemorrhage if the uterus is involved.

MECHANISMS OF TRAUMA

Abdominal Trauma

The extent of abdominal injury from trauma is largely dependent upon gestational age and whether the insult was blunt or penetrating. The bony pelvis serves to protect the uterus and fetus during the first trimester from all but the most severe injuries. Due to only minor anatomic changes, maternal injuries during this trimester approximate those of nonpregnant women.[11] As pregnancy progresses, both the nature of injury and its outcome may be altered because of associated anatomic changes.

Blunt

The primary cause of blunt abdominal trauma is motor vehicle accidents. However, battering also represents a significant source of trauma during pregnancy. Maternal death following severe blunt trauma is most frequently caused by head injury and exsanguination from rupture of a major blood vessel.[12] The most frequent cause of severe maternal injury in motor vehicle accidents is ejection from the vehicle. The leading cause of fetal death is maternal death. The most common fetal injury in severe cases is skull fracture with subsequent intracranial hemorrhage.[13] In less severe cases, the fetus is usually spared indirect injury because of the protective cushion of the amniotic fluid.

The leading cause of fetal death in cases of blunt abdominal trauma that the mother survives is placental abruption. When abruption occurs, it will most likely be within 48 hours after injury.[14] For this reason, patients with even minor injuries should be observed for signs and symptoms of abruption or preterm labor, including onset of vaginal bleeding, uterine irritability, pain, leaking of amniotic fluid, evidence of hypovolemia, or a change in fetal heart rate characteristics.[15] Late decelerations and an elevated baseline heart rate may be an early sign of significant abruption in trauma patients.[16] Therefore, continuous electronic fetal heart rate monitoring should be included in such observation protocols. For these reasons, the trend toward observation of these patients for approximately 24 hours, or until no bleeding or contractions are present, is judicious.

In the event of a motor vehicle accident, use of a seat belt with a shoulder harness decreases the risk of ejection from the vehicle and associated head trauma, thereby improving outcome for both mother and fetus. However, a seat belt worn improperly may contribute to abdominal injuries. The part of the belt that goes across the lap should be placed across the maternal thighs, underneath the fetus, rather than across the pregnant uterus.[3]

Certain abdominal structures become more vulnerable to blunt trauma with advanced gestation. The uterus compresses and displaces the liver and spleen, thereby increasing the risk of rupture.[17] The bladder is also displaced upward and is less protected from injury secondary to blunt trauma. Pelvic fracture may occur in severe cases of blunt trauma and may account for injury to the bladder as well as significant blood loss. The uterus is relatively resistant to blunt injury, with reports of uterine rupture being rather uncommon. Case reports indicate that uterine rupture most often occurs at a previous cesarean scar.[18]

Penetrating

Case reports exist describing a variety of objects responsible for penetrating injuries during pregnancy, including knives, bullets, spears, shrapnel, pitchforks, scythes, swords, and even animal horns.[3] The most frequent cause is a bullet wound. The rate of maternal mortality from gunshot wounds is fairly low, and the morbidity rate is proportional to the number of organs involved and to the location of the entrance wounds.[6] Of the reported cases occurring during the second half of pregnancy, the majority of fetuses were directly injured by the bullet.[4,12] Though maternal prognosis is excellent, fetal mortality rate is much higher—approximately 70% in one early report.[19] However, fetal gestational age at the time of delivery may have contributed to the high mortality rate, since preterm delivery occurred in a significant number of cases.

The posterior position of major vessels and the displacement of the intestines by the uterus provide protection to abdominal organs.[20] When the uterus is directly injured from a bullet, there is a diminished incidence of other visceral injuries because of this protective displacement. As with other cases of gunshot wounds to the abdomen, exploratory laparotomy is indicated.

Maternal and fetal prognosis is improved when the penetrating injury is a stab wound, since the injury is usually confined to the tract created by the knife.[21] Such wounds may occur in the upper or lower abdomen and require careful local exploration to determine if the peritoneal cavity has been penetrated. Peritoneal lavage may be performed to determine whether intraperitoneal hemorrhage is present. There is risk of pneumothorax and hemothorax with chest involvement.

Burns

Maternal and fetal prognosis after thermal burns varies depending upon percentage of body surface area involved, degree of the burn, and gestational age. Burns involving less than one third of the body surface area may not affect the pregnancy. With burns affecting greater than 60% of the body surface area, there is significant risk of maternal death.[22] Fetal survival generally accompanies maternal survival but is gestational age–dependent.

Routine burn care principles should be followed for the pregnant patient who is seriously burned but may include more vigorous fluid replacement, prompt correction of electrolyte imbalances, and meticulous attention to maternal oxygenation.[20] Interruption of pregnancy is attempted only if hypovolemia, hypoxia, or sepsis results in fetal compromise.[22]

Electrical burns, in the form of lightning strikes, have been reported to have generally good maternal and fetal prognosis. Asystole rather than ventricular fibrillation tends to follow lightning strikes, with a resumption of sinus rhythm because of the heart's automaticity.[23] Respiratory paralysis tends to outlast cardiac dysrhythmias, with anoxia being the primary cause of death. Immediate respiratory support is therefore essential.[7]

Pelvic Fractures

With pelvic fractures, displacement usually occurs in two places because of the rigid bony ring structure of the pelvis.[5] Retroperitoneal hemorrhage may be significant with such injury and requires careful monitoring. With engagement of the fetal head, pelvic fracture may also result in fetal skull fracture. Ultrasonography and radiography may be utilized to detect such injury.[3]

IMMEDIATE STABILIZATION

Both patient and professional expectations associated with pregnancy most often revolve around safe delivery of a healthy newborn. For this reason, when faced with caring for the seriously injured obstetric patient, professionals may find it difficult to identify priorities without confusing maternal and fetal needs. Yet immediate stabilization may well be the single most important factor in predicting outcome.

Though immediate stabilization of the pregnant woman is similar to that for other trauma victims, some differences do exist. Fluid resuscitation should be aggressive and accomplished with volume rather than vasopressors. Intravenous access with large-bore (16- to 18-gauge) catheters should be established early, and infusion of crystalloids, such as lactated Ringer's solution, is preferred.[20] Blood should be drawn for typing, cross-matching and diagnostic studies, including a complete blood count and platelet count.[24] Whenever possible, type-specific whole blood or packed red blood cells should be used to replace blood loss and therefore improve fetal oxygenation.[20] Type O, Rh-negative blood may be used without matching when type-specific blood is not immediately available. A pneumatic antishock garment—medical antishock trousers (MAST)—may be applied with the abdominal compartment left uninflated, in cases of severe hypotension. Oxygen at 10 to 12 L/min by tight-fitting mask should be administered to provide a maternal PO_2 greater than 60 mm Hg, which is recommended to maintain fetal status.[25] Supplementation of maternal oxygen does little for the normal mother since arterial blood is usually well saturated at room air, but fetal blood functions on a different oxyhemoglobin dissociation curve.[7] Increasing oxygen tension by oxygen administration may improve fetal oxygen saturation.[25]

Use of invasive hemodynamic monitoring may also be considered following immediate stabilization measures. Obstetric patients with massive blood loss and large transfusion requirements, such as those that may arise secondary to placental abruption or uterine rupture, may benefit from invasive monitoring.[26] Pulmonary artery catheterization allows for the assessment of cardiac function by providing a means for evaluation of preload, afterload, contractility, and heart rate, which are the determinants of cardiac output.

SETTING PRIORITIES

The acronym STABLE, described in Table 8-2, may be utilized when setting priorities in obstetric emergency situations. Each letter of the word represents an action to be initiated to facilitate successful stabilization. It represents a dynamic process and incorporates changing patient status.

The most common cause of fetal death is maternal death. Therefore, immediate stabilization measures are most appropriately directed toward the mother. Even when maternal death appears imminent, maternal resuscitation is always initiated until fetal status may be evaluated.

Table 8-2 Priorities for Obstetric Trauma Care: STABLE

Letter	Action	Description
S	Stay calm	Initiation of techniques to counteract sympathetic response
T	Triage	Assessment of airway, breathing, circulation
A	Assess	Rapid maternal assessment with emphasis on pulmonary, cardiovascular, and neurologic status
B	Baby	Assessment of fetal viability and gestational age
L	Launch	Implementation of protocols for continued care, including intravenous access, fluid and blood replacement, oxygen therapy, and laboratory tests
E	Evaluate-evacuate	Evaluation of patient responses and stability for transport, when applicable

Stay Calm

Anyone who has been involved in an emergency situation can appreciate how difficult it becomes to do that which at first seems so simple. Our natural sympathetic response to such stressful events, the release of epinephrine and norepinephrine, prepares us for what has been described as "fight or flight." However, such responses may lead to nonproductive professional behaviors during clinical emergencies. The ability to stay calm may be facilitated at the bedside by simple biofeedback techniques. It may be necessary, for example, to take a few slow deep breaths or to use conscious muscle relaxation in order to control the sympathetic surges that occur. Calmness, just like panic, is contagious, and a calm, focused, deliberate stabilization effort may yield better results for both patient and staff.

Triage

Immediate assessment of the pregnant trauma patient is similar to the primary survey utilized for other trauma victims. Airway, breathing, and circulation are priorities. If indicated, cardiopulmonary resuscitation is initiated, with the patient's uterus displaced laterally to avoid vena caval compression. It is imperative that each of these three parameters be adequately restored before initiation of secondary assessment and stabilization measures.

Assess

A head-to-toe assessment should follow primary triage measures with initial emphasis on pulmonary, cardiovascular, and neurologic status. This includes reassessment of adequacy of cardiac output, sufficiency of oxygenation, and neurologic evaluation for apparent injury and adequacy of compensatory central nervous system mechanisms. Assessment findings will enhance the ability of the stabilization team to identify the underlying cause of physiologic instability and set priorities for further intervention. A summary of immediate and additional maternal assessment parameters is presented in Table 8-3.

Baby

After initiation of maternal stabilization measures, two questions must be answered regarding fetal status. First, is the fetus alive, and, second, what is the best estimate of gestational age? The fetal heart rate may be determined by auscultation with a fetoscope or stethoscope, or its cardiac activity assessed by real-time ultrasonography. Gestational age may be estimated by historical data, fundal height measurement, or biometric assessment via ultrasonography. If the maternal condition remains unstable or worsens, this information may influence the medical plan of care. In the absence of acute maternal jeopardy, additional information regarding fetal status may be obtained. Continuous electronic

---

Table 8-3 Maternal Assessment Summary

Immediate	*Additional*
Airway-breathing-circulation	Electrocardiogram
Vital signs	Laboratory tests
Level of consciousness	Arterial blood gases
Breath sounds	Blood type and Rh status
Character, depth, symmetry, and	Complete blood count
regularity of respirations	Platelet count
Presence and quality of pulses	Kleihauer-Betke test
Skin color and temperature	Intake and output measurement
Capillary bed refill	Uterine activity:
	Contraction frequency, intensity, and duration
	Resting tone
	Presence and quality of vaginal bleeding and drainage
	Radiographs

monitoring of the fetal heart rate should be applied when it does not interfere with maternal resuscitation and stabilization activities. Measures to prolong the gestation, such as initiation of tocolysis, are contraindicated if maternal health would be jeopardized in any way. A summary of immediate and additional fetal assessment parameters is presented in Table 8-4.

Launch Protocols

After cardiopulmonary resuscitation has been initiated and an initial rapid maternal and fetal assessment completed, further nursing measures may be implemented.

Emergency care protocols may be beneficial in a stabilization setting to promote consistency in care and to decrease time delay between physician arrival and implementation of emergency care. Development of such protocols should take into account unique circumstances within different health care settings.

Evaluate and Evacuate

Evaluation should begin to determine the patient's response to stabilization measures and to facilitate additional care planning. The nurse should determine whether the patient's status is improving, unchanged, or deteriorating. If the status is improving, current protocols are most probably appropriate to the situation. If there has been no change or deterioration in status, additional or alternative protocols may be considered.

Stabilization is the single most important factor before transportation may be accomplished. Once evaluation shows improvement without major setbacks, the

---

Table 8-4 Fetal Assessment Summary

Immediate	Additional

Fetal heart rate:
  Auscultation via fetoscope/
    stethoscope
  Real-time ultrasonogram
Gestational age estimation:
  Last menstrual period
  Fundal height
  Ultrasonogram
	Continuous electronic fetal heart rate monitoring:
	  Baseline rate
	  Presence of accelerations
	  Presence and type of decelerations
	Biophysical profile
	Pulmonary maturation

patient may be considered, when applicable, for transport to another unit or institution that can better meet her needs. There are unique situations in which stabilization is not achieved but transport is nonetheless necessary because of the transferring institution's exhaustion of resources.

Transport of the patient should, however, reflect a continuation of ongoing stabilization procedures and protocols. When preparing a patient for transport, several questions may assist in determination of stability:

1. Is the patient's ventilation adequate?
2. Have vital signs continued to dramatically fluctuate?
3. Has level of consciousness changed?
4. Have medications required significant change or titration?
5. Is there a current need for transfusion?
6. Is delivery of the fetus imminent?

The goal of transport is the safe and timely movement of the patient to another location for care. It should be a smooth and timely continuation of the stabilization process. Personnel must display the capacity to remain calm and confident in their ability to establish priorities and implement appropriate care.

MEDICAL CONSIDERATIONS

Following stabilization measures, medical diagnostic studies may be indicated to determine the extent of injury. Peritoneal lavage, culdocentesis, and exploratory laparotomy to detect occult abdominal injuries represent examples of such evaluation. Computerized axial tomograms, radiographs, radioisotopic scans, and angiograms may also be useful in the evaluation of selected patients with blunt or penetrating trauma.[27]

CONCLUSION

Providing care for the pregnant trauma victim poses a unique challenge for health care professionals. Nurses must draw upon principles and clinical skills traditionally associated with obstetric and critical care specialities. The patient's physical as well as psychosocial needs must be considered when planning care. Fetal prognosis will best be facilitated through prompt, appropriate maternal support. Adherence to these important issues may enable us to better address the problems associated with trauma in pregnancy.

REFERENCES

1. Katz M. Maternal trauma during pregnancy. In: Creasy RK, Resnik R, eds. *Maternal Fetal Medicine: Principles and Practice.* Philadelphia: WB Saunders; 1984:772-780.
2. Buchsbaum HJ. *Trauma in Pregnancy.* Philadelphia: WB Saunders; 1979:vii. .
3. Buchsbaum HJ. *Trauma in Pregnancy.* Great Neck, NY: Medical Information Systems; 1986:1-10. American College of Obstetricians and Gynecologists Update. Vol 12.
4. Haycock CE. Injury during pregnancy. *Consultant.* 1982;22:269-276.
5. VanderVeer JB. Trauma during pregnancy. *Top Emerg Med.* 1984;16:72-81.
6. Auerback PS. Trauma in the pregnant patient. *Top Emerg Med.* 1979;1:133-147.
7. Neufield DG, Moore EE, Marx JA, Rosen P. Trauma in pregnancy. *Emerg Med Clin North Am.* 1987;5:623-640.
8. Barron WM. The pregnant surgical patient: medical evaluation and management. *Ann Intern Med.* 1984;101:683-691.
9. Framaszek JB. Trauma in pregnancy. *Top Emerg Med.* 1985;5:51-55.
10. Cruikshank DP. Anatomic and physiologic alterations of pregnancy that modify the response to trauma. In: Buchsbaum HJ, ed. *Trauma in Pregnancy.* Philadelphia: WB Saunders; 1979:21.
11. Haycock CE. Emergency care of the pregnant traumatized patient. *Emerg Med Clin North Am.* 1984;2:843-851.
12. Crosby WM. Traumatic injuries during pregnancy. *Clin Obstet Gynecol.* 1983;26:902-912.
13. Bremer C, Cassata L. Trauma in pregnancy. *Nurs Clin North Am.* 1986;21:705-716.
14. Higgins SE, Garite TJ. Late abruptio placenta in trauma patients: implication for monitoring. *Obstet Gynecol.* 1985;63:10-12.
15. Rothenberger D, Quattlebaum FW, Perry JF. Blunt maternal trauma: a review of 103 cases. *J Trauma.* 1978;18:173.
16. Freeman RK, Garite TJ, eds. *Fetal Heart Rate Monitoring.* Baltimore: Williams & Wilkins; 1981:69.
17. Foster CA. The pregnant trauma patient. *Nursing '84.* 1984;14:58-63.
18. Schrinsky DC, Benson RC. Rupture of the pregnant uterus: a review. *Obstet Gynecol Surv.* 1978;33:217.
19. Buchsbaum HJ, Caruso PA. Gunshot wound of the pregnant uterus. *Obstet Gynecol.* 1969;33:673-676.
20. Stauffer DM. The trauma patient who is pregnant. *J Emerg Nurs.* 1986;12:89-93.
21. VanderVeer JB. Trauma during pregnancy. *Top Emerg Med.* 1984;5:72-77.
22. Taylor JW, Plunkett GD, McManus WF, Pruitt BA Jr. Thermal injury during pregnancy. *Obstet Gynecol.* 1976;47:434-438.
23. Strasser EJ, Davis RM, Menchey MJ. Lightning injuries. *J Trauma.* 1977;17:315.
24. Newkirk EJ, Fry ME. Trauma during pregnancy. *Focus Crit Care.* 1985;12:30-39.
25. Witter FR, Neibyl JR. Drug intoxication and anaphylactic shock in the obstetric patient. In: Berkowitz RL, ed. *Critical Care of the Obstetric Patient.* New York: Churchill Livingstone; 1983:527-543.
26. Hankins GDV. Principles of hemodynamic monitoring. *Clin Perinatol.* 1986;13:765-777.
27. Sorensen VJ, Bivins BA, Obeid FN, Horst HM. Trauma in pregnancy. *Henry Ford Hosp Med J.* 1986;34:101-104.

Chapter 9

Diabetes Mellitus in Pregnancy

Lisa K. Mandeville

Diabetes was first recognized as a medical disorder by the Egyptians around 1500 BC. The name "diabetes," meaning "siphon," was given by Aretaeus of Cappadocia (AD 81–138), but the word "mellitus," meaning "honey," was not added until the 1700s.[1] Insulin was not identified and made commercially available until 1922; thus this age-old disorder of carbohydrate metabolism has had barely 70 years of treatment.

Approximately 2% to 3% of the population of the United States has diabetes, and of this group, 93% (5.07 million individuals in 1985) have type II non-insulin-dependent diabetes, and 7% (0.43 million in 1985) have type I insulin-dependent diabetes.[2] It is estimated, however, that only half of those currently affected have been diagnosed. In 1979 the National Diabetes Data Group defined gestational diabetes (GDM) as carbohydrate intolerance with onset or diagnosis occurring during pregnancy.[3]

Type I diabetes is characterized by the presence of the classic symptoms polyuria, polydipsia, and polyphagia. The patient with type I diabetes has elevated blood glucose, ketonuria, and rapid weight loss, in the absence of insulin therapy. Peak ages of onset are 11 to 14 years, although individuals of any age may develop the disorder. Type II diabetes is characterized by elevated blood glucose levels, but endogenous insulin levels are normal or excessive, and diet therapy typically restores euglycemia. These patients are frequently overweight (greater than 20% of ideal body weight), and peak onset occurs at age 51 to 55 years.

GDM frequently affects women over age 25, those who are overweight prior to pregnancy, or those with a strong family history of the condition; however, fully one half of GDM cannot be predicted by the presence of risk factors. Pregnancy acts as a stress test for diabetes, as up to 40% of women with GDM will develop type I or type II diabetes within a decade of the index pregnancy. (The identification of GDM may assist in predicting mature-onset diabetes or

161

make possible participation in weight reduction, exercise programs, and nutritional counseling, which may possibly prevent diabetes.)

Diabetes presents a clinical challenge to the perinatal nurse as advanced knowledge regarding the relationship between diabetic pathophysiology and the complex changes of pregnancy is mandatory for care of these patients. With routine screening for GDM, approximately 5% of the obstetric population will be identified. All levels of facilities must be prepared to provide clinical services for the GDM. Both type I (insulin dependent) and type II (generally insulin dependent during pregnancy) diabetics require specialized care and services and have a significantly higher incidence of complications that must be anticipated. It is therefore imperative that these patients receive obstetric care in a facility designed to provide comprehensive care to high-risk patients. The perinatal nurse likewise must be knowledgeable, skilled, and able to advise the diabetic when rendering nursing care.

PHYSIOLOGY OF GLUCOSE METABOLISM AND PATHOPHYSIOLOGY OF DIABETES MELLITUS

Glucose is an essential source of body cell energy and the sole fuel used by neural tissues, including the brain. Transformation of ingested carbohydrate (CHO) to glucose is a complex process that involves oxidation to produce carbon dioxide, water, and energy. This reaction is catabolic in nature because of its energy-liberating aspect and promotes the conversion of adenosine triphosphate (ATP) to adenosine diphosphate (ADP). The process is reversible, involving the anabolic or energy-requiring metabolism of glucose-6-phosphate and subsequent conversion of ADP to ATP.

Ingested carbohydrate is broken down by pancreatic and salivary enzymes and transported across the intestinal wall primarily as glucose, fructose, and galactose. These sugars enter the portal vein and cause a rise in blood glucose levels and subsequent stimulation of the pancreas to release insulin. The principal role of insulin is transport of glucose (the primary monosaccharide) across cell membranes, where its conversion to glucose-6-phosphate is catalyzed by the enzyme hexokinase. (In hepatic cells, the conversion occurs by the action of glucokinase.) Glucose-6-phosphate is then either converted to glycogen for storage or burned for energy.

It is in the fed state that glycogenesis (glycogen formation from glucose) occurs; during times of fasting, glycogenolysis (glycogen breakdown) occurs, resulting in production of glucose-6-phosphate. By the production of glucose-6-phosphatase, dephosphorylation can occur, releasing glucose for use elsewhere as a fuel source. Similarly, conversion of glucose into fatty acids and amino acids also occurs.

Along with insulin, the pancreatic islet of Langerhans cells secrete three other hormones: glucagon, somatostatin, and pancreatic polypeptide. Among the 1 to 2 million human islet cells in the pancreas, there are four basic types: A, B, D, and F cells. A cells secrete glucagon, which is a catabolic hormone and functions to liberate glucose. B cells secrete insulin, which functions as an anabolic hormone with an action reciprocal to that of glucagon. D cells secrete somatostatin, which probably has an overall islet cell regulation effect, and F cells secrete pancreatic polypeptide, the function of which remains unknown.

The synthesis of insulin occurs in the endoplasmic reticulum of the B cell and begins with the conversion of preproinsulin to proinsulin. Proinsulin is subsequently converted to equal amounts of insulin and a polypeptide called the connecting peptide, or C peptide, which is often measured as an indicator of endogenous insulin production in diabetics. Insulin is normally stored in granules within the B cells; upon stimulus the granules are moved to the cell surface membrane where they are released by the process of exocytosis.

Endogenous insulin has a circulating half-life of 5 minutes, with almost all insulin degradation occurring in the liver and kidneys. When exogenous insulin is intravenously injected, a maximal fall in the blood glucose level occurs at 30 minutes. Total blood glucose level is a function of glucose entering the circulation and glucose leaving it. As glucose is normally ingested, about 5% undergoes glycogenesis, 30% to 40% is converted to fat, and the rest is catabolized in other cells. During fasting periods, glycogenolysis and dephosphorylation of glucose-6-phosphate liberate glucose. When glycogen stores are exhausted because of extensive fasting, gluconeogenesis continues to occur.

Most people with type I diabetes exhibit an almost complete lack of insulin, and histologic examination of the pancreas usually reveals a marked reduction to a complete absence of B cells. Although type II diabetes has traditionally been explained by insulin resistance, both increases and decreases in B cell volume are found. Examination of the diabetic pancreas usually reveals the presence of inflammatory cells, a condition called insulitis. It is not known why this inflammatory response is seen at the time of diagnosis, but this inflammation may represent a type of chronic process consistent with end-stage destruction of B cells.

Early in the development of type I diabetes, the pancreas exhibits a decrease in insulin release. However, radioimmunoassay of proinsulin C peptide usually reveals increased levels in the first 3 to 6 months after diagnosis and with initiation of treatment, known as the "honeymoon" period. A subsequent decrease is seen, which usually falls to undetectable levels within 3 to 4 years. No evidence exists to correlate the change in C peptide levels during this initial period with diminished B cell mass or function.

The etiology of type I diabetes mellitus has yet to be explained and in all probability is multifactorial, but it is clearly related to B cell destruction. Viral induction has been suggested as an etiology since there is a seasonal variation in the diagnosis of diabetes[4]; viral infections such as mumps, congenital rubella, and those caused by coxsackievirus B4 have been implicated. Some drugs such as alloxan and streptozotocin cause diabetes in laboratory animals but have not been shown to do so in humans. Vacor, a pesticide, has been shown to cause diabetes in humans.[5] Diabetes may also have an immunologic etiology, as islet cell antibodies (ICA) are detected in most diabetics. The presence of ICA may, however, signal only susceptibility of autoimmune antibodies, as some subjects manifest ICA for long periods before clinical symptoms (hyperglycemia) appear. Also, since the typical insulitis of diabetes is characterized by infiltration of mononuclear cells, an immunologic injury may be involved.

Genetic factors must also be considered in the pathogenesis of diabetes. About 50% of identical twins are concordant for diabetes, although the resultant 50% (where only one twin has diabetes) suggests a multifactorial cause. Type I diabetics tend to have similar haplotypes, with 90% involving HLA-DR3 and HLA-DR4.

Type II diabetes, characterized by defective tissue sensitivity and insulin release, is probably also of multifactorial etiology. The onset is more prolonged than for type I and primarily affects patients over 20 years of age. It is associated with increased body weight; hereditary factors are also stronger among type II diabetics than among type I diabetics.

Normal Diabetogenic Effect of Pregnancy

Early in normal pregnancy, a state of hyperinsulinemia is observed, which is probably due to the combined effects of progesterone and estrogen. Levels of these sex steroids rise in early gestation and, among other actions, stimulate B cell hyperplasia, which increases insulin production and release and heightens tissue sensitivity to insulin. The anabolic effects of insulin result in deposition of subcutaneous fat and fat cell hypertrophy, the purpose of which may be to provide fuel stores for use later in pregnancy.

As gestation continues, increased tissue resistance is observed, with continued maternal hyperinsulinemia. Insulin antagonism is primarily caused by an increase in human placental lactogen (HPL), produced by the syncytiotrophoblast. This glycoprotein opposes the action of insulin in concert with other placental hormones such as progesterone, cortisol, and prolactin, and also promotes maternal lipolysis. The net outcome of these hormonal influences results in rapid storage of fuels during the fed state and insulin antagonism and accelerated metabolism in the fasting state. Thus nutrients are quickly stored and then liberated, to provide sufficient maternal intravascular fuel for fetal consumption.

Because of the diabetogenic effects of pregnancy, GDM may develop in previously normal women. There is, however, some evidence that GDM may merely represent undiagnosed or subclinical diabetes.[6] Among type II diabetics pregnancy most often demands exogenous insulin therapy to maintain near-normal blood glucose levels.

Pathophysiology of Diabetes Mellitus in Pregnancy

Early in gestation, the type I diabetic may require decreasing insulin doses as the hyperinsulinemic effects are exerted. Unless the blood glucose level is greatly altered in the type II diabetic, dietary therapy may prove to be sufficient during this time. GDM is not usually manifest in the first trimester as insulin antagonism is not significant until around the 26th week of gestation.[7] The rate of HPL production is directly related to placental mass, and as pregnancy progresses postprandial glucose levels increase. The fasting blood glucose level falls, however, presumably because of fetal-placental uptake. Plasma lipid levels, including free fatty acids, cholesterol, and triglyceride, generally remain unchanged in the type I diabetic until late in pregnancy when the levels increase. There are some studies that suggest that triglyceride levels increase and cholesterol levels decrease in the type II diabetic during pregnancy, although the significance of these changes is unknown.[8,9]

As accelerated fed and fasted states are observed with progressing gestation, the type I diabetic generally requires increasing insulin doses, and the type II diabetic exhibits progressive hyperglycemia that requires initiation of insulin therapy. During this time GDM also becomes manifest, requiring dietary therapy to correct postprandial hyperglycemia.

White's Classification of Diabetes in Pregnancy

Priscilla White[10] devised a classification system in 1949 for the identification of risk categories among pregnant diabetics. The system was subsequently revised in 1978[11] and is still useful today, as an increase in perinatal mortality has been associated with the advanced categories.[12] The system differentiates preexisting diabetes, insulin dependence and non–insulin dependence, duration of disease, and specific vascular complications of diabetes (Table 9-1).

Maternal Morbidity

When considered within a historical perspective, maternal morbidity and mortality have decreased significantly since the discovery and widespread use of

Table 9-1 Diabetes in Pregnancy Classification System

	Age at Onset	Duration of Disease	Vasculopathy
Gestational diabetes (GDM)*	During pregnancy	—	None
Class A[†]	Any	Variable	None
Class B[‡]	>20 years old	<10 years	None
Class C	<20 years old	10–19 years	None
Class D	<10 years old	>20 years	None
Class F	Any	Variable	Diabetic nephropathy
Class H	Any	Variable	Cardiopathy
Class R	Any	Variable	Proliferative retinopathy

*GDM may be insulin dependent or non-insulin dependent.
[†]Class A diabetics are non-insulin dependent.
[‡]Class B through R diabetics are insulin dependent.

insulin. Prior to the 1920s, prepubertal death was common among diabetic females. Of those who survived to childbearing age, many were anovulatory. Thus pregnancies among diabetics were rare, and among those who did conceive, maternal mortality was 35% to 50%. This incidence has decreased significantly during the past 60 years and is now reported as 0.5%,[13] but represents a 10-fold increase compared to the mortality rate for a general obstetric population.

Maternal morbidity is not increased among patients with GDM. In an extensive review of the literature published from 1965 to 1985, Cousins[14] concluded that pregnancy-induced hypertension (PIH), diabetic ketoacidosis (DKA), and pyelonephritis were not increased among those with GDM.

In type I and II diabetics maternal morbidity is increased. Hypertensive disease in general (both chronic hypertension and PIH) is increased among the advanced diabetic classifications D, F, and R, presumably because of the presence of vasculopathy among these patients. Although there appear to be no diabetes class distinctions when comparing the incidence of DKA and pyelonephritis, these disorders are seen more often in type I and II diabetics than in nondiabetics. The incidence of DKA is increased during pregnancy, partially because of accelerated fat breakdown enhancing ketone body formation. Further stimulus often occurs with an infection. Pyelonephritis also occurs more often among type I and II diabetics and was included as one of Pedersen's "prognostically bad signs of pregnancy" (PBSP) signaling increased perinatal mortality and morbidity.[15]

When diabetic nephropathy is present (class F), there appears to be a general acceleration of the process with advancing gestation.[16] Proteinuria and nephrotic syndromes increase during the last trimester, and hypertension may appear or accelerate. These changes frequently mandate early delivery of the fetus but do not appear to alter the natural course of nephropathy, as a conversion to prepregnancy renal status generally occurs in the postpartum period.[17] Similarly, pregnancy appears to temporarily worsen benign retinopathy in diabetic women, with a return to prepregnancy degree after delivery. Proliferative retinopathy (class R), however, may become progressive during pregnancy and may cause visual changes if the condition is not detected and treated.[18]

Fetal/Neonatal Morbidity and Mortality

It has been well established that maternal hyperglycemia stimulates fetal hyperinsulinemia that results in increased synthesis and deposition of fat. As the fetus experiences hyperglycemia and increased transfer of maternal amino acids, fetal B cell hyperplasia occurs, and insulin production increases. Insulin functions as an anabolic fetal growth hormone that stimulates fetal macrosomia, including accelerated body fat, organ mass, and muscle mass growth. Macrosomia is increased among all classes of diabetics and is most pronounced in untreated GDM. A higher rate of birth trauma that is due to unexpected macrosomia is observed among patients with insulin-dependent diabetes mellitus. The more common birth injuries include facial palsy, fractured clavicle, brachial plexus injuries, and ocular hemorrhage.

In 1964 the first article identifying a higher incidence of congenital anomalies among the infants of diabetic mothers (IDM) than among a general control population was published.[19] Of 853 such infants born between 1926 and 1963, 6.4% had major congenital anomalies, compared to 2.1% of 1265 control newborns. Since that time, multiple studies have confirmed three- to fourfold higher rates of malformations among IDM than among their nondiabetic counterparts.[20-22]

It has been suggested that in addition to metabolic derangements, early maternal hyperglycemia probably accounts for the increase in congenital anomalies seen in IDM. Although other possible etiologies, such as genetic factors,[21] hypoglycemia,[23,24] and vascular disease, have been studied, most evidence supports the teratogenic effects of hyperglycemia during the first 7 weeks of gestation.[25-28] Despite improvements in care and reduced perinatal mortality, congenital anomalies continue to affect 6% to 8% of all IDM and are significantly higher among type I diabetics who have elevated blood glucose levels during this early period of fetal organ formation. The incidence of congenital anomalies is probably related to hemoglobin A_{1c} (HgbA$_{1c}$) levels during the first trimester. Women with high HgbA$_{1c}$ levels in early pregnancy may be at risk for a maximal 50% incidence of congenital anomalies and also higher rates (up to 50%) of spontaneous abortion.[29] Congenital anomaly rates among IDM will decline only when prepregnancy normalization of blood glucose levels becomes standard. Although multiple organ systems may be involved with the malformations seen, neural tube defects, congenital heart disease, and musculoskeletal deformities are the most common.

Intrauterine fetal demise (IUFD) is increased and is usually of unexplained etiology. With intensified insulin therapy and antepartum testing schemes, the incidence of perinatal mortality for IDM has fallen from 600 per 1000 live births prior to insulin use to 20 to 40 per 1000 live births in the 1970s and 1980s.[30]

The incidence of respiratory distress syndrome (RDS), including hyaline membrane disease (HMD) and transient tachypnea of the newborn (TTN), is increased among IDM and has been attributed to delayed fetal lung maturation. Although these disorders are associated with prematurity, such infants have a higher probability as gestational age advances of developing some form of RDS.

Neonatal hypoglycemia is one of the cardinal signs of IDM and, along with other metabolic disturbances, is probably due to induced fetal hyperglycemia that stimulates elevated circulating insulin levels. At the time of birth, the fetal nutrient supply is acutely withdrawn as the umbilical cord is severed. Despite careful regulation of maternal blood glucose levels during the intrapartum period, fetal hypoglycemia may still occur. Chronic fetal pancreatic stimulation, which occurs in poorly controlled diabetes over long periods of time, produces fetal B cell hypertrophy and hyperplasia.

Hypocalcemia is frequently seen with IDM but may be partially associated with prematurity or fetal-neonatal asphyxia. Hyperbilirubinemia also occurs with more frequency among these infants and may also be related to prematurity, to elevated plasma erythropoietin levels stimulated by hyperinsulinemia, or to the polycythemia frequently seen in the IDM-complicated pregnancy.

PATIENT PRESENTATION: SCREENING FOR GESTATIONAL DIABETES

All women should be screened for diabetes during pregnancy. In the past only women with one or more risk factors for diabetes (such as age >25 years, obesity, previous unexplained IUFD, etc.) were screened; however, evidence has shown that selective screening omits identification of many women with GDM.[31,32] The screening procedure involves ingestion of 50 g of oral glucose without regard to time of day or oral intake.[33] Blood is drawn 1 hour following glucose ingestion for plasma glucose level determination. A threshold value of 135 mg/dL is considered a positive screen result[34] and should be followed by a standard 3-hour glucose tolerance test (GTT) as described by O'Sullivan et al.[35] To complete the GTT, patients should be placed on a carbohydrate-loading diet for 3 days prior to testing and should be tested for blood glucose levels at fasting and at 1, 2, and 3 hours following ingestion of 100 g of oral glucose. Two of the four values must exceed acceptable limits to constitute a positive GTT (see Table 9-2).

The optimal time for GDM screening is 24 to 28 gestational weeks, when the diabetogenic effect of pregnancy is clinically detectable. Patients with evidence of marked hyperglycemia should be screened at the earliest possible time. This may include women who became insulin dependent during a previous pregnancy, those with unexplained previous IUFD, or those exhibiting clinical parameters generally associated with diabetes, such as hydramnios of unexplained etiology or macrosomia revealed by ultrasonography. Patients who are screened early and have negative test results must be rescreened at 24 to 28 weeks to capture the diabetogenic effect of progressive pregnancy.

MANAGEMENT

Goals of Management

Prepregnancy

The role of prepregnancy preparation cannot be overemphasized for the diabetic woman. Indeed, all diabetics of childbearing age should receive information about the potential benefits of preparation and management. Evidence exists to support the hypothesis that euglycemia (normal blood glucose level) during the time of conception, implantation, and through the first 7 critical weeks of organogenesis prevents the occurrence of congenital anomalies.[36–40]

Table 9-2 Screening for Gestational Diabetes

	Pretest CHO Loading	Fasting at Test Time	Oral Glucose Load	Test Times	Maximal Values* (mg/dL)
Diabetes screening	No	No	50 g	1 hour post	135
3-hour GTT	Yes (3 days)	Yes	100 g	Fasting	105
				1 hour post	190
				2 hour post	165
				3 hour post	145

*All values are venous plasma.

Many diabetic women do not choose to maintain tight blood glucose control because of the financial, time, and life style costs of this intensified self-care. Unplanned pregnancies during these periods of chronically elevated blood glucose levels are particularly at risk for poor perinatal outcomes. The goals of patient care management involve promotion of factors that influence the achievement and maintenance of euglycemia.

During the prepregnant period it is also important to assess the diabetic woman for evidence of vasculopathy. Retinopathy screening should be done. The presence and degree of nephropathy is assessed via a 24-hour urine collection for protein and creatinine. Evidence of hypertension is carefully investigated, with initiation of antihypertensive therapy as necessary. Rubella immunity status can be determined, and the nonimmune woman vaccinated prior to conception. Prenatal vitamins containing folic acid may reduce the recurrence of neural tube defects.[41] The incidence of this group of malformations is significantly increased for women with diabetes, and vitamin supplements are commonly given once the patient begins contemplating pregnancy.

It is important to provide adequate contraception during this prepregnancy planning and preparation until euglycemia occurs and is demonstrated by blood glucose values within target ranges and HgbA$_{1c}$ less than or equal to 8.5%. Positive health behaviors are also encouraged during this time, such as smoking cessation. During the prepregnancy period patients are encouraged to maintain good records of menses to provide accurate information about the time of conception.

Antepartum

Continued maintenance of euglycemia is particularly important during the antepartum period. Abnormal blood glucose levels may increase the risks of maternal injury, which is possible during severe hypoglycemic periods or DKA. Nausea and vomiting associated with early pregnancy may contribute to the normal hyperinsulinemia observed during this time, causing hypoglycemia in the type 1 diabetic. Efforts must be made to reduce nausea and maintain adequate nutritional intake. Patients should intensify self-monitoring of blood glucose levels with more frequent determinations of blood glucose levels and also with more frequent evaluations of urinary ketones. Continued low blood glucose readings (less than 80 mg/dL) with increased amounts of urinary ketones, especially when combined with vomiting, place patients at risk of hypoglycemic reactions, and hospitalizations for parenteral therapy may become necessary.

If the woman has not received prepregnancy care and preparation, retinopathy and nephropathy screening is generally done during the first trimester. Patients with elevated proteinuria (greater than 300 mg in 24 hours), as determined by a 24-hour urine collection, or those with hypertension can monitor their blood pressure using a sphygmomanometer designed for home use. The patient should be given instructions for frequency of self–blood pressure recordings and also minimal and maximal cutoff levels. It is important to provide minimal cutoff levels to patients receiving antihypertensive drugs, to monitor for hypotension. See Chapter 3 for further information on hypertension in pregnancy.

Prenatal testing begins in early pregnancy to diagnose congenital anomalies. The maternal serum alpha-fetoprotein (MSAFP) level is determined between 15 and 20 gestational weeks to assess the risk of an open neural tube defect (NTD). The patient should receive an explanation of the test as well as the testing outcome. The false-positive rate of this test is very high. Of each 1000 women tested, 50 will have a positive test result indicating a possible open NTD; however, only 1 to 2 of those 50 women will actually have a fetus with an NTD. Inaccurate gestational dating is the most common reason for a falsely elevated MSAFP.

Ultrasonography is performed on all women who have diabetes during pregnancy to accurately assess gestational age, to monitor appropriate fetal growth, and to evaluate fetal structure for a congenital anomaly. Diabetic women are not at risk for a fetal chromosomal anomaly, so genetic testing is not indicated unless patient or family history or prenatal testing results indicate a potential problem.

Routine hospitalization is not generally practiced for pregnant diabetics during the antepartum period; however, hospitalization for complications may become necessary. Indications for hospitalizations are numerous; the more common reasons diabetics are admitted to the antepartum or intrapartum unit are listed in Table 9-3.

Depending upon the indication, these patients may require intensive nursing care, either for physiologic stabilization or for patient education needs, and frequently for both reasons. When processes occur that significantly alter blood

---

Table 9-3 Common Indications for Antepartum Admission of Pregnant Diabetics

1. Poorly controlled diabetes (frequent hypoglycemia, sustained hyperglycemia, or wide swings in blood glucose levels)
2. Apparent lack of self-care knowledge
3. Infections (upper respiratory infection, urinary tract infection, pyelonephritis)
4. Accelerating hypertension
5. Abnormal antepartum testing results
6. Diabetic ketoacidosis
7. Nonobstetric or diabetic indications (i.e., appendicitis)
8. Progressive cardiopathy

glucose levels, such as DKA or infections, intravenous insulin therapy may be required to increase blood glucose control.

Antepartum testing begins at 30 to 32 gestational weeks and comprises a number of tests to assess placental respiratory function and fetal response. The nonstress test (NST) is used most widely because of its ease of administration and ability to identify a healthy baby. The contraction stress test (CST), administered via exogenous oxytocin, nipple stimulation, or by spontaneous contractility, is the second most common method of antepartum testing. Biophysical profile (BPP) is evaluated with ultrasonography, and the newer doppler blood flow studies may provide fetal surveillance in the future. The NST, CST, and BPP are effective in identifying the healthy placenta and baby, but all three tests have high false-positive results. Further testing is usually indicated when an initial positive result (indicating decreased placental function) is observed. It is important to continue antepartum testing once the patient is hospitalized. Once- or twice-weekly testing schemes are implemented when the patient's condition remains stable. When the patient's condition is unstable, antepartum testing may become necessary on a daily basis or, occasionally, more often.

Tests for fetal lung maturity are done to assess the risks of HMD and other sequelae of prematurity. In most centers amniotic fluid is obtained by transabdominal amniocentesis and assessed for the lecithin and sphingomyelin ratio and the presence or absence of phosphatidylglycerol. The decision to deliver the diabetic woman is based on the counteropposing risks of delayed maturation (prematurity) and the increased risk of IUFD.

Intrapartum

The pregnant diabetic is at significant risk during the intrapartum period in terms of both maternal and fetal complications. The mother experiences the physiologic effects of labor, including the caloric expenditure of muscular contractions and changes in maternal hemodynamics. Subcutaneous insulin is not used during the intrapartum period because of the prolonged peak (3 to 4 hours) of even the shortest-acting insulin. Thus greater control of blood glucose levels is obtained via intravenous insulin. The patient receives nothing by mouth because of the ever-present risk of emergent operative delivery, which would require general anesthesia. Glucose intake must therefore be provided parenterally. Many diabetic women undergo induction of labor, exposing the mother to the physiologic effects associated with oxytocin infusion. Finally, the diabetic woman has a significantly greater chance of requiring a cesarean delivery, which carries the inherent risks of major surgery, than does the nondiabetic. Following delivery, the maternal effects of acute withdrawal of placental hormones are seen with decreasing insulin requirements and, frequently, hypoglycemia.

The infant of a woman with diabetes is at greater risk for development of neonatal hypoglycemia, polycythemia, hyperbilirubinemia, and RDS, occurrences that have been attributed to intrapartum management and mode of delivery. Some studies have supported the hypothesis that careful management of maternal blood glucose levels in the intrapartum period leads to a reduction in the incidence of neonatal hypoglycemia by turning off the fetus's excessive insulin production prior to birth.[42,43] In addition, fetal hyperinsulinemia may cause mild hypoxemia, which stimulates excessive erythropoiesis,[44] which leads to the increased rate of neonatal polycythemia seen among these infants.[45]The breakdown of this greater red cell volume makes hyperbilirubinemia more likely. Also, the presence of labor may have an effect; there is a higher incidence of hyperbilirubinemia in infants of women with diabetes who are born vaginally or whose mothers undergo cesarean delivery after labor than in those born by cesarean section without labor.[43]

The diabetic woman admitted for induction of labor is at greater risk than her nondiabetic counterpart for intrapartum fetal distress, and also for cesarean delivery for fetal distress.[46] Oftentimes, delivery (either by induced labor or cesarean section) may be indicated on the basis of poor antepartum testing results that are associated with a significant risk of decreased placental respiratory function and resultant fetal hypoxia and acidosis. Careful intrapartum fetal monitoring is indicated for the diabetic who is undergoing induction of labor. External appliances should be used until rupture of membranes is clinically indicated or occurs spontaneously. A fetal scalp electrode should be placed to directly monitor the fetal heart. Uterine contractions can be monitored indirectly by the external tocotransducer unless an intrauterine pressure catheter is indicated. When operative delivery is planned that is based on positive antepartum testing results (indicating possible uteroplacental or fetal compromise), the fetus should be monitored, as it may be at risk for morbidity in the interim preoperative stages.

Several investigators have suggested that maternal hyperglycemia increases placental lactate production, which is transferred to the fetus and leads to acidosis.[47,48] During labor, all efforts should be made to optimize uteroplacental perfusion. Because the diabetic has abnormal metabolic processes that encourage the development of acidosis, gaseous exchange within the spiral arteries becomes extremely important. A side-lying position is maintained throughout the intrapartum period to decrease vena caval and aortic compression by the uterus. Oxygen is administered when changes in maternal condition or fetal heart rate indicate compromise. Oxygen should be humidified and administered by tight face mask, and the rate of flow should be set at 8 to 10 L/min.

The administration of oxytocin increases the risk of uteroplacental insufficiency by producing or enhancing uterine contractility and decreased placental perfusion. Many diabetic women have oxytocin-induced labor once mature fetal lung profiles are obtained or when antepartum testing results indicate potential placental malfunction. Oxytocin should be used carefully in the diabetic and should always be administered by an infusion control device to allow precise titration. Monitoring must be upgraded to observe for early signs of fetal compromise.

Besides the careful intrapartum management required of all high-risk pregnant women, the diabetic also needs intensive control of her blood glucose level. This control is achieved by intravenous administration of separate solutions of insulin and glucose. Intermittent injections of subcutaneous insulin do not allow sufficient control of blood glucose levels during labor and may cause significant hypoglycemia after delivery. The initial doses and rate of change required by each patient are highly individualized. Generally, patients with higher beginning blood glucose levels will require higher initial insulin infusion rates.[49,50] Some type 1 diabetics may not even require intravenous insulin. The well-controlled type 1 diabetic generally requires insulin when induction of labor is started, but insulin needs may fall to zero once active labor is achieved.[51] Glucose needs, however, remain constant throughout labor at about 10 g/h.

Blood glucose target values for the intrapartum period are 70 to 100 mg/dL.[49-51] Symptomatic hypoglycemia and blood glucose values less than 50 mg/dL are to be avoided. During labor most patients require 0.5 to 2 units of insulin per hour to maintain target blood glucose values. See Table 9-4 for a protocol for intravenous insulin administration. The patient who is to be delivered by planned cesarean section should also have optimal blood glucose control prior to surgery to maximize fetal outcome and prevent anesthetic complications from abnormal blood glucose levels. The preoperative patient who has severe hyperglycemia or unstable blood glucose levels may benefit from intravenous insulin therapy, which provides a period of euglycemia immediately prior to delivery. The patient may be admitted up to 24 hours prior to surgery, and the protocol for intravenous insulin administration (Table 9-4) should be followed.

Postpartum

The immediate postpartum period is characterized by a profound decrease in insulin needs for the type I diabetic. Most patients may not require insulin for the first 24 hours and slowly increase their needs to prepregnancy levels within 7 days.[52] The diabetic is at much greater risk of infection than the nondiabetic during the postpartum period and should be monitored for signs and symptoms of endometritis and wound infections. The diabetic may be at greater risk for hemorrhage from uterine atony after maximal uterine muscle stretching caused by macrosomia and/or hydramnios. Careful attention to the amount and character of the lochia and to changes in vital signs may detect excessive blood loss.

Table 9-4 Protocol for Intravenous Insulin Administration

Important Points
1. Intravenous insulin is always administered via an infusion control device.
2. Only *regular* insulin (not NPH, Lente, or Ultralente) is administered intravenously.
3. Maximal hypoglycemic effect of each dose is reached in 30 minutes.
4. Normal saline (l000 mL) must be immediately available at all times in the event rapid fluid replacement without glucose or insulin is required (i.e., placental abruption, hypotension caused by epidural anesthesia).

Preparing the Solution
1. Mix 50 U of *regular* insulin in 500 mL lactated Ringer's solution or normal saline. This yields 1 U per l0 mL solution.
2. This preparation is fairly dilute and is useful for administering the small doses of insulin (0.5 U/h) that most patients require, yet only 30 mL total hourly intake will be given if a larger dose of 3 U/h is required.

Administration
1. Check capillary blood glucose level via finger pulp puncture.
2. Establish intravenous access with an 18-gauge catheter.
3. Start a mainline solution of 5% dextrose in lactated Ringer's solution at 125 mL/h.
4. Piggyback the insulin solution into the main line and maintain the infusion by a control device.
5. Begin infusion as ordered (usually 0.5 to 2 U/h).
6. Perform capillary blood glucose level determinations every hour during the first 4 hours of insulin therapy. Target blood glucose values for the intrapartum patient are 70 to 100 mg/dL. Once stable, blood glucose level determinations can be done every 2 hours. When the patient is unstable or approaching transition, resume hourly blood glucose level determinations.
7. Perform urinary ketone determinations hourly when the patient has an indwelling urinary catheter, or otherwise at each voiding.
8. As the insulin infusion dose is increased, decrease the rate of the mainline intravenous infusion to maintain a total hourly intake of 125 mL/h.
9. Discontinue intravenous insulin immediately prior to delivery.

Special Considerations:
1. Symptomatic hypoglycemia (anxiety; flushing; tremors; sweating; extreme hunger; numbing of tongue, lips, or fingertips)
   a. Check blood glucose level.
   b. Discontinue insulin.
   c. Increase infusion rate of mainline intravenous solution (5% dextrose).
   d. Obtain a consultation.
2. Hyperglycemia (flushing, headache, extreme fatigue)
   a. Check blood glucose level.
   b. Check for urinary ketones.
   c. Obtain a consultation.
3. Urinary ketones
   a. Check blood glucose level.
   b. Calculate intake and output totals.
   c. Check urine specific gravity.
   d. Obtain a consultation.

Nursing Care

The control of diabetes mellitus is achieved through particular attention to practices aimed at regulation of CHO metabolism. The blood glucose level is a result of CHO entering the system, insulin availability, and the influences of exercise, stress, and pregnancy. Euglycemia is achieved and maintained by the patient through attention to dietary intake, insulin self-administration, stress reduction, and exercise. The patient must be adept at self-monitoring of blood glucose levels to assess the effects of self-care activities and to make further self-care decisions. The most basic level of diabetes self-care is classified as "survival".[53] All patients placed on insulin therapy should have knowledge and skill concordant with survival techniques for home care. Most often these techniques can be taught on an outpatient basis; thus hospitalization may not be necessary to begin insulin therapy. Table 9-5 outlines the knowledge and skills consistent with survival-level self-care.

Table 9-5 Behavioral Outcomes of Survival Skills for Insulin-Dependent Diabetics

1. Self-blood glucose monitoring (SBGM):
   a. The patient accurately demonstrates SBGM using either a reflectance meter or visually compared oxidase reagent strips.
   b. The patient can distinguish normal from abnormal (both high and low) blood glucose values obtained by SBGM.
2. Nutrition:
   a. The patient can recite the general principles and importance of the diabetic diet.
   b. The patient demonstrates the ability to select appropriate food choices based on the prescribed diabetic diet.
   c. The patient can recite appropriate meal and snack timing.
3. Hypoglycemia:
   a. The patient can recite the general process and significance of hypoglycemia.
   b. The patient demonstrates knowledge of prevention, recognition, and appropriate treatment of hypoglycemia.
4. Diabetic ketoacidosis (DKA):
   a. The patient can recite the general process and significance of DKA in terms of both her own health and the health of the fetus.
   b. The patient demonstrates accurate urinary assessment for ketones.
   c. The patient can recite both routine and accelerated testing times for ketonuria.
   d. The patient can recite appropriate follow-up actions for evidence of ketonuria.
5. Insulin self-administration:
   a. The patient can recite the mechanism of action, times of onset, and duration of the type(s) of insulin that has been prescribed.
   b. The patient can prepare *any* dose of insulin, including mixing of insulins.
   c. The patient demonstrates knowledge and application of site selection and rotation.
   d. The patient recites appropriate administration times and correctly self-administers insulin.

At each hospitalization, the nurse must assess self-care knowledge, provide supplementary education as necessary, and document adequate performance and skill. These steps are necessary sometime during hospitalization whether the patient is admitted to the antepartum unit for pyelonephritis or to the intrapartum unit for labor and delivery. Nursing care of the pregnant diabetic is discussed below.

Assessment

a. general
- age, parity, estimated gestational age (EGA) (calculated by last menstrual period [LMP] and confirmed by ultrasonography at <20 weeks)
- significant medical problems (especially hypertension)
- past and current obstetric history
- complications occurring during this pregnancy
- medications
- social situation

b. diabetic
- age at onset of diabetes and duration

c. complications of diabetes (retinopathy, nephropathy)

d. self-care practices
- method of self–blood glucose monitoring (SBGM) and testing regimen; recent values of testing
- nutrition: daily calorie intake, number of snacks, timing of meals and snacks
- hypoglycemia: history and pattern of insulin reactions, knowledge of prevention and recognition. Does the patient have particular prereaction symptoms or does she experience hypoglycemia unawareness? Does she keep glucagon available? Who knows how to give her glucagon?
- DKA: history of DKA, knowledge about nature and prevention of DKA. Does the patient know how to check for urinary ketones? When does she check ketones? Determine recent values.
- insulin administration: type and dose of insulin, time and sites of injection. How does she determine where to give her insulin? Does she ever change her dose, and if so, how does she decide the amount of her new dose? Does she self-administer insulin, or does someone else give her insulin?

e. current status
- patient's chief complaint
- vital signs (temperature, pulse, respirations, blood pressure)
- uterine contractions, including time started and frequency
- rupture of membranes; if ruptured, color of fluid

- presence/absence of bleeding
- current blood glucose level and presence of urinary ketones and proteinuria
- fetal heart rate (apply external monitor and interpret tracing)
f. Further assessment is done in accordance with the patient's chief
complaint or as indicated by assessment findings.

Specific Interventions

Nursing care interventions are designed after assessment of the patient and formulation of a nursing diagnosis. Basic interventions for the pregnant diabetic are similar regardless of the patient's particular problem, and general guidelines are thus outlined below.

Self–Blood Glucose Monitoring. The development of oxidase reagent strips and reflectance meters has revolutionized diabetes care. The patient can determine blood glucose levels by finger puncture at any time and, therefore, can take charge of her diabetes care and learn the individual effects of different foods, exercise, and even emotional stress. Reflectance meters also are used in the hospital and provide instantaneous bedside blood glucose monitoring of the patient who requires only a fingerstick to obtain a specimen.

It is important to know the limitations of available equipment. Some monitors accurately read a small variation of blood glucose values (i.e., 40 to 400 mg/dL), while others read a greater range (i.e., 20 to 800 mg/dL). Blood glucose level determinations may be required every hour for the acutely ill or unstable patient, such as the diabetic in DKA or the patient receiving oxytocin for induction of labor. Other diabetics may require monitoring of blood glucose levels only at premeal times and bedtime. Whenever the patient's clinical situation permits, the diabetic should be encouraged to check her own blood glucose levels by performing SBGM, to assess the patient's knowledge of the technique and to encourage the patient to participate in her own care.

Some patients perform SBGM quite well using visually read oxidase reagent strips, and for this group reflectance meters may not be necessary. The type 1 diabetic or the patient who may have difficulty with testing procedures (such as timing or interpolation of the blood glucose value by comparison) will need a reflectance meter. Most meter brands have built-in timers, are simple to use, and provide a digital value readout; some even store values for later recall.

Blood glucose level determinations should be performed immediately when hyper- or hypoglycemia is clinically suspected. Target blood glucose values in pregnancy are 70 to 100 mg/dL preprandial and 70 to 120 mg/dL postprandial. It may take some time to reach target values with diabetics who are excessively hyperglycemic. Adaptation occurs with these patients, and hypoglycemic symptoms may appear with moderately high (100 to 200 mg/dL) values. A rapid fall in blood glucose level (from very high to moderate values) induces symptoms of insulin reaction, as will a low (usually less than 50 to 60 mg/dL) value. The patient with longstanding hyperglycemia takes longer to adjust to lower values. Patients with extreme hyperglycemia (400 to 1200 mg/dL), such as those in DKA, require prompt treatment to provide a rapid reduction in blood glucose level. Intravenous insulin is administered to promote a decline of 50 to 75 mg/dL blood glucose per hour (see "Acute Diabetic Ketoacidosis," below).

Intrapartum patients frequently exhibit a decrease in blood glucose level during labor. The well-controlled diabetic may need insulin early in labor but have gradually diminishing requirements until no insulin is needed during active labor of the first stage. The hyperglycemic diabetic may require insulin throughout labor to maintain a blood glucose level between 70 and 100 mg/dL. It is important to initially determine blood glucose levels every hour for the intrapartum diabetic, to carefully titrate glucose and insulin infusions.

Nutrition. Nutrition is a primary therapeutic intervention for the pregnant diabetic. During hospitalization, the nurse ensures that appropriate nutritional intake, whether food or intravenous solution, is provided in a timely manner. Timing of intake is particularly important in the maintenance of proper blood glucose levels. Once hospitalized, the patient is frequently changed to the hospital schedule of meal serving. Breakfast at 6:30 AM, lunch at 11:30 AM, and dinner at 4:30 PM is a common regimen for hospital kitchens, yet this plan is rarely followed by patients at home and enforces a 14-hour overnight fast. The patient's meal timing plan should be followed whenever possible.

Parenteral nutrition is oftentimes necessary when the patient is NPO for procedures (labor, cesarean section, etc.) or unable to take foods by mouth (vomiting, comatose, etc.). Attention to glucose intake is particularly important for the diabetic. Initiation of intravenous insulin may be necessary to promote careful regulation of blood glucose levels of the diabetic who receives parenteral nutrition.

A registered dietitian (RD) should be consulted at each hospitalization to monitor appropriate nutritional intake and to provide patient teaching for the diabetic. Follow-up education is reinforced by the nurse. Similarly, the nurse should inspect each meal tray given to a diabetic if the RD has not done so. Again, the therapeutic nature of the diabetic diet is an integral part of the total care of diabetes. It therefore requires the careful attention of a registered professional.

Symptomatic hypoglycemia should always be avoided by the diabetic pregnant women. Hypoglycemia probably has no directly deleterious effects on the fetus; however, maternal injury can occur with serious reactions. Most patients have warning signs prior to severe hypoglycemia, which may include tremors, sweating, extreme hunger, lack of muscular coordination, cramps, and numbness or tingling of lips, tongue, or fingertips. The patient may become unresponsive, with staring. Eventually, when untreated, the reaction results in lack of consciousness, convulsions, and death. A small group of patients have "hypoglycemia unawareness"; this may range from blunted or fewer warning signs to progressive hypoglycemia without warning. This condition has been associated with the use of human insulin.[54] It is particularly dangerous as the patient does not have sufficient time to institute appropriate treatment. For these patients, changing to beef or porcine insulins may reestablish hypoglycemic warning signs; otherwise, frequent blood glucose level monitoring (up to 8 to 10 times per day) becomes necessary. Small, frequent meals and raising daily blood glucose target values may prevent reactions.

Provision of glucose supplementation is the treatment for hypoglycemia. When the patient is alert and able to swallow, glucose-containing liquids are given, such as milk (14 ounces), juices (12 ounces), or soft drinks (10 ounces). A small snack of protein and carbohydrate can also be given to counter a subsequent drop in blood glucose levels that sometimes occurs after treatment. If the patient is unable to swallow, intravenous glucose (25 mg) or glucagon (1 mL) via intramuscular injection can be given. Blood glucose level determinations should be made at regular intervals to monitor for hyper- or hypoglycemia following treatment.

Diabetic Ketoacidosis. Most often DKA is a preventable process if the patient pays careful attention to predisposing factors, especially during exposure. Urinary ketones should be checked daily, preferably at the first morning voiding. Ketonuria in the presence of low to normal blood glucose levels is generally caused by nutritional deficits and is called starvation ketosis. When glucose is not available for intracellular metabolism, ketone body formation occurs as alternate fuel sources (fat) are sought. Dehydration may further accelerate ketogenesis. Thus when ketones are present with low to normal blood glucose levels, nutritional supplementation of fluids and glucose should be given.

Ketonuria with elevated blood glucose levels (usually greater than 200 mg/dL) is generally caused by insulin deficiency. Infections promote ketogenesis and hyperglycemia and cause progression to DKA. Thus ketonuria should be assessed frequently when the diabetic patient has a known or suspected infection. Early therapy with increased insulin administration, hydration (to dilute ketones), and prompt treatment of infections will generally prevent metabolic acidosis (see "Acute Diabetic Ketoacidosis," below).

Insulin Administration. Most pregnant diabetics receive a mixture of short- (regular) and intermediate- (NPH or Lente) acting insulins, given in two daily doses. Some diabetics require longer-acting Ultralente with three doses of regular at breakfast, lunch, and dinner. Regardless of insulin type, the knowledge of insulin peak times of effect is important to provide appropriate meal timing and to predict potential times of low blood glucose levels (see Table 9-6). Insulin needs change during pregnancy, and type 1 diabetics generally require a 200% to 300% increase in dose by the third trimester.

Insulin is a polypeptide with two amino acid chains. Because of small species-specific differences within amino acid composition, insulin is antigenic. Although these differences are not significant enough to alter the chemical effect of insulin, anti-insulin antibodies will form when humans receive animal-derived insulin. Commercial beef insulin is more antigenic than pork insulin; therefore, most patients will develop antibodies to it after prolonged use and will require higher doses to control blood glucose levels. Insulin produced by bacteria altered by recombinant DNA procedures is now available for commercial use.[55] This biosynthetic human insulin (BHI) is structurally more similar to endogenous human insulin, and fewer side effects are expected.

Acute Diabetic Ketoacidosis. DKA is associated with a significant risk of maternal and perinatal mortality. This acute form of decompensated diabetes is characterized by hyperglycemia and ketoacidosis and, when untreated, eventually leads to stupor, coma, and death. The pregnant diabetic is predisposed to DKA by virtue of enhanced ketogenesis that is due to insulin deficiency and reduced glucose utilization. Ketone clearance is diminished as peripheral tissue uptake is decreased. Increased production and decreased clearance lead to higher circulating ketone levels. Blood glucose levels are also higher in pregnancy as a result of the insulin antagonism of placental hormones. One of these hormones, progesterone, also directly increases respiratory function to clear excess carbon dioxide of fetal origin. Renal compensatory mechanisms excrete more bicarbonate ions, which stabilize the maternal pH and result in lower total bicarbonate levels (18 to 21 mEq/L)) and a poorly responsive pH system. Thus the pregnant diabetic has higher circulating glucose levels, enhanced ketogenesis, and minimal pH buffering ability. Stressors such as infections (which raise D KA-enhancing cortisol and catecholamines), de-

Table 9-6 Insulin Times of Action

Insulin Type	Start	Peak	Duration
Rapid acting			
Regular	1/2–1 hour	1–5 hour	6–8 hour
Intermediate acting			
NPH	1–2 hour	6–12 hour	18–26 hour
Lente	1–3 hour	6–12 hour	18–24 hour
Long acting			
Ultralente	4–6 hour	14–24 hour	28–36 hour

hydration, and insulin deficiency further promote the process of DKA. The hyperglycemic hyperosmolar state (HHS) is a form of decompensated diabetes similar to DKA with hyperglycemia but without ketoacidosis. This acute process can also progress to coma and death but is not seen with pregnant diabetics, presumably because of their ketosis-prone state.

As DKA develops, hyperglycemia and ketone production increase. An increase in plasma glucose levels increases serum osmolarity, causing a shift in body fluids from intracellular to extracellular compartments. As water moves out of the cell, hyponatremia occurs by dilution. Compensatory mechanisms produce polydipsia and glycosuria in an attempt to reduce serum osmolarity. As intravascular volume diminishes, urinary output decreases, blood urea nitrogen (BUN) and uric acid levels increase, and acute renal failure with oliguria can develop. Respiratory compensatory mechanisms produce hyperventilation to eliminate excess carbon dioxide. Further compensation occurs with buffering and excreting more hydrogen ions. If not corrected, acidosis continues, and death occurs.

DKA is associated with ritodrine hydrochloride administration,[56,57] presumably because of the hyperglycemic effects of this ß-sympathomimetic drug. Use of tocolytic agents in the diabetic mandates careful monitoring of blood glucose levels and ketonuria during administration.

The exact etiology of fetal death among women with DKA is unknown. Reports vary, but the incidence of IUFD with DKA may be as high as 90%.[58] Maternal metabolic acidosis may decrease uterine perfusion,[59] and decreased fetal heart rate variability with late decelerations is sometimes seen with DKA.[60]

When occurring among known type I diabetics, most episodes of DKA are preventable. Patients who are well prepared for self-care, including knowledge of prevention and early recognition of DKA, can make early contact with their health care providers when symptoms appear. Prompt attention to and treatment of infectious processes such as upper respiratory infections (URIs) and urinary tract infections (UTIs) among diabetics may prevent or reverse beginning ketoacidosis.

The goals of management of DKA are related to rapid correction of fluid, electrolyte, and glucose imbalances. Patients in DKA are frequently excessively dehydrated, and rapid fluid replacement will be necessary. Electrolyte stabilization is achieved by replacement of sodium (Na^+) and possibly sodium bicarbonate ($NaHCO_3$) and potassium (K^+). Blood glucose stabilization is achieved with low-dose continuous intravenous insulin. A bolus intravenous injection is frequently given at the start of therapy. Glucose-containing solutions are given intravenously once blood glucose levels reach 200 mg/dL.

The patient in DKA generally presents with nausea and vomiting and may have abdominal pain. Recent polydipsia and polyuria are generally reported, but the patient may be excessively dehydrated at presentation, with dry mucous membranes, poor skin turgor, and decreased urinary output. A decreasing level of consciousness (LOC) is common and is caused by decreased cerebral blood flow or cerebral edema. As excess carbon dioxide is being blown off, the patient may have typical Kussmaul (labored) respirations, and the breath may be "fruity" from excessive acetone.

Nursing care for the pregnant patient in acute DKA is outlined below.

1. Assessment
   a. Rapid assessment of the patient is vital.
   b. Obtain past history of diabetes, including type and complications (nephropathy, retinopathy).
   c. Determine insulin type, dose, and regimen; last dose (time and amount), and oral intake (time and amount).
   d. Obtain vital signs (temperature, pulse, respirations, blood pressure).
   e. Auscultate breath sounds, and note character of respirations.
   f. Apply external fetal heart rate monitor and interpret tracing; note uterine activity.
   g. Establish LOC (alert, obtunded, stuporous, or comatose).
2. Laboratory tests
   a. Check blood glucose level via finger pulp puncture and assess urine for ketones, immediately.
   b. Send specimens for determination of blood gases; levels of glucose, serum ketones, Na^+, K^+, chloride (CL^-), carbon dioxide, BUN, and uric acid; and serum osmolarity.
3. Specific interventions
   a. Maintain airway (especially important for comatose patient).
   b. Give oxygen via tight face mask at 6 to 8 L/min.
   c. Start intravenous line with large-bore (at least 18-gauge) catheter.
   d. Infuse normal saline (NS), generally 1 to 2 L during the first hour, then at 200 to 250 mL/h. Watch for pulmonary edema. Begin 5% to 10% dextrose in water once blood glucose level is 200 mg/dL.
   e. Monitor fetal heart rate and uterine activity continuously.
   f. Institute maternal cardiac monitoring.
   g. Administer intravenous insulin via infusion control device as outlined in the protocol for intravenous insulin (Table 9-4). An initial bolus intravenous dose of 25 to 100 U may be given, followed by constant infusion of 3 to 12 U/h. Adequate insulin doses should promote decrease of 50 to 75 mg/dL in the blood glucose level each hour.
   h. Hemodynamic monitoring may be needed to assist in replacement of fluids (especially for the hypertensive or class F diabetic).
   i. Insert a nasogastric tube if patient is comatose, stuporous, or obtunded.
   j. K^+ replacement is generally started with the second liter of fluids if K^+

<3 mEq/L and is administered at 20 to 40 mEq/h as long as urinary output is >40 mL per hour.

k. Bicarbonate therapy may be necessary (generally if arterial pH <7.1).General guideline doses:
   • if pH <7.10, add 44.6 mEq NaHCO$_3$ to 1000 mL NS.
   • if pH <7.00, add 89.2 mEq NaHCO$_3$ to 1000 mL NS.
   • if pH >7.20, stop NaHCO$_3$ administration.

l. Place Foley catheter and maintain hourly intake and output documentation. Check urine every hour for glucose, ketones, and specific gravity.

4. Cautions

a. Symptomatic hypoglycemia is to be avoided and usually does not occur when 5% to 10% dextrose in water is started once the blood glucose level falls to 200 mg/dL. Treatment for symptomatic hypoglycemia should include 50% dextrose intravenously.

b. Cerebral edema can occur as fluid shifts when blood glucose levels fall quickly. Prevent hypoglycemia. Monitor patient for decreasing LOC.

c. Pulmonary edema may occur by excessive fluid replacement. Monitor intake and output carefully, and auscultate breath sounds every hour. Use hemodynamic monitoring as necessary.

d. Hypo- or hyperkalemia may occur as osmotic diuresis moves fluids between compartments. A fall in the K$^+$ level is usually not seen immediately but may occur 1 to 4 hours after therapy is started. The patient should be placed on a cardiac monitor and observed for dysrhythmias. Watch for clinical signs of hypokalemia (muscle flaccidity or paralysis, including respiratory muscle involvement). Maintain K$^+$ level at 3–6 mEq/L.

e. Infection is the most frequent catalyst for DKA. Suspect respiratory or urinary tract infections. Send cultures (including blood) as necessary. Watch for increasing temperature as the patient is rehydrated.

f. Evaluate the fetal heart rate tracing carefully for nonreassuring signs. Continue oxygen and encourage a lateral tilt position to improve uteroplacental perfusion.

REFERENCES

1. Hazlett BE. Historical perspective: the discovery of insulin. In: Davidson JK, ed. *Clinical Diabetes Mellitus. A Problem Oriented Approach.* New York: Thieme;1986:2-10.
2. Davidson JK, ed. Non-insulin-dependent diabetes mellitus. In: Davidson JK, ed. *Clinical Diabetes Mellitus. A Problem Oriented Approach.* New York: Thieme;1986:11-25.
3. National Diabetes Data Group. Classification and diagnosis of diabetes mellitus and other categories of glucose intolerance. *Diabetes.* 1979;28:1039-1057.
4. Gamble DR. The epidemiology of insulin dependent diabetes, with particular reference to the relationship of virus infection to its etiology. *Epidemiol Rev.* 1980;2:49-70.
5. Karam JH, Lewitt PA, Young CW, et al. Insulopenic diabetes after rodenticide (Vacor) ingestion. A unique model of acquired diabetes in man. *Diabetes.* 1980;29:971-978.
6. Harris MI. Gestational diabetes may represent discovery of preexisting glucose intolerance. *Diabetes Care.* 1988;11:402-411.
7. Kyle GC. Diabetes and pregnancy. *Ann Intern Med.* 1963;55:1-82.
8. Knopp RH, Chapman M, Bergelin R, Wahl PW, Warth MR, Irvine S. Relationships of lipoprotein lipids to mild fasting hyperglycemia and diabetes in pregnancy. *Diabetes Care.* 1980;3:416-420.
9. Hollingsworth DR, Grundy SM. Pregnancy-associated hypertriglyceridemia in normal and diabetic women. Differences in insulin-dependent and non-insulin-dependent, and gestational diabetes. *Diabetes.* 1982;31:1092-1097.
10. White P. Pregnancy complicating diabetes. *Am J Med.* 1949;7:609-616.
11. White P. Classification of obstetric diabetes. *Am J Obstet Gynecol.* 1978;130:228-230.
12. Gabbe SG. Application of scientific rationale to the management of the pregnant diabetic. *Semin Perinatol.* 1978;2:361-371.
13. Gabbe SG, Mestman J, Hibbard L. Maternal mortality in diabetes mellitus: an 18 year survey. *Obstet Gynecol.* 1976;5:549-551.
14. Cousins L. Pregnancy complications among diabetic women: review 1965–1985. *Obstet Gynecol Surv.* 1987;42:140-149.
15. Pedersen J, Pedersen LM. Prognosis of the outcome of pregnancies in diabetics. A new classification *Acta Endocrinol.* 1965;50:70-78.
16. Hayslett JP, Reece EA. Effect of diabetic nephropathy on pregnancy. *Am J Kidney Dis.* 1987;9:344-349.
17. Kitzmiller JL, Brown ER, Phillippe M, et al. Diabetic nephropathy and perinatal outcome. *Am J Obstet Gynecol.* 1981;141:741-751.
18. Dibble CM, Kochenour NK, Worley RJ, Tyler FH, Swartz M. Effect of pregnancy on diabetic retinopathy. *Obstet Gynecol.* 1982;6:699-704.
19. Pedersen LM, Tygstrup I, Pedersen J. Congenital malformations in newborn infants of diabetic women. Correlation with maternal diabetic vascular complications. *Lancet.* 1964;1:1124-1126.
20. Kucera J. Rate and type of congenital anomalies among offspring of diabetic women. *J Reprod Med.* 1971;7:61-70.
21. Chung CS, Myrianthopoulos NC. Factors affecting risks of congenital malformations: report from the collaborative perinatal project. *Birth Defects.* 1975;11:23-28.
22. Diamond MP, Salyer SL, Fields LM, Boehm FH. Improving care of the insulin requiring pregnant diabetic at a tertiary care center: A preliminary report. *J Tenn Med Assoc.* 1983;76(7):439-444.
23. Smithberg M, Rummer MN. Teratogenic effects of hypoglycemia treatments in inbred strains of mice. *Am J Anat.* 1963;113:479-489.

24. Horii K, Watanabe G, Ingalls TH. Experimental diabetes in pregnant mice. Prevention of congenital malformations in offspring by insulin. *Diabetes.* 1966;15:194-204.
25. Cockroft DL, Coppola PT. Teratogenic effects of excess glucose on head-fold rat embryos in culture. *Teratology.* 1977;16:141-146.
26. Sadler TW. Effects of maternal diabetes on early embryogenesis, II: hyperglycemia-induced exencephaly. *Teratology.* 1950;4:349-351.
27. Miller E, Hare JW, Cloherty JP, et al. Elevated maternal hemoglobin A_{1c} in early pregnancy and major congenital anomalies in infants of diabetic mothers. *N Engl J Med.* 1981;304:1331-1334.
28. Naftolin F, Diamond MP, Pinter E, Reese EA, Sanyal MK. A hypothesis concerning the general basis of organogenetic congenital anomalies. *Am J Obstet Gynecol.* 1987;157:1-4.
29. Key TC, Guiffrida R, Moore TR. Predictive value of early pregnancy glycohemoglobin in the insulin-treated diabetic patient. *Am J Obstet Gynecol.* 1987;156:1096-1100.
30. Golde S, Platt L. Antepartum testing in diabetes. *Clin Obstet Gynecol.* 1985;28:516-527.
31. Freinkel N, Josimovich J. Conference Planning Committee: American Diabetes Workshop-Conference on Gestational Diabetes. Summary and recommendations. *Diabetes Care.* 1980;3:499-501.
32. Lavin JP. Screening of high-risk and general populations for gestational diabetes. Clinical application and cost analysis. *Diabetes.* 1985;34:24-27.
33. Coustan DR, Widness JA, Carpenter MW, Rotondo L, Pratt DC, Oh W. Should the fifty-gram, one-hour plasma glucose screening test for gestational diabetes be administered in the fasting or fed state? *Am J Obstet Gynecol.* 1986;154:1031-1035.
34. Carpenter MW, Coustan DR. Criteria for screening tests for gestational diabetes. *Am J Obstet Gynecol.* 1982;7:768-773.
35. O'Sullivan JB, Mahan CM, Charles D, Dandrow RV. Screening criteria for high-risk gestational diabetic patients. *Am J Obstet Gynecol.* 1973;5:895-900.
36. Steel JM, Parboosingh J, Cole RA, Duncan LJP. Prepregnancy counseling: a logical prelude to the management of the pregnant diabetic woman. *Diabetes Care.* 1980;3:371-373.
37. Steel JM, Johnstone FD, Smith AF, Duncan LJP. Five years experience of a prepregnancy clinic for insulin-dependent diabetics. *Br Med J.* 1982;31:353-356.
38. Fuhrman K, Reiher H, Semmler K, Fischer F, Fischer M, Glockner E. Prevention of congenital malformations in infants of insulin-dependent diabetic mothers. *Diabetes Care.* 1983;6:219-223.
39. Goldman JA, Dicker D, Feldberg D, Yeshaya A, Samuel N, Karp M. Pregnancy outcome in patients with insulin-dependent diabetes mellitus with preconceptional diabetic control: a comparative study. *Am J Obstet Gynecol.* 1986;155:293-297.
40. Jensen BM, Kuhl C, Molstead-Pedersen L, Saurbrey N, Fog-Pedersen J. Preconceptual treatment with insulin infusion pumps in insulin-dependent diabetic women with particular reference to prevention of congenital malformations. *Acta Endocrinol.* 1986;277:81-85.
41. Smithells RW, Seller MJ, Harris R, et al. Further experience of vitamin supplementation for prevention of neural tube defect recurrences. *Lancet.* 1983;1:1027-1031.
42. Light II, Keenan WJ, Sutherland JM. Maternal intravenous glucose administration as a cause of hypoglycemia in the infant of the diabetic mother. *Am J Obstet Gynecol.* 1972;4:345-350.
43. Miodovnik M, Mimouni F, Tsang RC, et al. Management of the insulin-dependent diabetic during labor and delivery. *Am J Perinatol.* 1987;4:106-114.
44. Widness JA, Susa JB, Garcia JF, et al. Increased erythropoiesis and elevated erythropoietin in infants born to diabetic mothers and in hyperinsulinemic rhesus fetuses. *J Clin Invest.* 1981;67:637-642.
45. Mimouni F, Miodovnik M, Siddiqi TA, Butler JB, Holroyde J, Tsang RC. Neonatal polycythemia in infants of insulin-dependent diabetic mothers. *Obstet Gynecol.* 1986;68:370-372.

46. Olofsson P, Ingemarsson I, Solum T. Fetal distress during labour in diabetic pregnancy. *Br J Obstet Gynaecol.* 1986;93:1067-1071.
47. Datta S, Kitzmiller JL. Anesthetic and obstetric management of diabetic pregnant women. *Clin Perinatol.* 1982;9:153-156.
48. Hay WW Jr, Sparks JW. Placental, fetal and neonatal carbohydrate metabolism. *Clin Obstet Gynecol.* 1985;28:473-485.
49. Caplan RH, Pagliara AS, Begiun EA, et al. Constant intravenous insulin infusion during labor and delivery in diabetes mellitus. *Diabetes Care.* 1982;5:6-10.
50. Golde SH, Good-Anderson B, Montoro M, Artal R. Insulin requirements during labor: a reappraisal. *Am J Obstet Gynecol.* 1982;5:556-559.
51. Jovanovic L, Peterson CM. Insulin and glucose requirements during the first stage of labor in insulin-dependent diabetic women. *Am J Med.* 1983;4:607-612.
52. Rayburn W, Piehl E, Lewis E, Schork A, Sereika S, Zabrensky K. Changes in insulin therapy during pregnancy. *Am J Perinatol.* 1985;2:271-275.
53. American Diabetes Association and American Association of Diabetes Educators. *Guidelines for Diabetes Care.* New York: American Diabetes Association; 1981.
54. Teuscher A, Berger WG. Hypoglycemia unawareness in diabetics transferred from beef/porcine insulin to human insulin. *Lancet.* 1987;2:382-385.
55. Department of Health and Human Services. Human insulin receives FDA approval. *FDA Drug Bull.* 1982;12(3):18-19.
56. Halpren EW, Soifer NE, Haenel LC, Manara LR, Belsky DH. Ketoacidosis secondary to oral ritodrine use in a gestational diabetic patient: report of a case. *J Am Osteopath Assoc.* 1988;88:241-244.
57. Mordes D. Dangers of intravenous ritodrine in diabetic patients. *JAMA.* 1982;8:973-975.
58. Kitzmiller JL. Diabetic ketoacidosis and pregnancy. *Contemp OB/GYN.* 1982;l:141.
59. Blechner JN, Slenger VG, Prystowksy H. Blood flow to the human uterus during maternal metabolic acidosis. *Am J Obstet Gynecol.* 1975;121:789-792.
60. Hughes AB. Fetal heart rate changes during diabetic ketosis. *Acta Obstet Gynecol Scand.* 1987;66:71-73.

SUGGESTED READING

Davidson JK, ed. *Clinical Diabetes Mellitus: A Problem Oriented Approach.* New York: Thieme; 1986.

Dyck PJ, Thomas PK, Asbury AK, Winegrad AI, Porte D. *Diabetic Neuropathy.* Philadelphia: WB Saunders; 1987.

Hollingsworth DR. Maternal metabolism in normal pregnancy and pregnancy complicated by diabetes mellitus. *Clin Obstet Gynecol.* 1985; 28:457-472.

Ober C, Simpson JL. Diabetes mellitus: preventing anomalies through maternal metabolic intervention. *Clin Obstet Gynecol.* 1986;3:558-568.

Radder JK, Lemkes HHPJ, Krans HMJ. *Pathogenesis and Treatment of Diabetes Mellitus.* Boston: Martinus Nijhoff Publishers; 1986.

Reece EA, Hobbins JC. Diabetic embryopathy: pathogenesis, prenatal diagnosis and prevention. *Obstet Gynecol Survey.* 1986;6:325-335.

Schade DS, Eaton RP, Alberti KGMM, Johnston DG. *Diabetic Coma: Ketoacidotic and Hyperosmolar.* Albuquerque, NM: University of New Mexico Press; 1981.

Steel JM. Prepregnancy counseling and contraception in the insulin-dependent diabetic patient. *Clin Obstet Gynecol.* 1985;3:553-566.

Waife SO, ed. *Diabetes Mellitus.* 8th ed. Indianapolis, IN: Lilly Research Laboratories; 1980.

Chapter 10

Cancers in Pregnancy

Mary Lou Adams

Cancer is a devastating disease both physically and emotionally. The impact may be all the more great when the individual with cancer is pregnant. Approximately 12.8% of all cancers occur during the childbearing years.[1] The incidence of cancer during pregnancy is estimated to be 1 in every 1000 pregnancies.[2] Of every 118 women found to have cancer, one is also pregnant.[3] These figures indicate that health care professionals who work with obstetric patients should be aware of the effect that cancer has on pregnancy, and of the unique problems that may be associated with cancer during pregnancy.

It was previously thought that cancer that developed in the pregnant female was more aggressive than cancer in the nonpregnant female. A delay in diagnosis during pregnancy was believed to be responsible for this hypothesis. Symptoms of cancer may be dismissed in the pregnant patient and attributed to the pregnancy. The theory that cancer during pregnancy is more aggressive was supported by the mother's immunologic tolerance of the fetus's foreign body. It was believed that the same responses that allow the fetus to survive also allowed rapid progression of neoplastic diseases.[1] This theory began to lose support as more information became available. The incidence of cancer in pregnant women is not significantly different from the incidence of cancer in nonpregnant women of the same age group.[4] In contrast, patients who receive immunosuppressive drugs on a regular basis have a much higher incidence of cancer than the general public.[4]

Although pregnancy does not seem to affect cancer adversely, cancer may have adverse effects on a pregnancy. The rate of spontaneous abortion is not significantly higher in patients with cancer when compared to the national average of 10%. The rate of premature births also seems to be similar in the two groups.[4] However, many of the medical complications associated with cancer may affect the growth and development of the fetus adversely. For example, the common problems of anemia, thrombocytopenia, and leukopenia that are associ-

189

ated with leukemia may cause similar and more severe problems in the developing fetus.

Another important concern is that of metastasis of maternal cancer to the fetus. Potter and Schoeneman[5] reviewed 24 cases of transplacental metastasis to either the fetus or the placenta, or both. Malignant melanoma was involved in 11 of these cases. Of the remaining cases, breast cancer occurred in 4 cases; stomach cancer in 2 cases; lung cancer in 2; and lymphosarcoma, sarcoma, adrenal carcinoma, ethmoid cancer, and ovarian cancer each occurred in 1 case. All 18 placentas that were examined showed metastasis. Eight cases of fetal metastasis were found. Six of these infants died after birth, and two with melanoma showed regression of the tumor and survived. At the time of delivery all of the patients who exhibited metastasis to the fetus and placenta had disseminated disease that had started before the pregnancy or early in the pregnancy.[5] This particular review, however, has been controversial since its publication.

Donegan[6] found only 44 reported cases of metastasis of maternal cancer between 1866 and 1981. Once again, malignant melanoma was the most common form of cancer, followed by leukemias, lymphomas, and breast cancers. All of these patients also had extensive metastatic involvement. Thirty-five cases involved placental tissue, twelve involved the fetus, and only three had both placental and fetal involvement.[6]

Most sources agree that the placental villi appear to be barriers against neoplastic spread. This belief stems from the observation that an involved placenta that did not exhibit villous invasion was usually accompanied by an unaffected fetus.[6] Since this phenomenon does not occur often, there may exist other protective means that have not been detected. This small risk of transplacental metastasis does not seem to warrant therapeutic abortion. However, microscopic examination of the placenta and careful assessment of the neonate should be done.

Since cancer occurs most frequently in the very old and the very young, the incidence of cancer during the childbearing years is rather low in comparison to other age groups. The adverse effects that cancer has on pregnancy have been addressed briefly. Most of the detrimental effects upon the fetus result from the treatment modalities utilized in the treatment of cancer.

TREATMENT MODALITIES—EMBRYOLOGIC AND FETAL EFFECTS

The most commonly used methods in the treatment of neoplastic diseases are surgery, chemotherapy, and radiation. Each of these modalities may result in complications of the pregnancy. Since the surgeries required for the different types of cancer differ greatly with the type and extent of cancer, these will be discussed in conjunction with the specific cancers. The use of chemotherapy or radiation to treat cancer may introduce multiple problems to the pregnant woman of which health care providers must be aware.

Chemotherapy

The use of chemotherapy in the treatment of cancer has drastically improved the survival rate. During pregnancy, the risks to the fetus must be weighed against the potential gain for the mother. The risk of complications, such as fetal anomalies, premature birth, and hemorrhage, is approximately 12.7% when the mother receives chemotherapy during pregnancy.[7] The effect of chemotherapeutic agents depends on several factors, such as dose, gestational age, and duration of administration. The effect of these drugs is more devastating during the first trimester, especially during the period of organogenesis (2 to 7 weeks). Unfortunately, this may also be the period of time when a woman does not know she is pregnant. In general, therapeutic abortion is usually advised when a woman becomes pregnant while on chemotherapeutic agents or when a woman is pregnant at the time of diagnosis and requires chemotherapy as treatment or palliation. However, Schapira and Chudley[7] reported a case in which a 21-year-old with a diagnosis of hystiocytic lymphoma received combination chemotherapy for 16 weeks prior to conception and throughout the pregnancy, which ended in the delivery of a normal male infant. Gililland and Weinstein[8] reviewed cases in which women received chemotherapeutic agents during pregnancy. Upon evaluation of their results, they strongly discouraged the use of the following agents during pregnancy: aminopterin, busulfan, chlorambucil, fluorouracil, cytoxan, methotrexate, and thioguanine.[8] Even though therapeutic abortion is recommended, one must always consider the possibility that the patient may choose not to terminate the pregnancy.

Chemotherapy may leave the patient feeling worse than she did before the initiation of treatment. Nursing interventions may serve to decrease the number and severity of these side effects. The nurse must have a working knowledge of the side effects most common to the drugs being administered to the patient. Patient education must occur before chemotherapy is initiated to decrease anxiety and alert the patient to anticipated side effects. The nurse must conduct an ongoing assessment of the patient to identify actual and potential problems, support systems for the client, and the learning needs of the client.[9]

Since the therapeutic index of most chemotherapeutic agents is fairly narrow, toxicity is not uncommon and can result in many complications. Chemotherapy is most effective on rapidly dividing cells; therefore, the bone marrow, the gastrointestinal tract, and the hair follicles are the areas at greatest risk for toxicity.

Bone marrow depression occurs quite frequently during chemotherapy. The extent of bone marrow suppression and the blood components that will be affected are dependent on the particular agent(s) utilized and the dosages required. One factor to be considered is the half-life of the different blood components. The half-life of red blood cells is approximately 120 days, compared to 5 to 7 days and 6 hours, respectively, for platelets and granulocytes.[10] Therefore, effects on erythroblast stem cells may not become clinically evident unless long-term therapy is required.

It is imperative to monitor the blood components of all patients receiving chemotherapeutic agents. This information becomes critical as the pregnant patient approaches delivery. Since bleeding tendencies may be affected adversely, nursing care immediately after delivery is focused on the prevention of hemorrhage. Nursing assessment of bleeding prior to, during, and after delivery must be done frequently and at regular intervals. Fundal massage to maintain uterine tone is also done. The neonate's blood components should also be monitored since many of these agents can cross the placenta and cause similar problems in the fetus.

The cells of the gastrointestinal (GI) tract may also be affected by chemotherapy. This GI involvement may take many forms, one of which is stomatitis. Nursing care must be aimed at reducing the risk of infection, relieving pain in the case of stomatitis, and maintaining nutrition and hydration for the patient. The nurse should instruct the patient to keep her mouth free of exudate, to brush frequently with a soft-bristle toothbrush, and to gargle frequently with normal saline.[11] These measures may minimize the problems associated with stomatitis.

Nausea and vomiting are probably the most common side effects of chemotherapy. It is believed that the cause is direct stimulation of the chemoreceptor trigger zone of the central nervous system.[10] Local irritation frequently occurs and may add to these problems. The incidence of nausea and vomiting varies with the agents used. A working knowledge of the side effects of these drugs is helpful to educate and assist patients. Antiemetics may be helpful when administered 30 to 60 minutes before the administration of chemotherapeutic agents but do not completely resolve the problem.[10] The use of marijuana has shown some promise but is still under investigation.[10] Nurses can assist patients in scheduling meals to avoid a full stomach at the peak times of chemotherapy. These nursing measures may minimize the effects on the GI tract.

Because of the action of chemotherapy on hair follicles, alopecia often results. Hair loss usually occurs after 1 to 2 weeks and reaches its maximum after 1 to 2 months.[10] Regrowth occurs after most agents have been discontinued. Nursing actions include education and support. The patient needs to receive information regarding the probability of hair loss, the use of aids (i.e., wigs), and the probability of regrowth. The patient also needs to understand that initially hair that regrows may be of a different texture or color from the original hair. This change is usually temporary. Because of the body image changes that usually accompany hair loss, the patient will need emotional support and encouragement.

Some measures may also minimize the hair loss. These measures include gentle scalp care, scalp tourniquets left in place 5 to 10 minutes after the intravenous push administration of some agents, and the application of ice bags 5 minutes before and 10 to 15 minutes after the intravenous administration. However, the risk of metastatic spread to the scalp precludes the use of these measures in cases such as leukemia or other cancers with widespread metastasis.[10]

The pregnant patient receiving chemotherapy may be very concerned regarding whether to breastfeed. This decision must be made by evaluating each chemotherapeutic agent individually. Insufficient data to support or preclude breastfeeding are common with agents such as vincristine, thioguanine, and doxorubicin.[12(pp154,471,434)] Other agents, such as methotrexate, are excreted in breast milk in very small quantities, and breastfeeding is not recommended as there are insufficient data on consumption of these small quantities.[12(p284)] In summary, each agent must be considered individually before a recommendation can be made to the patient.

Chemotherapeutic agents carry with them many potential and actual complications that can affect both the pregnant woman and her unborn child. Nurses have the opportunity to make a significant difference in the patient's mental and physical outcome.

Radiation Therapy

Awareness of the effects of radiation exposure increased drastically after the use of atomic bombs during World War II. Much of the information received focused on the effects of in utero exposure to radiation. It is universally accepted that pregnant women should avoid all unnecessary exposure. Some radiation exposure is unavoidable, including exposure to radiation from the ground, building materials, and outer space.[13]

Pregnancy is one of the major contraindications to radiotherapy. Approximately 1% of all pregnant women receive abdominal radiography for one reason or another.[14] Chromosomes are the major target of radiation, resulting in injury or death of the cell. The cells often repair themselves before replicating. Therefore, rapidly dividing cells are the most sensitive to radiation.[13] The developing embryo and fetus are most susceptible to radiation damage.

The effects of in utero exposure to radiation have been determined by studying the effects of radiation on animals, on the children of Japanese survivors who were pregnant at the time of the atomic bomb explosions, and on fetuses of patients requiring radiotherapy during pregnancy. Congenital anomalies and growth retardation are the most common results of in utero exposure in animals.[13] Studies of radiation exposure after the atomic bomb explosions showed a direct correlation between central nervous system abnormalities and the exposure dose.[15] Other researchers also found that as the in utero exposure increased, the incidence of childhood cancer in the offspring also increased.[16]

The effect of radiation on the embryo/fetus is dependent on the period of time after conception that the exposure occurs. During the first week after conception (preimplantation), the embryo is quite sensitive to the fatal effects of radiation. This sensitivity usually results in spontaneous abortion. If the pregnancy continues, there is a smaller risk of teratogenic effects. During the period of organogenesis (2 to 7 weeks), the fetus is very sensitive to the teratogenic effects of radiation, which can result in growth retardation, congenital anomalies, death, or neoplastic effects. During the fetal period (8 to 40 weeks), there is a decreased amount of radiosensitivity to teratogenic effects, but the risk of growth retardation continues.[14] Unfortunately, many of the adverse effects occur before the woman is aware that she is pregnant. The risks and benefits must be weighed when considering radiation exposure for a pregnant woman.

The radiation dose that is considered safe is very controversial. Most authorities have agreed that a dose of 10 rads (radiation absorbed dose) or less to an embryo or fetus probably results in few if any adverse effects.[14] Necessary radiation doses for cancer treatment vary greatly and range from 2200 rads to 7000 rads and beyond.[17] This total dose should be administered in divided doses. Total exposure and fetal exposure are vastly different, depending on the area irradiated and the measures taken to decrease fetal exposure. In Hiroshima, an in utero dose of approximately 10 to 19 rads before the 18th week of gestation resulted in abnormally small head circumferences and mental retardation; however, in Nagasaki no effect was observed in an exposure dose of less than 150 rads.[17] Estimating the dose of radiation to which the fetus is exposed is difficult. The accuracy level should be assumed to be ± 15%. Most abdominal radiography delivers a dose of less than 5 rads. Therapeutic abortion may be recommended when the dose exceeds 10 rads.[18] Measures may be taken to reduce in utero exposure. Radiographs may be canceled or delayed. When they must be done, an abdominal shield should be used if at all possible. These same considerations apply if the mother is to receive radiation therapy for cancer.

Radiation therapy may result in several adverse effects. Cells that are more vascular, well oxygenated, and divide rapidly are the most sensitive to radiation.[19] The sites most commonly affected include the skin, the GI tract, and the bone marrow.

Skin reactions occur due to breakdown of epidermal basal cells, which results in local inflammation. This problem is usually limited to the irradiated area and begins to appear after 2 to 3 weeks of treatment.[19] Reactions range from hair loss in the involved area to severe blistering. Radiation burns are rare today because of the advanced technology and understanding of radiotherapy.[19]

Nurses can assist the patient in minimizing these complications. The patient should limit her direct exposure to the sun and avoid trauma to that area. Mild soap should be used, and oils and perfumes should be avoided. Loose clothing provides comfort and decreases irritation.[19]

Irritation of the GI mucosa is another complication of radiation treatment. The outcome depends on the irradiated area (i.e., mouth, esophagus). Radiation of the oral cavity may result in soreness, taste changes, and dysphagia. The nurse can encourage good oral care to decrease the potential for these problems. Over-the-counter mouthwashes and spicy foods should be avoided. A mixture of 1 teaspoon of baking soda and 1 cup of water can be used as a mouthwash.[19] Lip balm, ice chips, and sugarless candy keep the mucous membranes moist, which helps prevent breakdown. The patient receiving radiotherapy or chemotherapy is at risk for oral candidiasis and should be instructed on the signs and symptoms of thrush, primarily the appearance of white patches in the mouth that leave reddened, irritated areas when removed.

When the GI tract is involved in the irradiated area, nausea, vomiting, and diarrhea may result. When this occurs, the patient's intake and output should be monitored. An increased calorie intake usually is required for these patients. Hydration is assessed by checking skin turgor regularly. In many instances, intravenous therapy will be necessary. Antiemetics may prove helpful for nausea. Lomotil, Kaopectate, or Imodium may provide partial or total relief for patients experiencing diarrhea.[19] Dairy products may intensify diarrhea and should be avoided. Foods high in potassium (i.e., bananas) should be encouraged for patients experiencing diarrhea.

Bone marrow and lymphoid tissue are also radiosensitive. The effect will depend on the radiation dose and the size of the area irradiated. Leukocytes and platelets are most frequently affected; therefore, monitoring the patient's complete blood count and platelet count is important.[19] These counts become especially important for the pregnant patient who is approaching her due date. Radiation therapy may be temporarily discontinued or modified for these patients. Excellent nursing care is critical for the patient's well-being. Postpartum bleeding must be controlled, and episiotomy care or incisional care (cesarean sections) must be done frequently. Any temperature greater than 101° F requires investigation.[19] The neonate's blood counts must be checked after delivery since the mother's hematologic status can affect the fetus's status. The role of radiation therapy in the treatment of neoplastic diseases is quite valuable but carries with it multiple complications; good nursing care can act to improve the patient's outcome.

BREAST CANCER DURING PREGNANCY

Breast cancer is the most commonly occurring cancer in women and also the cause of the most deaths.[1] Breast cancer occurs most often in women approaching menopause. One percent to 3% of all cases of breast cancer occur during pregnancy or lactation. It is estimated that 1 of every 3200 pregnancies is accompanied by breast cancer, making it the most common neoplastic disease to occur in pregnancy.[4] Although breast cancer is less common in young women, the disease process is often very aggressive. In general, tumors that are negative for estrogen receptors (ER) are generally more aggressive than ER-positive tumors and carry a higher recurrence rate and a poorer prognosis. Younger women develop ER-negative tumors more frequently than older women; therefore, breast cancer in the younger population (childbearing years) must be diagnosed quickly and treated promptly.[20]

It is interesting to note that women who have had children, especially those who breastfed their children, have a decreased incidence of developing breast cancer.[4] This information suggests that pregnancy or lactation confers some type of protection from breast cancer.

At one time it was thought that breast cancer in pregnant women held a poorer prognosis than that occurring in the nonpregnant population.[3] This theory was rationalized by the many breast changes that occur during pregnancy. These changes include increased vascularity, hormonal stimulation, decreased immune response, and increased lymphatic permeability.[6] However, studies have shown no significant difference between the survival rates for pregnant women with breast cancer when compared to a nonpregnant control group who were matched for age and stage of the disease.[21]

It is currently believed that the theory that breast cancer in pregnant women is more aggressive stemmed from the fact that pregnant women are often diagnosed later than nonpregnant women. This fact, along with the finding that younger women more often have the aggressive ER-negative tumors, explains why breast cancer during pregnancy carries a poorer prognosis.[20] The delay in diagnosis is probably due in part to the physiologic changes occurring in pregnant women. These factors include age, hormonal changes, and breast enlargement.[22] Both the patient and the health care provider can be at fault for this delay in diagnosis, since many changes that may be indicative of breast cancer may be attributed to pregnancy. The breast exam is complicated by enlargement of the breast during pregnancy, making palpation very difficult, especially when the mass is small. Diagnosis may be delayed until there are skin changes or discharge, which often accompanies a poorer prognosis.[23] Applewhite and colleagues[24] believed that the delay in diagnosis was at least three times longer in pregnant women than in nonpregnant women. This additional time before diagnosis allows the disease to progress and results in the appearance of a more aggressive cancer in pregnant women. It is unjustifiable to attribute breast masses to pregnancy without further investigation.[1]

In a recent study evaluating breast cancer in pregnancy, 178 women were evaluated. One hundred and twenty-one of these women were diagnosed during pregnancy (first group), compared to 57 who were diagnosed and treated prior to pregnancy (second group). The pregnant women from the first group were consistently diagnosed with a more advanced stage of the disease. Seventy-two percent of the pregnant women had nodal involvement at the time of diagnosis, compared to 51% of the women from the second group. The 5-year survival rates were 37% for the first group versus 69% for the second group. These major differences are believed to have occurred because of delayed diagnosis in the first group of women.[25]

Early diagnosis is the key to survival for these women. If any uncertainty about a breast mass exists, biopsy under local anesthesia should be done. Some sources recommend needle aspiration of the mass first to distinguish between cystic and solid lesions, before continuing on with biopsy.[1] Both methods pose minimal risks to the fetus. Mammography may be performed with proper shielding but is not reliable because of the increased density of the breast tissue during pregnancy.[23] Once diagnosis has been made and staging has been completed, treatment should begin.

In general, treatment depends on both the stage of the disease and the gestation of the pregnancy (Table 10-1). In the early stages of the disease, modified radical mastectomy is the treatment of choice. This treatment modality removes the breast and the axillary nodes.[3] The risk of spontaneous abortion is minimal (approximately 1%). When the patient is close to term, the surgery may be delayed until delivery has taken place. When there is no nodal involvement, no further treatment is necessary. Therapeutic abortion does not prolong survival.[17]

For stage II or III, adjuvant chemotherapy after mastectomy is recommended for nodal involvement. When the pregnancy is in the first or second trimester, therapeutic abortion is usually advised because of the possible dangers chemotherapy poses to the developing fetus.[20] When the pregnancy is in the third trimester, evaluating the number of involved nodes is decisive in determining whether treatment can wait until after delivery.[23]

For stage IV breast cancer, treatment is palliative since the 5-year survival rate is zero. Once again, therapeutic abortion will not improve prognosis but may be considered because of the poor prognosis and the ability to provide palliative measures.[6] Since treatment is only palliative, the mother may choose to delay treatment in order to have a viable infant. Because of the prognosis, the mother may choose a therapeutic abortion since the infant would soon be motherless.

Radiation to the breast is generally not used during pregnancy. Even in the last half of the pregnancy, the risks outweigh the benefits. The risks to the fetus are lower in the last half of pregnancy, but the uterus is higher in the abdomen and

Table 10-1 Characteristics of the Different Stages of Breast Cancer

Stage I   1. a) tumor 2 cm or less, fixed or not to underlying pectoral muscle, b) nonpalpable axillary nodes that are negative [without growth], c) without distant metastasis

Stage II   1. a) primary tumor, b) positive [with growth] movable axillary nodes, c) without distant metastasis

             2. a) tumor 2 cm or less, b) positive movable axillary nodes, c) without distant metastasis

             3. a) tumor greater than 2 cm and less than 5 cm, b) nonpalpable nodes, or movable axillary nodes [either positive or negative], c) without distant metastasis

Stage III   1. a) tumor 2 cm or less, b) positive axillary nodes, fixed to other nodes or structures, c) without distant metastasis

             2. a) tumor greater than 2 cm and less than 5 cm, b) positive axillary nodes, fixed to other nodes or structures, c) without distant metastasis

             3. a) tumor greater than 5 cm whether fixed to underlying tissue or not, b) nonpalpable axillary nodes or movable axillary nodes [either positive or negative], c) without distant metastasis

Stage IV   1. a) tumor with extension to chest wall [excluding pectoral muscle] or skin, b) negative or positive axillary nodes, c) with or without distant metastasis

             2. a) any size tumor, b) positive axillary movable nodes and fixed to other nodes or structures, c) with or without distant metastasis

             3. a) any size tumor, b) positive or negative movable axillary nodes, fixed or not, c) with distant metastasis

Source: Adapted from *Cancer Principles and Practice of Oncology*, ed. 3 (pp 1211-1212) by VT DeVita, S Hellman, and SA Rosenburg with permission of JB Lippincott Company, ©1989.

---

would receive a higher dose of radiation.[1] Therefore, radiation therapy is generally delayed until after delivery.

Overall, pregnancy has no adverse effect on breast cancer. At one time women with breast cancer were advised against becoming pregnant. In recent years, pregnancy has been shown to have no effect on the progression or recurrence of breast cancer; therefore, this recommendation has changed.[1] Some recommend putting off future pregnancies 3 years for those with negative nodes (the most common time for recurrence).[3] It is important to note that some studies suggest that women who become pregnant after treatment exhibit improved outcome, with higher 10-year survival rates.[23,26] This may be the result of estriol (the estrogen derivative that is elevated during pregnancy), since estriol competes for estrogen-binding sites.[26] Estriol inhibits mammary carcinogenesis in rats and may be a protective agent against cancer of the breast in women.[22,26] However, a successful pregnancy after treatment does not imply a guaranteed nonrecurrence. Hormonal therapy may be helpful for those women with ER-positive tumors and would also require pregnancy termination. Since the effects of hormonal therapy are not known, mechanical means of contraception are generally recommended.[23]

The issue of breastfeeding is controversial. Breast cancer in mice is caused by a virus that passes through breast milk. There is no such evidence in humans, but this argument generally discourages breastfeeding.[3]

Breast cancer is the most common type of cancer occurring during pregnancy and can be traumatic for the mother and the baby. The most important concept is prenatal screening for early detection. All masses must be suspected. The nurse is in a position to help the patient understand the disease entity, the treatments available, and their effects, and ventilate her feelings with regard to this disease.

CERVICAL CANCER DURING PREGNANCY

Cervical cancer is the second most common type of cancer during pregnancy. The incidence of cervical dysplasia is the same in pregnant women as in nonpregnant women.[27] Cervical cancer affects one of every 1240 pregnancies, and approximately 2.7% to 3.5% of all cervical cancers occur during pregnancy. The average age for carcinoma in situ during pregnancy is 29.9 years; the average age for invasive carcinoma of the cervix is 33.8 years.[28] Benedet and coworkers[29] suggest that abnormal Pap smears during pregnancy are fairly common but that only a few are invasive. The prevalence of cervical dysplasia and carcinoma in situ is two to three times higher in black women than in white women.[28]

Many cervical changes occur during pregnancy. These include eversion of the squamocolumnar junction, increased vascularity, and softening. These factors may exaggerate the appearance of neoplasia and make overdiagnosis more common than underdiagnosis.[28]

All pregnant women should have a cytologic examination of the cervix. Symptoms seem to be the same as in nonpregnant women. Most women with carcinoma in situ are asymptomatic, whereas women with invasive carcinoma usually present with abnormal vaginal bleeding (63%), vaginal discharge (13%), postcoital bleeding (4%), and pelvic pain (2%). Eighteen percent are asymptomatic.[28]

If the patient has an abnormal Pap smear, a colposcopy should be done. Colposcopy, a procedure that involves examination of the cervix, vagina, and vulva using a magnifying instrument, has replaced cervical conization as the method of choice to investigate an abnormal Pap smear.[27] Although conization has a higher rate of accuracy, the complication rate is 20% to 30%. These complications include postoperative hemorrhage, premature onset of labor, cervical incompetence, and cervical dystocia and are eliminated when colposcopy is used.[29] Pritchard and colleagues[30] felt that conization was less reliable during pregnancy since the epithelium cannot be sufficiently excised because of the increased risk to the fetus of blood loss and of abortion or premature labor. Hannigan et al.[31] studied the effects of conization in the second trimester and found that the risk of fetal wastage was 19.1%. They recommended the use of conization only when colposcopically directed biopsy reveals microinvasion or when the Pap smear results suggest invasive disease. Mitchell and Capizzi[4] agreed that cone biopsies should be done to confirm the diagnosis of invasive carcinoma and to determine the degree of invasion. Once the diagnosis has been made, a decision about the treatment regimen must be made.

Treatment decisions are based on the stage of the disease and the trimester of the pregnancy. Since cervical cancer usually progresses slowly, early stages may be treated conservatively. If mild to moderate dysplasia is found in the specimens obtained via colposcopically directed biopsy, the pregnancy is continued with reevaluation at 4 weeks for mild dysplasia and at three 4-week intervals for moderate dysplasia. If no progression is found, the patient is allowed to deliver vaginally and is re-evaluated postpartum. When severe dysplasia or carcinoma in situ is detected, the patient is followed with repeat Pap smears every 4 weeks until delivery and re-evaluated during the postpartum period.[4] This Pap smear can be done at the routine 6-week postpartum checkup, and the colposcopic exam at 12 weeks.[27] Treatment during the postpartum period is conventional, such as cryosurgery or laser therapy.[28] Hysterectomy is reserved for those patients with persistent disease.

Invasive carcinoma of the cervix demands immediate treatment. Conization during pregnancy would be accepted for these patients, but studies have shown that 50% of patients treated with conization during pregnancy have residual carcinoma in postpartum hysterectomy specimens.[1] When the disease is diagnosed in the first or second trimester, the patient is treated as though she were not pregnant because of the poor prognosis associated with invasive carcinoma of the cervix. The treatment usually consists of radical hysterectomy with pelvic lymph node dissection or radiation therapy.[32] After 20 weeks of gestation the mother may chose to await fetal maturity and have a cesarean section followed by a hysterectomy and nodal dissection.[27]

More advanced stages are often treated with radiation. Radiation may also be used as an alternative to surgery for early stages.[28] Spontaneous abortion usually occurs with external therapy about 20 to 50 days after initiation of therapy. Once again, during the late second or third trimester delivery can precede treatment, and radiation can be started on the seventh postpartum day.[28] Vaginal delivery in the presence of invasive carcinoma of the cervix is controversial. Early studies suggested a poorer prognosis with a vaginal delivery; however, more recent studies have failed to show this correlation.[27] Mitchell and Capizzi[4] support the theory that vaginal delivery should be avoided since it may lead to severe hemorrhage.

The prognosis for cervical cancer in pregnancy depends on the stage of the disease. Carcinoma in situ carries a very good prognosis, with recurrences in only 1.5% of the cases. Invasive carcinoma has a survival rate of 73.2% in those treated in the first trimester and 36.5% in those treated after delivery.[1] The key to an optimal outcome is early diagnosis. Since cervical cancer is a fairly slow-progressing disease, every woman should be strongly encouraged to have annual Pap smears. Each pregnant woman should receive a cytologic evaluation, and appropriate treatment should be carried out for all abnormal findings.

OVARIAN CANCER DURING PREGNANCY

Ovarian cancer occurs in approximately every 18,000 to 25,000 deliveries.[33,34] Women between the ages of 40 and 65 are most frequently affected, thereby decreasing the incidence in pregnancy.[35] Ovarian cancer has a very poor prognosis, with only 10% of women surviving for 10 years or longer.[36] It has been suggested that pregnancy may protect against the development of ovarian cancer since there is an inverse relationship between family size and mortality from ovarian cancer. An increased mortality in single women and a decreased mortality in Catholic women have added to this theory. The etiology of this protectant factor is unknown; however, several hypotheses have been proposed, such as the suppression of ovulation, hormonal changes, and immunologic changes associated with pregnancy.[36] Ballard[37] reported that only 2.2% of ovarian tumors diagnosed during pregnancy are malignant. This compares favorably to the 15% to 20% malignancy rate found in nonpregnant women.[1]

Ovarian cancer is usually diagnosed by exploratory laparoscopy. Ultrasonography has also been used to aid in the diagnostic process. Diagnosis during pregnancy may be made difficult because of the enlargement of the uterus. Another factor that adds to the difficulty of diagnosis is the fact that patients with ovarian cancer are often asymptomatic. When symptoms do occur, the disease has often progressed to the point at which a cure is improbable. These symptoms include abdominal pain, pelvic fullness, ascites, abnormal uterine bleeding, a palpable mass, and urinary complaints.[35]

Diagnosis and estimation of involvement is determined by an exploratory laparoscopy.[35] The treatment of choice is usually surgery followed by radiation or chemotherapy. Because of the poor prognosis, prompt treatment is imperative. Most sources recommend total abdominal hysterectomy, salpingo-oophorectomy, and postoperative radiation.[32] A unilateral oophorectomy may be considered when (1) the woman is young and desires more children, (2) the tumor is well encapsulated, (3) there is a negative peritoneal cytology workup, and (4) the tumor has a low histologic grade.[6] This mode of treatment would also allow the pregnancy to continue.

Ovarian cancer has a high mortality rate. Early diagnosis and aggressive treatment are the keys to a favorable outcome for the mother. Because of the poor prognosis, the fetus becomes a secondary consideration. This mother will often lose her child and her fertility, and often her life.

MELANOMA DURING PREGNANCY

Melanoma originates from melanocytes, which arise from the epidermis or the pigmented area of the eye, and is not always malignant.[4] It often materializes from an already present mole. Since the incidence of melanoma is highest in the third and fourth decade, melanoma occurs during the childbearing years.[1] Because of the pigmentary changes that normally occur during pregnancy as a result of an increased level of melanocyte-stimulating substance, many believe that the incidence of melanoma during pregnancy is drastically increased.[38] Reintgen et al.[39] studied 58 women who were diagnosed with malignant melanoma during pregnancy and 43 women who became pregnant within 5 years of the diagnosis. Both groups were compared with a control group. They found no significant difference with regard to survival between those who were pregnant at the time of diagnosis and the control group. The same held true for those who had subsequent pregnancies after their diagnosis. However, the actuarial disease-free interval was significantly shorter for those women diagnosed during pregnancy when compared to their control group.[39] The results are inconclusive as to the effect of pregnancy on malignant melanoma.

Shiu et al.[40] reviewed 251 cases of malignant melanoma treated with surgery and found no difference between nulliparous, parous, nonpregnant, and pregnant women with stage I melanoma. They did find a significantly lower survival rate for pregnant and parous women who had experienced activation during a pregnancy (29%), when compared to nulliparous and other parous women (55% and 51%, respectively).[37]

Krebs[3] suggests that survival rates are not significantly different in pregnant and nonpregnant women when they are matched for the stage of the disease. She does acknowledge that pregnant women present more often with melanoma on the trunk area than nonpregnant women.[3] This location is often the most advanced at the time of diagnosis.

Many other factors suggested a hormonal influence on the development and progression of melanoma. Overall, premenopausal women have a higher survival rate than postmenopausal women.[41] Also, multiparous women seem to have an increased survival rate over nulliparous women.[42] The results of a study conducted by Sutherland and coworkers[43] suggested a worse prognosis when the melanoma was diagnosed during pregnancy, or when it was initiated or stimulated by pregnancy.

There is a 50% to 80% cure rate when surgical excision is done and the melanoma has only invaded the dermis superficially, without lymph node involvement. However, this rate decreased to <20% when the lymph nodes or the lowest one third of the dermis was involved.[4] Early diagnosis is critical in improving the prognosis.

The symptoms associated with malignant melanoma include darkening, irregularity, and elevation of a mole. Bleeding and ulceration are usually late signs. A biopsy should be done on any suspicious area. Once the diagnosis of malignant melanoma has been made, one should attempt to discover the extent of involvement. Malignant melanoma usually involves the viscera, especially the liver, lungs, bones, brain, pericardium, and pleura. Death from metastatic malignant melanoma frequently occurs in 6 to 12 months.[4]

After diagnosis, treatment begins immediately, regardless of the pregnancy, because of the rapid progression of this disease. Treatment includes a wide dissection (at least 3 cm) of the involved area and dissection of the clinically involved lymph nodes. Prophylactic regional lymph node dissection is controversial.[1]

Chemotherapy is used for advanced melanoma. Because of the effects of chemotherapy on a developing fetus, therapeutic abortion is recommended when the pregnancy is in its first or second trimester. In the advanced stages of the disease, chemotherapy is only palliative and may be delayed to await viability if the mother desires. If this is the mother's request, the infant and placenta should be closely examined after delivery because of the risk of metastasis.[5]

Attempts to improve prognosis by endocrine manipulation have been unsuccessful. There is no evidence that abortion, oophorectomy, adrenalectomy, or hypophysectomy are of any benefit to the pregnant woman with melanoma.[40] Immunotherapy has shown some promise with regard to the treatment of malignant melanoma.[4]

The prognosis for the pregnant woman with stage I malignant melanoma is the same as for the nonpregnant woman. This may be because there is an increased chance of total removal of the melanoma in stage I.[40] There is a lower 5-year survival rate for pregnant women with nodal involvement when compared to nonpregnant women. Because of the question of hormonal involvement, some recommend no future pregnancies, while others recommend no pregnancies for 3 to 5 years. Nonhormonal methods of birth control are usually preferred, particularly for those patients treated for more advanced stages.[40]

Malignant melanoma is a dismal disease. The trauma of this disease may be greater, both physically and mentally, for the pregnant woman. The woman must receive accurate information and support so that she may make a knowledgeable decision about her future and that of her baby.

CONCLUSION

Although cancer is not as common during pregnancy as other medical complications, it nonetheless occurs and requires specialized nursing care to optimize the outcome. Cancer carries with it a grim connotation that may be magnified in the case of the pregnant woman. Many ethical decisions often must be made by the patient and her health care providers. It is the nurse's role to ensure that the patient receives accurate information to make her decisions.

These decisions must be respected and supported. The patient must be mentally and physically prepared for the treatment modality chosen. Potential and actual problems are dealt with on an individual basis. Ideally, the outcome would be a cancer-free mother and a healthy baby. Nursing care of the pregnant patient with cancer must be directed toward providing quality nursing care to achieve an optimal outcome for all involved.

REFERENCES

1. Donegan WL. Cancer and pregnancy. *CA*. 1983;33:194-214.
2. Nesbitt JC, Moise KJ, Sawyers JC. Colorectal carcinoma in pregnancy. *Arch Surg*. 1985;120:636-640.
3. Krebs LU. Pregnancy and cancer. *Semin Oncol Nurs*. 1985;1:35-412.
4. Mitchell MS, Capizzi RL. Neoplastic diseases. In: Burrow GN, Ferrie TF, eds. *Medical Complications during Pregnancy*. Philadelphia: WB Saunders; 1988:540-569.
5. Potter JF, Schoeneman M. Metastasis of maternal cancer to the placenta and fetus. *Cancer*. 1970;25:380-388.
6. Donegan WC. Cancer. In: Danforth DN, Scott JR, eds. *Obstetrics and Gynecology*. 5th ed. Philadelphia: JB Lippincott; 1986:575.
7. Schapira DV, Chudley AE. Successful pregnancy following continuous treatment with combination chemotherapy before conception and throughout pregnancy. *Cancer*. 1985;54:800-803.

8. Gililland J, Weinstein L. The effects of cancer chemotherapeutic agents on the developing fetus. *Obstet Gynecol Surv.* 1983;38:6-13.

9. Engelking CH, Steele NE. A model for pretreatment nursing assessment of patients receiving cancer chemotherapy. *Cancer Nurs.* 1984;7:203-212.

10. Dorr RT, Fritz WL, eds. Common toxicities. In: *Cancer Chemotherapy Handbook..* New York: Elsevier North Holland; 1980:102-115.

11. Walter J. Care of the patient receiving antineoplastic drugs. *Nurs Clin North Am.* 1982;17:607-629.

12. Briggs GC, Freeman RK, Yaffe SJ. *Drugs in Pregnancy and Lactation.* Baltimore: Williams & Wilkins; 1986:471, 434, 154.

13. Jankowski CB. Radiation and pregnancy. Putting the risks in proportion. *Am J Nurs.* 1986;86:260-265.

14. Mossman KL, Hill LT. Radiation risks in pregnancy. *Obstet Gynecol.* 1982;60:237-242

15. Plummer G. Abnormalities occurring in children exposed in utero to the atomic bomb in Hiroshima. *Pediatrics.* 1952;10:687-693.

16. Sweet DL, Kinzie J. Consequences of radiotherapy and antineoplastic therapy for the fetus. *J Reprod Med.* 1976;17:241-246.

17. Anderson JM. Mammary cancers and pregnancy. *Br Med J.* 1979;1:1124-1127.

18. Yasko JM, Greene P. Coping with problems related to cancer and cancer treatment. *CA.* 1987;37:106-125.

19. Petton S. Your role in radiation therapy. *RN.* 1985;48:32-37.

20. Nugent P, O'Connell TX. Breast cancer and pregnancy. *Arch Surg.* 1985;120:1221-1224.

21. Ribeiro GG, Palmer MK. Breast carcinoma associated with pregnancy: a clinician's dilemma. *Br Med J.* 1977;2:1524-1527.

22. Max MH, Klamer TW. Pregnancy and breast cancer. *South Med J.* 1983;76:1088-1090.

23. Onion P. Breast cancer prognosis with pregnancy. *Am J Nurs.* 1984;84:1126-1128.

24. Applewhite RR, Smith LR, DiVincenti F. Carcinoma of the breast associated with pregnancy and lactation. *Am Surg.* 1973;33:101-104.

25. Ribeiro G, Jones DA, Jones M. Carcinoma of the breast associated with pregnancy. *Br J Surg.* 1986;73:607-609.

26. Harvey J, Rosen PP, Ashikari R, Robbins GF, Kinne DW. The effect of pregnancy on the prognosis of carcinoma of the breast following radical mastectomy. *Surg Gynecol Obstet.* 1981;153:723-725.

27. McGee JE. Management of cervical dysplasia in pregnancy. *Nurse Pract.* 1987;12:34-42.

28. Hacker NF, Berek JS, Lagasse LD, Charles EH, Savage EW, Moore JG. Carcinoma of the cervix associated with pregnancy. *Obstet Gynecol.* 1982;59:735-747.

29. Benedet JL, Selke PA, Nickerson, KG. Colposcopic evaluation of abnormal Papanicolaou smears in pregnancy. *Am J Obstet Gynecol.* 1987;157:932-937.

30. Pritchard JA, McDonald PC, Gant NF, eds. *Williams Obstetrics.* 17th ed. Norwalk, CT: Appleton-Century-Crofts; 1985:493.

31. Hannigan EV, Whitehouse HH, Atkinson WD, Becker SN. Cone biopsy during pregnancy. *Obstet Gynecol.* 1982;60:450-455.

32. DeVita VT Jr, Hellman S, Rosenburg SA, eds. *Cancer Principles and Practice of Oncology.* Philadelphia: JB Lippincott ;1985:1039.

33. Munnell EW. Primary ovarian tumors in pregnancy. *Clin Obstet Gynecol.* 1973;41:211.

34. Chung A, Birnbaum SJ. Ovarian cancer associated with pregnancy. *Obstet Gynecol.* 1973;41:211-214.

35. Dugan KK. The bleak outlook on ovarian cancer. *Am J Nurs.* 1985;85:144-147.

36. Beral V, Fraser P, Chilvers C. Does pregnancy protect against ovarian cancer? *Lancet.* 1978;1:1003.

37. Ballard CA. Ovarian tumors associated with pregnancy termination patients. *Am J Obstet Gynecol.* 1984;149:384-387.
38. Riberti C, Marola G, Bertani A. Malignant melanoma: the adverse effect of pregnancy. *Br J Plast Surg.* 1981;34:338-339.
39. Reintgen D, McCarty KS Jr, Vollmer R, Cox E, Seigler HF. Malignant melanoma and pregnancy. *Cancer.* 1985;55:1340-1344.
40. Shiu MH, Schottenfeld D, Maclean B, Fortner JG. Adverse effect of pregnancy on melanoma. A reappraisal. *Cancer.* 1976;37:181-187.
41. Shaw HM, Milton GW, Farago G, McCarthy WH. Endocrine influence on survival from malignant melanoma. *Cancer.* 1978;42:669-677.
42. Hersey P, Stone DE, Morgan G, McCarthy WH, Milton GW. Previous pregnancy as a protective factor against death from melanoma. *Lancet.* 1977;1:451-452.
43. Sutherland CM, Loutfi A, Mather FJ, Carter RD, Krementz ET. Effect of pregnancy upon malignant melanoma. *Surg Gynecol Obstet.* 1983;157:443-446.

List of Abbreviations

ACOG	=	American College of Obstetricians and Gynecologists
ACTH	=	adrenocorticotropic hormone
ADP	=	adenosine diphosphate
aPTT	=	activated prothrombin time
ARDS	=	adult respiratory distress syndrome
AT III	=	antithrombin III
ATN	=	acute tubular necrosis
ATP	=	adenosine triphosphate
BHI	=	biosynthetic human insulin
BPP	=	biophysical profile
BUN	=	blood urea nitrogen
CAT	=	computerized axial tomography
CBC	=	complete blood count
CHO	=	carbohydrate
CNS	=	central nervous system
CO	=	cardiac output
COP	=	colloid osmotic (or oncotic) pressure
CPAP	=	continuous positive airway pressure
CST	=	contraction stress test
CVA	=	cerebrovascular accident
CVP	=	central venous pressure
DIC	=	disseminated intravascular coagulation
DKA	=	diabetic ketoacidosis
ECG	=	electrocardiogram

FDP	=	fibrin degradation products
FSH	=	follicle-stimulating hormone
FSP	=	fibrin split product
GDM	=	gestational diabetes mellitus
GFR	=	glomerular filtration rate
GI	=	gastrointestinal
g	=	gram(s)
GTT	=	glucose tolerance test
HbS-S	=	homozygous sickle cell anemia
HCG	=	human chorionic gonadotropin
HCS	=	human chorionic somatotropin
HELLP	=	hemolysis, elevated liver enzyme levels, and low platelet count
HgbA$_{1c}$	=	hemoglobin A$_{1c}$
HHS	=	hyperglycemic hyperosmolar state
HPL	=	human placental lactogen
ICA	=	islet cell antibodies
IDM	=	infants of diabetic mothers
IUFD	=	intrauterine fetal demise
IUGR	=	intrauterine growth retardation
K^{+}	=	potassium
L/S	=	lecithin/sphingomyelin ratio
LH	=	luteinizing hormone
LOC	=	level of consciousness
LV	=	left ventricle
LVEDP	=	left ventricular end diastolic pressure
LVSWI	=	left ventricular stroke work index
MAHA	=	microangiopathic hemolytic anemia
MAP	=	mean arterial blood pressure
MAST	=	medical antishock trousers
MgSO$_4$	=	magnesium sulfate
mL	=	milliliter(s)
mm Hg	=	millimeters of mercury
MSAFP	=	maternal serum alpha-fetoprotein
MSH	=	melanocyte-stimulating hormone

Na^+	=	sodium
$NaHCO_3$	=	sodium bicarbonate
NS	=	normal saline
NST	=	nonstress test
NTD	=	neural tube defect
PA	=	pulmonary artery
PaO_2	=	arterial oxygen
PAC	=	pulmonary artery catheter
$PaCO_2$	=	arterial carbon dioxide
PAD	=	pulmonary artery diastolic
PAP	=	pulmonary artery pressure
PAWP	=	pulmonary artery wedge pressure
PBSP	=	prognostically bad signs of pregnancy
PCWP	=	pulmonary capillary wedge pressure
PEEP	=	positive end expiratory pressure
PG	=	phosphatidylglycerol
PIH	=	pregnancy-induced hypertension
PT	=	prothrombin time
PTT	=	partial thromboplastin time
PVR	=	pulmonary vascular resistance
RA	=	right atrium
rads	=	radiation absorbed dose
RBC	=	red blood cells
RDS	=	respiratory distress syndrome
RPF	=	renal plasma flow
RV	=	right ventricle
SBGM	=	self–blood glucose monitoring
SGOT	=	serum glutamic-oxaloacetic transaminase
SGPT	=	serum glutamic pyruvic transaminase
SV	=	stroke volume
SVO_2	=	venous oxygen saturation
SVR	=	systemic vascular resistance
TED hose	=	antithrombus hose
TTN	=	transient tachypnea of the newborn
UBF	=	uterine blood flow
URI	=	upper respiratory infection
UTI	=	urinary tract infection

Index